Dear Se,
Thankyou For
being everyone. shero.
Love, Hoda.

RISING FROM

TAHRIR

HODA RASHAD

To Ismail Nourel Din whose bravery inspired
me every step of the way.
It inspires me still.

ACKNOWLEDGMENTS

Without God's blessings I would not be present in Egypt when these historical events took place and I would not have had the opportunity nor the strength to share this story. Without His divine power our plans are sketched in sand and the lightest breeze can pose the greatest challenge.

I would like to thank my husband who distracted the kids, cooked for me and offered his undying support to me and this project. Without him, I would have never been able to complete the work or cover its expenses.

My father was the first person to suggest that this book should be written and then dedicated all of our conversations to date to pushing me towards completing it. One of my major motivations became to make him proud and that is a magical carrot that only a parent can offer.

My mother's love, words of faith and utter wisdom kept me from giving up on myself and losing sight of the book's goal and the importance of its message.

On a parallel platform I am fortunate enough to have a second mother (my mother-in-law) who offered her powerful and practical maternal support by making herself available in every warm way. During almost every interview I conducted for the book, my children were left in her loving care and possibly did not even notice my absence.

Religious scholar, Moez Masoud, someone I now consider a true ally and friend, stood by me when there was no concrete concept to the book and few characters to include. An unknown and inexperienced writer, I had no way of landing the initial phone calls with people like Mohamed Diab, Layla Marzouk and Mustafa El Naggar, let alone the six-hour-long interviews that he set up for me with them. This book exists largely because he believed in it.

Similarly, activist, friend and generally amazing woman Yasmin Galal provided the necessary introductions to members of the Muslim Brotherhood and the Sixth of April Youth Opposition Movement.

Very early on in the process, an American freelance editor, Taylor Ray, was introduced to me by our remarkable, mutual friend Joel Orr. Based on his kind recommendation, she took on a consulting role—without requesting any form of payment—and provided vital preliminary editing and guidance throughout the process of writing and publication; she also was the source of several revitalizing pep talks.

Dr. Mohamed Tag El Din, a close friend and supporter of both my husband and I as well as our spiritual guide and confidante. We could not have survived as a team without him. We consider him a member of our family in every sense of the word.

To all these beautiful souls mentioned above, I cannot thank you enough for your contributions to this book and my attempt to share a face of our beloved and beautiful Egypt that few non-Egyptians have seen or heard about. My gratitude is endless and my wording of it an immense understatement.

INTRODUCTION

In any historic political event, dramatic things happen. But a chronology of those events never tells us what it was *like* to be there. It doesn't answer why things happened the way they did. It neither gives us insight into what people heard versus what they were thinking, nor gives us a sense of what the air felt like in a particular instant.

Rising from Tahrir presents the Egyptian revolution through the experiences of ten main characters before, during and after the protests that started on January the 25th of 2011. The story itself is an adaptation of their accounts, extracted from over 40 hours of recorded conversations between the writer and 9 of the characters, the writer's story being the tenth account that stitches all the others together. Parts 1 and 2 are told in the first person as the characters tell their stories to the reader directly, while in part 3, the author's voice takes over and the remainder of the book's storyline is told in the third person.

As such, this book gives readers a glimpse into the unique lives, histories, opinions and actions that collided to define a new Egypt. It shares the experiences of very different and key people, offering a deeper sense of the root causes and inner workings of the Egyptian revolution, without delving into a political analysis of the situation. As a result, this collection of personal narratives provide the reader with the "vocabulary" and terminology needed to decipher the uprising.

Timeline of the revolution:
June 26, 2010: The public and fatal beating of young business-man Khaled Saeed at the hands of Alexandrian police sparks early protests.

January 14, 2011: Tunisian President Zein El Abideen ben Ali, is the first Arab leader to step down prompted by the intense protests dubbed the **"Tunisian Jasmine Revolution"** that marked the beginning of the Arab Spring.

January 25, 2011: Egyptian Revolution – Day 1 – Day of Rage
National holiday for Egypt's police. Thousands of people march in Tahrir Square, Cairo. Police use water cannons and tear gas to disperse the crowds and fail.

January 26, 2011: Egyptian Revolution – Day 2 – Protesters defy ban
Egyptian authorities impose a ban on protests but demonstrations continue in Cairo, Alexandria, Suez and beyond. Social networking sites Facebook and Twitter are closed down in Egypt.

January 27, 2011: Egyptian Revolution – Day 3 – Opposition leader Dr. Mohamed El Baradei returns to Egypt
Mohamed El Baradei, Nobel laureate and critic of the Mubarak regime, returns to Egypt to support the protests and his followers. Google executive Wael Ghonim is reported missing by his family.

January 28, 2011: Egyptian Revolution – Day 4 – Friday of Anger – Army rolls in
Internet and mobile phone networks blocked and police violently attack protestors in an attempt to end the uprising. Egyptian army deployed throughout the main cities.

January 29, 2011: Egyptian Revolution – Day 5 – Mubarak fires entire cabinet
Unrest grows, dozens of people reported dead. Mubarak tries to calm anger by dismissing his government.

January 30, 2011: Egyptian Revolution – Day 6 – Tourists begin exodus

More and more tourists begin to leave the growing unrest as Egyptian army blocks roads to the pyramids.

January 31, 2011: Egyptian Revolution – Day 7 – Army holds its fire

Egypt's army says it will not use force against peaceful protesters and guarantees freedom of expression.

February 1, 2011: Egyptian Revolution – Day 8 – One Million Man March

Emboldened by the army's restraint, more than a million people take to the streets. Mubarak announces in a televised address that he will not run for another term and offers talks with the opposition. The majority of protestors appear to leave the square with a false sense of victory.

February 2, 2011: Egyptian Revolution – Day 9 – The regime strikes back – "The Battle of the Camel"

"Mubarak loyalists" on camel and horseback, attempting to impersonate the camel and horseback tour guides from the Pyramids, attack remaining protestors in the square and violent clashes ensue. Signs emerge that the Egyptian economy is buckling under the strain. Internet services are at least partially restored in Cairo after a five-day blackout aimed at stymieing protests.

February 3, 2011: Egyptian Revolution – Day 10 – Heavy gunfire in Tahrir Square

Bursts of heavy gunfire aimed at anti-government demonstrators in Tahrir Square, leave at least five people dead and dozens wounded.

February 4, 2011: Egyptian Revolution – Day 11 – Protests continue

Hundreds of thousands of anti-government protesters gather in Cairo's Tahrir Square for what they have termed the "Day of Departure." Chants urge Hosni Mubarak to leave.

February 5, 2011: Egyptian Revolution – Day 12 – Mubarak clears out his party

Mubarak removes leaders from his party, including his son Gamal, in a renewed bid to appease the protesters. However, he remains at the head of the NDP and the country.

February 6, 2011: Egyptian Revolution – Day 13 – Muslim Brotherhood joins the table

Talks begin between the regime and opposition parties including the Muslim Brotherhood, a group which had previously been banned from Egyptian politics.

February 7, 2011: Egyptian Revolution – Day 14 – Google executive Wael Ghonim's release boosts protester morale

Google executive Wael Ghonim is released from detention and reveals to the media that, as the administrator of the Facebook page "We Are All Khaled Saeed," he played a major role in organizing protests online. The news brings fresh fervor into the demonstrations.

February 8, 2011: Egyptian Revolution – Day 15 – Protests Continue

Massive protestor-encampment is visible in Tahrir Square in addition to protesters in the capital also gathering and chanting outside parliament. Cairo witnesses possibly the biggest crowd of demonstrators, including Egyptians who have returned from abroad and other newcomers mobilized by the release of activist Wael Ghonim.

Vice President Omar Suleiman announces a slew of constitutional and legislative reforms, to be undertaken by yet to be formed committees.

February 9: Egyptian Revolution – Day 16 – Labor union strikes raise fears over Suez Canal

Labor unions join protesters in the street, calling for Mubarak to step down as massive strikes take place across Egypt. With the unrest hammering the Egyptian economy, strikes by Suez Canal workers lead to rises in gas prices across the globe.

February 10: Egyptian Revolution – Day 17 – Mubarak's presidency on its last legs

Fervent speculation from the army, regime leaders and the US lead protesters to believe Mubarak will not last another day in power. However, millions are disappointed as he addresses the nation and declares that he will not step down.

February 11: Egyptian Revolution – Day 18 – VP Omar Suleiman announces that Mubarak has handed over power to the Supreme Council of the Armed Forces (SCAF)

After 30 years in complete control of Egypt, Hosni Mubarak is finally forced out of office and the army takes power.

PRELUDE

He who stands for nothing will fall for anything.

—*Alexander Hamilton*

HODA RASHAD

had given up on trying to sleep. No matter how hard I tried, I could not fall into that peaceful slumber. The house would not stop speaking to me. "Are those your plane tickets on the dresser?" it seemed to say. "Are you really taking the children away from these walls? From their room…from my kitchen? Have you no roots in the backyard where you played and sang and watched them ride their bikes? Will you lock your home into years of silence, like you've done before? I thought you had returned. I'd hoped you would stay."

I know that houses cannot speak.

But when you are a dual national citizen, your family and homelands—and all that lies between those two categories—are in an emotional, lifelong tug of war. The house had been impersonating our extended family in Egypt, and it was doing a good job.

The truth is, as a dual national, you are not comfortable anywhere. What's more, when you choose your companion for this lifetime, as I had done, you end up selecting someone who shares your background—and therefore belongs nowhere, too. You may have found common ground in each other, but no "ground" on which either of you are entirely at home.

That was the case with my husband and me. I had been in college in Egypt with my family when I met him. My father had made the move back from Boston after landing a job with GTE as an American expat in Cairo in 1984. It was the perfect scenario for an American Egyptian with two young girls, fleeing the horrors of prom night with all the implications it held for a family of Middle Eastern origins.

My sister had struggled with the transition, but I found it exciting and had a relatively smooth ride. I enjoyed Egypt. I had a lot in common with its people. There was a large part of me that was obviously Middle Eastern.

Still, when the time came to marry, I fell for an American Egyptian, like myself. Basil caught my eye and heart immediately. I could switch between Arabic and English with ease when I spoke to him, and he wouldn't miss a joke or a nuance on either front. He had come to Cairo at the age of twenty-five from the Bible Belt, to finish college and get to better know his roots.

Throughout our engagement and first few years of marriage, he tried to be happy at work in Egypt and fulfill his promise to my father to set up a life for us there. He tried so hard, but was unable to acquire the skills it took to deal with all the frustrations and disappointments of professional life in a "third world" country.

What a terrible classification that is. It implies that we had all competed in some imaginary race and come in third. How inane. There is no such thing as a "third world" person or a "third world" soul, so there should never be a "third world" country.

There is, however, an entirely different set of dimensions and variables that come with every geographical location, its culture, religion, and struggle. These elements require skills to help one survive. Basil had acquired the survival skills a man his age needed for the United States, but Cairo was an entirely different ballgame. Business deals were paperless, based on "one's word" or a mere handshake, and men were often judged by their lineage before their performances were even considered.

We spent four years trying to make it in Cairo and prove to our families that we appreciated our heritage enough to put some time into the betterment of their motherland. But in the end the tragedies outweighed the triumphs, and Basil found a career in America that served us better as a family.

When I was eight months pregnant with our second child, and had been in the States for close to four years, the collapse of the housing market and the ensuing economic crisis caused our landlord to default on the house we were renting in Fremont, California. One day, a bank employee visited and told us that he needed to take pictures of the property for its foreclosure documentation. We had just moved in four months earlier, and were fresh out of cash and energy.

Basil suggested that the kids and I spend the first year of the new baby's life in Cairo. Our son would learn Arabic and I would have help with the baby. We would save loads of money between living rent-free and the fact that one American dollar was worth six Egyptian pounds.

As an added benefit, we got to stay in our own house. It was a tradition for families who could afford it in Egypt to buy and set up their children's first home when they get married to give them a decent head start on life. Basil had initially tried to decline this offer from both of our parents and convince our families we would be fine on our own, especially since we were not sure yet which country we would end up settling into.

My father completely rejected that notion. In fact, it was a deal-breaker, and he made that clear. "A good home for you both will keep you coming back here," he told us. "In time you will find that this is where you belong." His tone told us this was an offer we couldn't refuse.

We decided it was easier to allow them to break their banks than it was to break their hearts, so we agreed to the home. While it was being built, we stayed in family-owned apartments, and by the time it was complete we had decided to move to the States. We had since gone back and forth for short visits to Egypt, only staying in the house for a few months at a time.

There was no doubt that it was an excellent option to have when America's economic slump hit. Basil had just initiated his own software start-up in California, and the Bay Area was expensive. Two months after the baby was born, we put all our belongings in storage. Basil would make the Holiday Inn Extended Stay in Fremont his home until we were able to reunite as a family on American soil again.

When we arrived in Cairo, it was a relief to open up the beautiful, rent-free house and show my then-five-year-old son his awesome room with the bunk bed and all his toys from back home shipped in and set up neatly on shelves. Our son had a "transplant" childhood, where we kept transporting him and his belongings back and forth between cultures. He had become a cultural nomad like us—another dual creature with an identity crisis.

Our home in Egypt was in a suburb with a yard and a park and a good school within twenty minutes. In short, we were enjoying a style of life to which roughly only 1 percent of the Egyptian population had access. The suburb was twenty-five minutes outside of the city, so we were far from the pollution and the traffic yet close to our parents' homes. It was a safe haven for the kids and me until things picked up financially. Basil traveled back and forth between Egypt and San Francisco every six to eight weeks.

There were some challenges and adjustments, and I missed my husband and having a complete family unit, but on the whole I was enjoying the experience. I was able to go back to work as an educational consultant even though the baby was only three months old, because my mother-in-law had offered to take care of her during the day.

Six months into the new school year, in January 2011, the Egyptian revolution exploded. Less than six months later, in June, my bags were packed and the kids and I were all set to move back to California. We fled the States because of our personal financial crisis, and we were fleeing Egypt because it was at war with itself.

I felt like a traitor and a weakling. Were we any different than all the other families who did whatever optimized their survival? Or were we supposed to stay where my sister had settled with her family and my parents had retired? The dual national is a creature most likely to flee because he or she has an alternative.

There was little police presence across Egypt, since the regime fell six months before and the suburb that was once considered conveniently secluded was now dangerously in the middle of nowhere. I could no longer stay in the house because it was dangerous. If our home were to be attacked by the increasing number of looters in Cairo, there was literally no law enforcement entity to call for help. I could no longer drive the kids around alone on the isolated roads that lead to our house. I could not afford another home in Cairo.

There was a lot I could no longer do independently from my husband.

My only option, had I decided to stay, was to move the children and myself into a room in my parents' or my in-laws' houses. We would have been a burden to them, and the children would lose their space and sense of stability. This was unacceptable; we had to leave. Our families did not argue with our decision. With their hearts heavy, they pushed us toward what was safer and more stable: America.

The house did not share their common sense.

It seemed to stare at me from my own eyes in the wedding picture in the hallway. Every room I entered was a reminder of what I had there.

Since I was not going to sleep, I finished up on some last-minute-items I needed to pack. I tucked away my laptop and the forty-plus hours of taped interviews I had gathered from activists and citizens for this book. I had made the decision to document the stories of the brave people I'd had the honor to be in contact with before, during, and after the revolution. Their personal stories, pieced together, told the multilayered tale of a nation worthy of the world's respect.

I hoped that the variety of individual experiences I would chronicle would bring together a complex mosaic of viewpoints, and serve as a "behind the scenes" version of what the whole world had so eagerly followed through the media.

Promising to write about what I had seen and experienced this last year was the only guilt-fighting mechanism I had. Maybe my dual existence would serve as one extra little bridge between these two Eastern and Western cultures that seldom understood each other.

The world needed to know that Egypt was not a third-rate country, but it did receive third-rate treatment for the last thirty years. It was now bravely turning that around. One thing was unfortunately evident now. Egypt would not be "first" in anything else globally for a long time to come. It needed time and maybe even a few miracles to recover. Its own people had begun to lose sight of what the revolution was all about. The struggle to exist in a crumbling country numbed their senses and they began to fall into disunity.

Both pro- and anti-revolution groups began to search for conspiracy theories that would enable them to assign fault and find a root cause for their current financial and emotional pain. It was like a wounded person picking at his own scab because it looked so ugly. The more he picked away at it, the less chance there was for him to ever become whole again. It was painful to watch and experience, and even more painful to be a part of.

We were all guilty of being angry at each other.

But Egypt needed us now more than ever. I needed us to find clarity amid the mess and find love at a time when hate was rampant. Like an ailing parent, the country needed all of her children to bury the hatchet and focus on the nursing process.

In fact, the country needed all of its citizens—those who lived within her boundaries and those who sought their livelihoods elsewhere.

"I will not forget Egypt," I told the house. "And I will not forget you."

PART ONE

A CULTURE OF
RESISTANCE

CHAPTER ONE

MOHAMED DIAB, 33, SCREENWRITER AND FILM DIRECTOR

1.

We Egyptians have an innate talent for discussing and debating politics and breaking news; as a young Egyptian in my thirties, I was no different. I loved to partake in analyzing all things political. The only problem was, around here, one could only analyze the political situation to death within the confines of one's home, lest it lead to one's actual death.

One of the paradoxes of Egyptian society has always been that children in every household are bred on a combination of government opposition mixed with fear. This lethal combo, carefully woven in as part of the former regime's plan, results in a constant underlying feeling of fear, shame, and helplessness.

The helplessness chains you to the bed when you feel the urge to rage against the system.

The fear keeps you from walking out the door.

Fear of Amn El-Dawla, the nation's internal police force, is woven into your panic system throughout your life. You might be willing to bear arms to free Iraq but unwilling to set foot in a local demonstration against your own police units. Very few citizens would dare to oppose the government publicly; it was a death wish. And I certainly did not have one.

I studied business in college and underwent a series of struggles like every young Egyptian in my age group. I was the embodiment of depressed and repressed Egyptian youth. Even my selected major was the stereotypical specialization in Cairo of those who did not know what to do with their lives: commerce was the easiest college faculty to get accepted into, and the courses were not necessarily beyond the scope of average intelligence. I knew this well. There was no internal denial. I knew I was getting by, and I was consciously fighting against the image I had of myself.

I had no hope for my country's future and constantly revisited the common and sad Egyptian dream to live abroad anywhere beyond Egypt. Sometimes I thought it through on paper. I would map out the pros and cons into mini-alternative scenarios to my current situation. The scenarios often spun into stories. The stories grew into tales. The practice of writing these tales was a release, and that release swelled into a talent that would later give birth to a dream.

However, initially the focus was to travel down the "typical" road financially fortunate young men of my age and income level traveled on in Egypt. I graduated college unceremoniously. I landed jobs and worked different positions with no real sense of commitment. I kept initiating and abruptly dropping projects. I was a pathological entrepreneur, you might say, with no specific goal or direction. I was constantly dissatisfied and at wits' end at what to do with my lack of fulfillment. Like a knife in my gut, it slowed me down and made life quite painful.

After a failed attempt to immigrate to America, I ended up an employee in Cairo's multinational Citibank. Originally from Ismailia, a small governorate along the west bank of the Suez Canal, the Citibank position in Egypt's capital offered stability and a good income.

The bank also offered extensive training and an environment for positive personal growth. So positive, in fact, that the company had high turnover. Apparently employees tended to receive the necessary training that convinced them that they needed to do more with their lives than just work at a bank.

So following in that tradition and feeling the urge of my pregnant dream, I quit my job at the bank and began studying writing. The endeavor would ironically send me to the States to study at New York's Film Academy for two years.

That could have been it for me. I could have stayed in the States. I could have grabbed the chance to forget about my frustrations and transplant my life to a different venue. But I was determined to go back. To "make it" in Egypt made emotional sense to me. It gave my writing a mission statement.

I returned to Egypt confident and unwavering. The following few years bore several mini-victories, as I wrote the screenplays to four movies that were successful in the Egyptian box office. Confident in my own abilities, I married the woman I love, and added "husband" to my resume.

I made my directorial debut in 2010, with the controversial film *678* about sexual harassment in Egypt, and was tangled up in the positive and negative press I had received shortly before the revolution exploded. By then I had become a recognizable figure for many people, not only as a director but also as an activist for women's rights. As a result, I had thousands of followers in the social media universe.

Things were turning around slowly. The despair about Egypt's state of continuous decline was turning into a driving force, and the internal conversations in my mind began to lean toward opposing the forces that controlled the country. News of my wife's pregnancy created a sense of urgency.

I wanted to provide a homeland I could explain to this child I did not yet know. The current situation gave me no positive vocabulary to describe Egypt, however I did not allow myself to exude anything but positivity to the public that had found truth in my words.

I was married to an American Egyptian who had spent the bulk of her years on American soil. She was in a constant state of cultural shock that spilled into our everyday conversations and became a regular source of disagreements. Her complaining echoed my own sentiments, the traffic, the pollution, the difficulty of the most benign of tasks due to mere inefficacy... it seemed all too exhausting to my already troubled mind.

We instilled a new household rule that stated that complaints about Egypt in my presence were only allowed four times a day. (That included comparisons between America and Egypt.)

I couldn't blame my wife. Her complaints were often accurate, and a true reflection of her agonizing double experience. She had two homelands she loved dearly for different reasons. This was a typical feeling for dual national Egyptians who carried around with them a sense of failure when it came to Egypt in that place regular Egyptians reserved for helplessness and shame.

My own brother ended up writing the screenplay for one of the biggest blockbuster hits of recent Egyptian cinema about this American/Egyptian dilemma. The film *Black Honey* tackled dual citizens' love/hate relationship with what Egypt had to offer its countrymen at the time. It's a must-see for anyone who doesn't understand what it is like to love a country, yet grieve for its inability to catch up to the rest of the modern world.

When I became aware of Egyptian opposition leader Dr. Mohamed El Baradei in 2010, I had already been writing for locally known opposition papers such as the *Destour* (*"The Constitution"*), however attending gatherings at which El Baradei spoke made me officially a member of the opposition. My close friend Amr Salama (a film director) and I began to feel hopeful. El Baradei was not necessarily addressing all of our issues to a T, as they say, but he offered us an alternative scenario where political discourse and action were possible and within reach.

He spoke of our right to a democracy and how there was a methodology behind attaining it. He spoke of the role of local businessmen in moving the country forward and how our collective duty was to come together against corruption.

We wanted to be part of this new possibility. So Amr and I started to create online promotional videos for El Baradei when regular, state-run, television channels refused to air his views. This was my very first step in doing something directly to fight the system. That knife in my gut began to slowly ease its way out.

Another possibly counterintuitive way of opposing the status quo was the effort to include in my movies a somewhat positive depiction of Egyptian police officers. I was attempting to be optimistic in my message. I was hoping that somehow this bringing forward of the "good" officers out there may inspire the prevalent negative elements to improve their acts. I was not being hypocritical. I firmly believed that not all officers were "bad." They certainly should not be labeled as representatives of the government and the decision-making process.

Accordingly, my childhood fear of Amn El-Dawla was temporarily appeased when they became fans of my movies. I felt secure that my opposition efforts would not be misconstrued and that at least they, the officers, had seen my work and knew where I was coming from.

I was *safely* opposing. It was a delicate balancing act for those who had the best of intentions for our beloved country.

෴ ෴

If I had to pinpoint when I officially became part of the Egyptian Revolution, I would say that it was when I joined the Facebook page "Kolona Khaled Saeed" ("We Are All Khaled Saeed"), which was built to commemorate an innocent young Egyptian who suffered immense torture before dying at the hands of Egyptian police in June of 2010.

The pure injustice of his story moved me. He was seized in an internet café on bogus charges and beat to death in the middle of a street. I lost touch with that ever-present feeling of "helplessness" and began to share and voice opinions online. I could no longer be comfortable in a system that let this story happen. Khaled's painful death brought the knife right into my gut again, and the discomfort made me see that my work in film was falling short of what needed to be done.

I met a surprisingly passionate young man named Wael Ghonim at a gathering at El Baradei's home. Wael, who was head of marketing at Google Middle East and North Africa, appeared intelligent, focused, and aligned with me emotionally. We often discussed issues presented on the "Kolona Khaled Saeed" page. Amr Salama, Wael, and I became buddies, and our meetings quickly took on a Boy-Scout sort of excitement that often accompanies ventures into unchartered territories. And this was what any kind of political activism for young adults in Egypt was at that time—completely unchartered territories.

Wael's background in IT and his position at Google, coupled with the movie experience Amr and I brought to the table, made us a good media team. In essence, I believe we met the highest caliber of Egyptian youth during those early El Baradei days. Everyone who attended his sessions was nursing a budding project or involved in one way or another in an initiative of change. Our gatherings in El Baradei's home became circles of hope and sources of energy that fueled us for the remainder of the workweek.

Looking back, these gatherings were incubators for Egypt's young future politicians. We may have disagreed on some of El Baradei's issues or priorities, but El Baradei was definitely one of the main catalysts that brought mechanization to our still political waters and pumped them toward their destined channels.

Then the Church of the Saints in Alexandria was bombed on January 1, 2011 (at the alleged hands of Muslims). This shocking event, which killed twenty-three people and injured nearly one hundred others, shattered our momentum and brought it to a screeching halt. The religious break-up that the media had taught us to anticipate and dread in recent years burst to the surface, and I felt the walls closing in on me. What I had accomplished so far seemed so small compared to the larger forces at work.

Many Facebook accounts, as well as the "Kolona Khaled Saeed" page, began bearing messages of hatred and accusation between Christian and Muslim Egyptians. It was another symptom of Hosni Mubarak's divisive regime. Egypt had been home to Christians and Muslims for decades, but at the hands of a tyrant who only knew how to nurture a hateful environment, the seeds of conflict had been sown. The Mubarak regime was one of hunger and ignorance and bred nothing but envy and hate.

I felt myself sink to the bottom. I had as little hope as I'd ever had in my life in us being able to create a different Egypt than the one we had now.

My Facebook status on the third of January read: "1) I can either give in to all the pressures around me and leave Egypt to join the generation that might be known in history as the one that turned its back on the country; or 2) I can try one more time, give it my all, and possibly join a generation remembered for turning Egypt around. "

I actually wrote these options onto my Facebook page. (Modern history will be collected off of tweets, text messages, and Facebook pages: Is that not something to marvel at?)

The Facebook page "Kolona Khaled Saeed" posted a suggestion to its two hundred fifty thousand members: a peaceful protest denouncing what happened to the Christians should take place on January 7. Members were called to a public mourning, in which participants would gather silently, dressed in black at night on the Kasr El Nile Bridge that leads to Midan El Tahrir ("Liberation Square").

I was relieved that some plan was in place, and I excitedly assigned myself a role in this noble nighttime protest. I circulated videos Amr and I had made to paint a clear picture of why all Egyptians should show solidarity with our Christian brethren.

On the night of the protest, on my way to the bridge, it dawned on me that I wasn't really seeing any people heading there with me. Pedestrians to my right and left wore regular clothing and chatted among themselves. When I reached the end of the bridge and headed toward the Saad Zaghlool Statue, the official meeting point, it became apparent that only 250 people had showed up. I would later learn that the maximum number of people who gathered in Cairo that day was estimated at a meager five hundred.

I stayed only half an hour and then all of us slowly started to slip away, sadly heading back to our homes and into our beds. In my bed that night, with my pregnant wife sleeping next to me, the chains of helplessness dangled menacingly, their shackles open and ready.

Then a complete miracle appeared, almost out of nowhere. On the 14th of January, a mere week after the failed mourning/ protest, beautiful Tunisia brushed oppression off its shoulders and sent out the brightest beacon of hope to hit the Arab world in over fifty years.

It is my belief that Egypt had been ready for its revolution for at least ten years. But it took Tunis to make the chains that shackled every Egyptian simultaneously open and fall to the ground. The resounding clank awoke the entire nation.

On that glorious day, my Facebook status read: "Our ordeal appears to be as good as over. It is now only a matter of time. A call to all hypocrites who have benefitted from the status quo; please start to slowly side with the righteous now, to secure a future in this, soon to be blessed, free country for your families and loved ones."

My prophecy took very little time to materialize. I believe that any official holiday that followed Tunisia's liberation would have resulted in mass demonstrations. However, as part of the almighty's well-crafted screenplay, the upcoming historic holiday of the 25th of January just happened to be "Police Day", a national holiday—and the designated day for a mass protest against the current regime.

The Facebook page "Kolona Khaled Saeed" started a massive campaign calling on all Egyptian Facebook users to come forward in resistance, and started to send mass e-mails to mailboxes registered under Arabic names, as well. The message was for Egyptians to take to the streets on January 25th, and gain back what was rightfully theirs from a government that had overstayed its welcome.

The page listed its first goal to be to remove the Minister of Interior Affairs, believed by most Egyptians to be the source of all torture and violence in Egyptian prisons.

I made videos encouraging people to participate. I wrote an article in the *Fajr* opposition newspaper inviting people to imagine what it would be like to be a Tunisian today who hadn't participated in the Jasmine Revolution. Wouldn't they have been dying to be part of it? Wouldn't they have wanted to proudly tell the tale to their children and grandchildren? I warned them to not make the same mistake. The article appealed to all Egyptians to go out in defiance on the twenty-fifth, lest they miss creating history like those Tunisians who opted to stay home.

Then I noticed something curious. The administrator of the Khaled Saeed page (still anonymous at the time) appeared to have access to my Facebook page. He or she seemed to share and/or copy all my links and post them to the Khaled Saeed page as soon as I posted them. It occurred to me that I probably knew this person, and he or she was on my contact list. I found it interesting, but knew that it would take a while for someone running such a powerful opposition page to gain the necessary confidence to reveal his/her identity, especially to a public person like me.

So on a whim, I posted to my page: "To the administrator of the Khaled Saeed page. I have a feeling you are an acquaintance of mine. If you value my opinion, please do not focus the demonstrations on police hatred or removing certain members of government. Instead follow Tunisia's road map and focus on the 'head' of the system."

Later I would learn that the page's incognito administrator was none other than Wael Ghonim, and that he had read my message and assumed that I knew his identity and that I was being secretive to preserve *his* anonymity. He explained that he and Mostafa El Naggar (one of the most important orchestrators of the page) went back and forth on whether or not to call their initiative a "revolution." They viewed it as a powerful word—and a grave responsibility. They struggled with the notion of placing the ceiling of their demands at the removal of the Minister of Interior Affairs or whether they should dare to go to the very top and target Mubarak himself. They worried about protestor safety and pushing the regime too far. However, they also worried that meager numbers would show up making their demands all too ridiculous.

I don't know if my statement made a difference. They were the ones calling the shots in terms of where protesters should meet, and they were the ones giving the designated days of protest names such as "The Friday of Anger" and "The Tuesday of 1 Million." I believe that their confidence in what to *call* it and what to *demand* swelled with the eruption of passion that took place before them on the streets of Cairo and all around the country.

Indeed, on the twenty-fifth, Wael, Amr, Mostafa, and I witnessed a volcano of Egyptians who hit the ground chanting *"Al shaab yoreed isqat el nizam"* ("The people demand the fall of the regime!") spontaneously, in unison, *without being directed.*

I turned to my friends with confidence and restated my Facebook posting: "Our ordeal is over. It is a mere matter of time." But even then, Wael did not come forward and admit that he was the administrator of the Khaled Saeed page. He was still very afraid. His fear was so great that earlier that day, when I called him (confident that he could not change my fortitude in going to the demonstrations even if he wanted to), he put on an act to deter me from going to the protests, saying that they might not be all that important.

∽ ∽

On the 25th of January in juxtaposition to the scant five hundred people who turned up for the "Mourning Protests," one hundred thousand Egyptians took to the streets to call for the end of Mubarak's decaying regime. It was a sight that hit every Egyptian seated in his living room straight on the head, forcing him or her to take that head and move it out of the house where it could speak its mind once and for all.

The community of Tahrir Square, especially on the 25th of January, was as close to utopian as I believe is humanly possible. One must remember that the hundred thousand who turned up that Tuesday were mostly educated people, with access to the Internet. Their message would *later* bring in the masses, but this very first group was the core of "good" and "decent" Egyptians. *They* sang the songs that moved the population onto the dance floor as the battle began to take form.

If a protester attempted to light a fire, you would see a random veiled woman jump out and remind him, *"Silmia, silmia!"* ("Peaceful, peaceful!"), and the man would immediately heed her admonition. You would also see women in jeans and T-shirts standing side by side with male protesters and treated with care and respect. In a different setting in Egypt, with such a mix of economic levels and different beliefs, women dressed in such attire would often be stared at, perhaps be on the receiving end of some sexist comments and in some rare cases harassed.

It dawned on me that these people had gathered here because of love—love for each other and for their country.

In the past, Mubarak's regime had kept us compliant through hate. We hated the regime, but we also hated each other for accepting it. We hated the thieves who took our money, but the hatred justified us doing the same to each other. Egyptian thieves were always able to sleep through the night with a clear conscience because they believed the very people they stole from were thieves as well. Sexual harassers felt no shame or guilt because they believed all women were whores who deserved it.

The waving of Egyptian flags that Tuesday fanned the flames of the strong current of emotion that led protesters from the safety of their homes to the square. They were united in the dream of a country they could love the way their parents had. They longed for an Egypt that was proud of them—and that they could be proud of.

Police did not attack the flag-bearing crowds, at least not at first. They followed orders to let the protests happen. But you could see the surprise in their eyes as the square filled and the voices rocked the concrete. In the beginning the ratio of police to protesters was two hundred to one, but that quickly changed. As protesters flocked to the square, police were pushed out, but sadly, the day still ended with savage beatings from the police shortly before midnight.

The numbers decreased on the Wednesday and Thursday of the first week of protests, but swelled again on Friday. In the Middle East, Friday and Saturday are the official weekend days, as opposed to the West's Saturday and Sunday. It would become apparent as the weeks passed that the strategy of the revolution, loosely coordinated by the Khaled Saeed page, focused on Tuesdays and Fridays as days of significance.

The first Thursday, January 27, marked an event that shook and motivated me to the core. Wael Ghonim, our friend from the El Baradei meetings, was reported missing by his wife and family. Apparently, he had left for the protests and never returned home. At that point, still unaware of Wael's position in the Khaled Saeed page, my responsibility in the movement suddenly expanded, as I felt the urgency of having a strategy for these dangerous times. The fight had just begun to turn ominously ugly, and fear motivated me to intensify my role.

My routine was to protest by day and write articles and appear on television broadcasts by night. The goal was to use my celebrity to keep the message alive. People like me were not running the show by any means. We were merely suggesting directions, and the *people* made the decision to follow them or not.

Every day on the ground was a surprise to all those involved. The spontaneity and harmony of the crowds dictated the scene and claimed the spoils. But Friday, January 28, stands out as one of the most violent days of the revolution—and one of the worst days in Egyptian history.

❧   ❧

As I left my house that Friday, I kissed my wife and burst into tears, overwhelmed by the apprehension of what was about to take place.

All signs that day pointed toward a violent confrontation, which the Khaled Saeed page labeled *Yowm El Ghadab* ("The Friday of Anger"). Announcements were made on state-run media that the government would be cutting off all cell phone and internet services.

They were preparing to beat us in the dark.

My tears were not merely because of the personal danger I might face, but rather a show of mourning in advance for the lives that I knew would inevitably be lost.

I remembered an article I wrote for the *Fajr* newspaper on the twenty-fourth that was written in a note-like format to my parents and friends. It explained the reasons why I thought participation in the demonstrations was necessary, and how I would be intentionally disobeying all the rules that my parents had put in place for my safety throughout my life. It outlined how I was willing to die that day.

On the morning of Yowm El Ghadab, I knew that my words in that article would be tested, and I knew that this time, all those on the way to Liberation Square were risking their lives, whether they were aware of that or not. The government had already issued a warning to people not to attempt to participate in the protest after the Friday prayers.

Knowing that the prayers would draw people in the hundreds, as they did every week, put the police at a disadvantage from the start. They could not openly keep people from praying, but by allowing them to pray they automatically had a crowd amassed. Once out of their homes, the people were unlikely to go home without attempting to emulate the beautiful, brave miracle they had seen on their television sets January 25th.

The government's decision to cut off cell phone services and the Internet was considered brazen. Though the government would claim that this decision was a "normal" security measure that was within its "rights.", citizens were highly offended.

Consequently, as if on cue, most Egyptians became defiant. The fear barrier was broken then and there, and there was no going back.

But if we were going forward, what were we going toward? To many of us, we were headed into a void.

The unknown.

I was in my thirties and all I had ever known was Egypt's Mubarak. What else was out there? Would things get better or worse? If they got worse, would it be perceived as my fault, or maybe the fault of everyone who promoted and pushed this course of action?

These questions flashed through my head as I got closer to the square and started to notice the sea of people moving with me. I brushed my fears aside, knowing for certain that this was a defining moment in Egyptian history, and that those who chose to be absent would later on regret it.

As the day unfolded I could clearly see it morph into a milestone in the series of events that made the revolution what it was. I met up with my close friend Moez Masoud, a well-known religious scholar and television-show host. He had returned from Cambridge, where he was completing work on his thesis, to take part in the demonstrations. The twenty-eighth would be his first day to participate.

The demonstrations quickly took a dramatically violent turn as police started to assault demonstrators. Tear gas fumes were thick and regularly replenished. Though this would later be considered the first day that the police were officially defeated in the square, the night would see a lot of deaths and injury before that final outcome was achieved.

Anti-riot forces would soon realize that instead of acting as a deterrent, the gas, rubber bullets, and live ammunition seemed to compel people to continue. News started to spread that buildings housing the National Democratic Party and police stations across governorates in Egypt were being burned to the ground.

News of violence beyond Tahrir prompted me to call home from the nearest landline I could find. My wife was crying hysterically and said that all homes in our area were being attacked by looters. Unable to leave at that specific moment—because of the threat of snipers—Moez and I found reporters on the scene and decided to make use of our celebrity. We described to the satellite channel what was happening and hoped that being public figures lent authenticity to what we were reporting.

I also described my phone call to my wife to viewers and accused the government and the National Democratic Party of intentionally letting security measures slip in residential neighborhoods to convince people that the demonstrations were resulting in a shortage of police and a security crisis.

Indeed, the day's events were *designed* to create a sense of fear and chaos to make citizens long for the serenity of civic compliance. The speed at which rumors of kidnappings, rapes, and worse traveled by word of mouth rivaled that of Facebook and text messages. Citizens who were on the outskirts of the protests, in terms of their participation and level of involvement, and glued to television sets across Egypt, succeeded in creating the biggest mass panic attack this country had ever seen.

In Tahrir, we were not buying it. Moez and I remained in the square until news of a television appearance by the president motivated us to find a way to view it firsthand. We headed for Moez's empty house. (He'd evacuated his family to his mother-in-law's as a safety measure before he left for the protests.)

As Mubarak spoke of the democratic existence he had set up for us, and we had abused, Egyptians lost their lives in the hundreds on Egypt's streets, as police liberally employed live ammunition. Sunrise marked the end of one of the most vicious nights in Egyptian history. However, it also recorded the first signs of the impending triumph of the Egyptians. Their will to take over the square, with all the symbolism it represented, began to dwarf the forces of riot police.

What had happened in Tunis on the fourteenth happened on the twenty-eighth in Egypt—the obvious dismantling of the governing system. We all expected the president to announce his abdication the very next day.

Community committees for safety began to form and Egyptian citizens took to the streets to guard property and organize traffic as a tense sense of ownership began to spread. Come Saturday morning, international analysts and journalists alike would spend the bulk of their time on the air debating one vital issue of the Friday of Anger: Was the burning of NDP buildings and police stations in tandem all over the country, within hours of each other, planned or spontaneous?

I believe it was neither.

The people were angry and the evidence of victory was fluid. Protestors who experienced tear gas, rubber bullets, live ammunition, and death in battle for the first time in their lives hungered for signs that their fight was accomplishing something. So, for example, when people in Ismailia heard of the Suez NDP being burned, they felt the need to do the same as a way of planting their struggle's figurative flag on an imaginary frontier.

Similarly, police stations were an easily identifiable personification of the system, which made them vulnerable targets. The government's attempt to stamp out the revolt made the fires spread to its own governing body, and it began to lose ground with the same speed that the martyrs' souls lost their bodies.

As news of the lack of police in the square spread, and with it the stories of those who lost their lives, limbs, or loved ones over the twenty-four hours of the Friday of Anger, people began to leave their homes and head to the square. The twenty-ninth was witnessing quite a buildup.

Local, state-run media falsified the numbers on the streets to make them appear insignificant and began to spread more lies about protesters being paid to demolish the country. So-called "foreign agents" and the "Muslim Brotherhood" became patsies. The stories spun so far-fetched and hysterical, especially when juxtaposed with relatively accurate international news channels' reports, that the local media started to lose all credibility. Some protests and demonstrations were actually directly focusing on dismantling Egypt's journalists' union since it was a living, breathing symbol of corruption and lies.

The government instructed local, state-run media to propagandize that protesters should accept whatever the president had offered in his speech. They began to spread the rumor that the crowds in Tahrir were violent and unsafe, including to protesters. They entertained theories of people being spies and having "foreign agendas."

They offered advice for protesters seeking safety and gave them hypothetical exit routes, implying that they were stuck against their will in Liberation Square.

I was going crazy with all the ways I wanted to refute their bogus information. But with the Internet gone and us physically stuck in the square, there was little to be done until we found the next journalist on location.

The El Arabiya television station was actually located in Tahrir. Moez and I decided to go there and see how we could get some information out.

MOHAMED SHAWKY, 26, MUSLIM BROTHERHOOD/ SIXTH OF APRIL ACTIVIST

2.

My name is Mohamed Shawky. I am twenty-six years old. I have been married for three years, and I am the father of Eiad, who is two years old. I have a bachelor's degree in social services, but I work in e-marketing for Lowein Coffee House.

I am a member of the Muslim Brotherhood, a political opposition party, and this party has given my life purpose.

That statement alone, before January 25, 2011, would have been grounds for extensive torture sessions.

I grew up in a small rural town called Mansoura, and the Brotherhood had a strong presence there. The Brotherhood has a strong presence everywhere in Egypt. *We* come from all professions; from physicians to garbage collectors, the variety and scope are endless.

When I joined in 2000, I was not into politics, and that was not what the Brotherhood was offering me at the time. You see, the Brotherhood is about more than just politics, and contrary to common beliefs, it is not solely religious, either. The Brotherhood offered the means to be involved in something that made my life of value to those around me, as opposed to benefitting just my immediate family and me. It had its own literature that prospective members were required to read, and for me, *that* was the first educational experience about which I was ever passionate.

The Muslim Brotherhood was the closest I had ever gotten to a Social Security-type setup in the sense that American people understand it. My Egyptian national ID did not grant me any rights— apart from the right to be arrested for no reason and receive no medical care and no unemployment compensation. My own citizenship offered me no security whatsoever as a young man.

The Brotherhood, on the other hand, offered opportunity, mentorship, and spiritual guidance to those who wished to join. You could be active with the organization in a plethora of fields ranging from development to the arts.

The core of its ideology is the Islamic religion but believe me, that is not a limitation to its members. The way the Brotherhood sees it, Islam is a way of life. It is highly adaptable and applicable to modern life—*if* you know what is to be done with it. I am a firm believer in this, though I know it scares some people.

Did we discuss Israel and Palestine in our meetings? Of course. That is a topic you are raised to empathize with in every household in the Middle East, even in Israel itself. The Brotherhood discussed Jerusalem often and held members together with the emotional unity that topic presented. That doesn't mean I am one who hates those of the Jewish faith and wishes them harm. They are our cousins. It does mean, however, that I see fault in the current set-up the State of Israel has presented Palestinians, and I wish that my own country gave us voice to discuss it in the international political arena.

The Brotherhood does not conduct suicide bombings or any other kind of violence, not just because it is wrong but also simply because we don't have to. Please, do not confuse us with the Gamaat Islamiya ("The Muslim Group"), a bastardized offshoot of the Brotherhood. We are no more related to that group than Frankenstein was to mankind.

Bombings and violence are for the desperate, those who have no other route. Our group has enough members to comprise the population of a small country, and have been around since 1923, when Egypt was a kingdom, so we have other avenues, believe me. The only reason why one's membership in the Brotherhood was not always publicly divulged was to protect those in lower ranks from the regime and ensure the longevity of their productivity within the group.

We are interested in a true *political* presence that is out in the open. That is why from the very beginning, it was all about Maglis El Shaab ("The People's Assembly") and how we could get the majority of seats in it. This was the first step to raising awareness in how a seat based on votes equaled a voice in the country. To have a voice was to have a say in things, and therefore meant you could protect your own rights. That basic message was revolutionary in Egypt at the time.

Look at me in my blue jeans and T-shirt. I would not catch your attention if I were standing among those waiting for a bus.

I love my wife and care for the kind of world I offer my son.

I am not apathetic and I believe that one person *can* make a difference no matter his faith or background.

I am not a terrorist.

I am a young man with beliefs.

I believe in the Egyptian people and their ability to be free, proud, and productive.

In 2000, I was a kid, but I already knew that Mubarak's Egypt, and even as far back as Nasser's Egypt, had no room for political participation by regular citizens. The Egyptians would say, *"Imshi ganb el heit"* ("Walk as close to the wall as possible") so that you would not be exposed to the government's long-reaching arm. In other words, lay low, stay out of sight. We had reached a level of fear and compliance that we were now told to walk *inside* the wall to ensure our safety. It was better if we basically ceased to exist altogether.

You did not want your name in a file with Amn El-Dawla. Just a few papers in that file would land you behind bars indefinitely. Muslim Brotherhood ties were the worst you could get caught with.

The government hated the Brotherhood with a vengeance. It hated the Brotherhood's organized ranks and personal funding abilities. But most of all, it hated that the Brotherhood's main focus was to spread "awareness."

The Brotherhood taught its members that there was a big difference between being *God-fearing* men and simply *fearing* men. It taught us that a good Muslim sought the advancement of his/her community through grassroots involvement and outreach to the impoverished. With the Brotherhood, I felt like a citizen, and was willing to do whatever I could to further their cause.

∽ ∽

There was an intricate system for every wannabe member of the Brotherhood. First, you got educated. There were levels akin to a K-12 system through which prospective members had to complete before being allowed further access to the organization's activities.

With the completion of each curriculum level, you moved up a notch until you attained an actual position. Positions were divided from micro to macro, by area, town, governorate, and so on. You could be active in improving Egypt at any level to which you earned the right to commit yourself, in whatever field you were best skilled in.

Through this effort, you brought yourself closer to God's purpose for your existence. You were his ambassador on earth and your time a gift from the almighty for the purpose of helping all those around you. Nothing was considered too small a task or of lesser value than anything else.

And, so I stood proud on my college campus in 2005 with Brotherhood-related fliers in hand, willing to risk my reputation as a bright, energetic, and accomplished student. I already had a presence in the Student Union and was head of what we called a "student family" on campus. I helped put together student-led art galleries and set up recreational and educational field trips for the different faculties in my college. I wasn't one to just sit there and focus solely on academics. You could say I stood to lose my standing with the faculty *and* the students by my insistence on taking my active nature to a different level.

The Muslim Brotherhood has three axes of involvement: the spiritual and prayer, morality and behavior, and political movement.

My college days were divided between attending classes and catching Brotherhood meetings. Between the three axes, I was attending close to a meeting a day, and hence was earning a parallel degree in activism, Brotherhood-style.

It became obvious to me that even within university walls, the administrators started to catch up on the identities of Brotherhood students, and slowly made sure that they were left out of activities and events. That motivated me further. Their resistance was proof that the system was biased. That was unacceptable to me.

Just completely unacceptable.

Any individual who worked hard to achieve something he/she believed in, that benefitted others and harmed no one, should not be silenced just because he/she chose to do things differently and dared to be vocal about it.

This driving force led me straight to my first arrest. I had been promoted up the Brotherhood ranks to a security officer within my college department. That meant that I was responsible for the safety of other Brotherhood members in this department.

One day, when we were trying to market a fundraiser for the Brotherhood, I noticed that another member was being careless. We had been trained not to stand alone while distributing fliers, or stand in the same area for a long period of time, lest we draw attention to ourselves and get caught. This particular member had been doing just that.

As I approached to tell him he was being watched and he should get rid of the fliers he had on him, two university security guards approached, grabbed us, and escorted us off campus to where a police truck was waiting. Campus security guards in universities across Egypt were known to shamelessly act as the government's informants, and they enjoyed the power of their positions.

I remember thinking to myself, they did it all too quickly...no one saw us get arrested. The Brotherhood had no knowledge of the arrest and couldn't help to get us out. My parents were unaware of my affiliation to the group or the potentially dangerous activities in which I participated. Even if they had known, I spent weekdays in the college dormitory, and it would take them a few days to find out that I never made it back to my room.

As the police aggressively pushed us into the truck, my heart was beating hard in my throat and my knees were literally knocking together. It was only four o'clock in the afternoon.

The truck stopped in front of a large, ominous building downtown. We were partly pushed and dragged up the steps to a reception area, where the officers quickly separated us. I was taken to a room that resembled the interrogation rooms you see in the movies. It had a table in the middle and a large mirror on the wall.

I was left there for at least three hours.

During that period, I had enough time to talk myself through what I would say. I reminded myself that I was an "A" student who had never been caught doing anything wrong before. All I had to do was stick with the story that this was my first time, and that I didn't realize the implications of giving out those particular fliers.

I remembered that my wallet was full of business cards of Brotherhood members and my cell phone was full of their numbers. I even had some pictures saved to the phone that could get me in trouble. I requested to go to the bathroom. It was about three hours into my detainment, so it didn't look too suspicious.

In the bathroom I quickly deleted all numbers and pictures from my phone and cut up the business cards and flushed them down the toilet. I did this with record speed. So fast, in fact, that I realized that now my phone appeared conspicuously empty. I started to save whatever numbers I had committed to memory, so I could at least claim I had a new phone and I didn't have my complete contact list saved yet.

Back in the room, I figured that I was probably being watched through the mirror. I quickly decided that instead of just sitting there I should take out my books and work on my assignments. I figured it would help calm me down and it would support my image as a hard-working student. An officer quickly came in and shouted, "What the hell do you think you are doing?" I answered, "Studying until I am allowed to go. When do you think that will be?" The officer laughed and said something to the effect of, "When hell freezes."

The next officer to enter the room was a serious but non-threatening man. His requests were simple: He wanted names and locations of meetings and any information about future Brotherhood plans.

"The Muslim Brotherhood has a presence on campus?" I asked in a shrill voice. "Is that what you thought I was doing? Working for them?" I looked at him in a panicked, desperate manner and added, "I...I am a student in the social services department. You will ruin my reputation with these allegations. You will ruin me!"

The officer was surprised by my reaction and seemed to believe me. His eyes showed he had no reason not to believe my account of being involved in the fundraiser as a first-timer. His tone became noticeably calmer, but he kept me in the room till 3:00 am none-theless and repeated the same questions across the 10 hours I spent in the holding room. I stuck to my story.

When I was finally released in the early hours of dawn, I met with my friend—the guy I was arrested with—at the front steps of the Amn El-Dawla building. He was standing with his parents, who were in tears. They had been looking for us all night after they had heard from someone at school that we were seen with university security.

Assuming the worst, they came to the Amn El-Dawla building and were told that we were not inside. Not knowing where else to search, they desperately sat on the steps until the wee hours of the morning, when we finally walked out.

When I walked into my dorm room, I fell into bed without changing my clothes and with my book bag still on my shoulder.

The last thought to cross my mind was that I really should tell my parents what I was doing.

〜 〜

My parents' interrogation was in some ways worse than what happened at Amn El-Dawla. My heart was broken by the expression on my father's face. He was stricken with what appeared to be a mixture of panic and disappointment in my choices. Whenever they were unhappy with me, I felt my resolve stumble a little. I did not want to burden them.

My father would not address me directly. Instead he faced my mother and said, "Your son is now with the Brotherhood. The police will take him from you and you will never see him again. They will take him from you, torture and maim him, and you will have a cripple as your son. Is that what you want for him?"

My mother's face lost all its color and she grabbed onto my arm and said, "Please son, have mercy on our hearts. We are too old for this."

I gently took her hand off of my arm, held it in my hand, and looked her in the eyes and said, "Mother, don't tell me not to do something because it is dangerous. Tell me not to do it because it is wrong. Is it wrong, Mother? Is it wrong to want something better? Is it?" She looked away silently, and in her silence was my answer.

My father failed to come up with an adequate answer, too, and gave up. He never spoke to me about it again. He deferred the discussion to his prayers and filed his worries with God.

My parents reluctantly gave in and prayed for my safety, and I was immensely thankful for their stance. A fellow Brotherhood member's father used to hang him from his feet from a hook in the ceiling formerly used to hold a chandelier. The father thought it better that *he* hurt his son with his own hands than have Amn El-Dawla do it.

For me, it was simple. There was a ceiling to what the government could do to me, no matter how ugly it was. Their worst was something I believed I could handle.

I would rationalize it to myself: If they killed me, I would go straight to heaven. If they put me in jail, it was an opportunity from God to prove my devotion to him. If they beat me up, well…I could just as well get beaten up walking down the street, so there was no sense living my life trying to avoid a beating.

So I continued my involvement in the Brotherhood, and started to educate myself beyond its teachings and readings. I began to find material by El Baradei online. A budding leader of change who was highly accomplished in the United States, El Baradei was an example of how far Egyptians could go when given a chance and the proper environment. I found his words, on citizen's rights and our potential as a nation if we are led properly, refreshingly logical and inspiring.

When I listened to him, I could see a clear path to my efforts. I felt that the end goal was within reach. It comforted me that someone of his stature and level of education believed there was hope for Egypt. I started to read about other opposition movements dedicated to change. Many members of the Brotherhood were affiliated with other groups as well. I made a mental note to expand my scope if I found a group that inspired me.

I ended up marrying into the Brotherhood, which was not uncommon for members. The daughter of a senior member became my wife as soon as I graduated from college. I fell deeply in love with her. She was the beautiful grouping of everything I ever wanted in a woman. The fact that she was from a Brotherhood family was like icing on the cake.

We were blessed with our son, Eiad, within the first year of our marriage and moved to Cairo together as a family.

In Cairo, my involvement was as active as ever. By 2006, I had heard of the *Kefaya* ("Enough") movement and was mesmerized by the courageous concept of protesting in the streets. I watched in envy on TV as Kefaya members were dragged in defiance across the pavement with their self-placed black duct tape across their mouths, with the word "Kefaya" written on them, signifying the silencing of truth by the government.

The Brotherhood at that point refused the idea of chanting, "Down, down with Hosni Mubarak," because its religious ideology prohibited public insults against a Muslim head of state. Still, to me, what Kefaya was doing appeared liberating. I wanted the opportunity to scream it from the top of my lungs in the streets; how cathartic that would be!

I had so much to scream about. I had witnessed firsthand the rigged assembly elections, in which a Brotherhood candidate would have forty thousand votes guaranteed and then fail against the National Democratic Party's candidate by fifty thousand votes in an area that only had forty-five thousand people.

I had seen my own father's name signed on a voting attendance roster when I knew he did not vote that day. I had even seen the names of individuals who had passed away signed onto voting attendance rosters. I had seen a friend die from injuries sustained in a police beating during the 2005 farce of a presidential election. His bloodied face never left my memory, especially when the presidential elections ended with Hosni Mubarak winning a ridiculous 99.9-percent majority. To protest in the street was the next level, and I was entirely ready for it.

In 2008, the "Sixth of April" movement came to the forefront and caught my eye immediately. At this point Facebook and Twitter were necessary tools for any activist worth his salt. One of the main speakers for the Sixth of April movement was a young woman named Israa Abd El Fatah, and her YouTube videos would circulate on Facebook and Twitter shaming and motivating young men into "growing a spine," so to speak.

Israa seemed to be the online representative for the core cause of Sixth of April movement, which was the workers' strike in the small, rural town of Mahala, which protested against insanely low salaries and recent rises in food and bread prices. She told us tales of the Mahala people's bravery and the brutality of police against them. She chided the people of Cairo for being disconnected and lacking the sense of solidarity needed for this country to progress.

In her videos, she appeared small and her background surroundings humble, but her words would jump out of the screen and into your head, and you couldn't help but be haunted by them through the night.

I thought of her words when I hugged my son, Eiad, and sang to him at night. I thought of her words when I caught the bus to work in the morning and watched the hustle and bustle of Cairo from the window. Her voice became my motivation, and I joined the Cairo branch of the Sixth of April movement. This branch called itself the "Sixth of April Youth Opposition Movement."

My dream of joining live protests started to become part of my regular reality. At that time, a typical protest meant one thousand of us against ten thousand riot police. Being hit by batons and tear gassed became part of the "workweek," and my wife grew accustom to the sight of my bruised face and messed-up clothes. Because of her family background, she took it all in stride.

I juggled work, family, and my struggle to be part of a better Egypt. My activism resume at this point included some minor detainments during recent protests and a relatively popular blog. I was the man I wanted to be and, though the apparent futility of the fight brought me down at times, my spirit was renewed with every new friend that joined our Facebook page or a new member in one of our meetings.

∞ ∞

The Mahala protests that had inspired the Sixth of April movement became an example of the cycle activists went through with the Egyptian governmental system. Though at face value, the movement took a step forward in raising the Egyptian people's expectations of what kind of civil disobedience is possible, it fell short in terms of the "real" results it accomplished.

The prime minister himself played a role in the government's sham, which portrayed the workers winning and their salaries increased. This was done because news of these protests had reached the international political arena, and the government was under pressure to act like *some* exercise of democratic response had taken place.

However, whatever the government raised in workers' salaries, it consequently exacted in taxes and increased prices, rendering any relief nonexistent. Furthermore, it sent the indirect message to the people of Mahala that the government was prepared to play the game, and the activists would lose the fight and a few lives and limbs in the process.

This gave birth to the sole strategy of the Sixth of April movement, which was for its core members' numbers to multiply online rapidly. The idea was, the larger our number, and the bigger our protests, the harder it would be for the world to look away. At one point, when the numbers online started to look impressive, a female member from the group built up the courage to suggest that the online group hold its first face-to-face meeting.

These early meetings focused on planning organized protests in front of official buildings demanding that the government free the Mahala activists who were still in custody. Some of the detainees had been granted court orders for their release, but the prisons brazenly refused to let them out.

To show that the spirit was shared across Egypt, Sixth of April branches started opening up beyond Cairo and Mahala, into other governorates and small towns throughout the country. Mini-protests would sprout here and there in the name of the movement, and civic activism began to slowly become something that Egyptians at least heard about, even if they did not yet have a full understanding of it.

To bring in more and more people, the group decided that raising awareness of the scope of the government's corruption was key. My role was to be part of a core group that uncovered corruption wherever I could find it. In that sense I became a rogue reporter, camera in hand, and a slew of online articles as my signature participatory course of action.

For some naïve reason, I didn't feel the threat of an arrest looming. The government did not appear to mind Sixth of April movement too much. It treated the group as a minor nuisance. Every time the regime saw the movement gathering its members, it would scatter them apart with a somewhat lazy show of force, but no real arrests were initially made.

Apart from El Baradei being the group's unofficial "guru," and his teachings ingrained into their creed, Sixth of April had no announced goal. It appeared to the non-discerning eye to be disorganized and nomadic in its affiliations. At times it would participate in the Brotherhood's movements, at other times with a women's rights cause, and then it would take to the streets to support El Baradei's reformist coalition protests. It seemed spread too thin to have any real effect on the status quo.

As an activist, it paid off in these times to be affiliated to the Brotherhood. Though it was the most dangerous association you could have, it had a lot of pull. An obvious example was El Baradei's attempt to gather signatures for his seven demands for political reform, which were widely published in independent Egyptian newspapers.

El Baradei gathered an impressive two hundred thousand signatures, which included ID numbers that showed that people stood behind their signatures by letting their identities be known. When the Brotherhood agreed to support these seven demands by actively taking part in the signature-gathering process, it collected eight hundred thousand more signatures in a mere couple of months.

Nevertheless, personally, it felt like a natural evolution to slowly shift from my Mansoura Brotherhood days into a lower-profile Sixth of April activist. That seemed a less dangerous position to be in as a married man and father, and at the same time it did not compromise my non-liberal Brotherhood values too much. Sixth of April was open to all faiths, and did not attach itself to a single ideology, which in and of itself showed a newfound degree of flexibility on my end.

I had settled into my Cairo identity for the time being and was just starting to get comfortable when the tragedy of young Alexandrian Khaled Saeed took place.

A horrific head shot of his severely beaten face had surfaced online. El Baradei had personally sympathized with the case, and

Khaled became the embodiment of the torturous course that was the Egyptian experience.

Activists organized their own funeral for Khaled after police had forced his family to bury him in silence with no one in attendance. They lined the shores of Alexandria's main beach promenades, and in Cairo they lined the shores of the Nile for miles and miles. Young men and women held the Quran and the Bible and prayed until they received word by phone to leave their prayers and group together in protest.

Thousands protested in Khaled's neighborhood, and emotions were inflamed at the sight of his broken-down family, mauled with grief. The two officers involved in the beatings had been heckling the family publicly, and claimed that Khaled was a drug dealer, who choked on a marijuana joint when attempting to conceal evidence from police. Many of the chants vehemently called for justice from the corrupt Alexandrian police force.

A Facebook page called "Kolona Khaled Saeed" emerged with a strong presence online. It became an online podium for my posts about government corruption, and I frequented it regularly. It played an educational role for regular readers. Members of the page exchanged articles and video links. We posted meetings for different groups, announced our minor triumphs, and shared our many defeats.

We had found our form of group therapy, but we were doing much more than just letting off steam.

∾   ∾

In 2010 my pet corruption-fighting project was the upcoming parliamentary elections. The Brotherhood was pushing forward solid candidates that had their own following, and we were confident that we could win a fair share of seats.

I was all set with my camera and some fake documents, to get me into the voting halls. My target location was the Hadayek El Obba voting zone in central Cairo, set up within a high-school building. I didn't want to miss anything, so at 7:00 a.m. I was already at my post at the door, and I intended to stay there until 7:00 p.m. I clicked away as the day progressed. I took pictures of anything I thought was unusual. I was uploading the images from my phone directly to my online blog in case I got arrested before I reached my home.

There was a reason I had forged my way into the voting stalls without a voter ID. Obtaining this ID entailed a process so tedious and bureaucratic that it successfully deterred people from voting. Egypt had reached such a state of electoral apathy that only 10 percent of the population was actively registered to vote.

As the day appeared to come to an end and the sun was going down, I witnessed firsthand the government serpent's arrival to swallow the people's voices. A truck full of plainclothes, thuggish characters arrived at the building. The license plates of the trunk at the front and back were covered in newspaper. The characters ran into the building, and the police quickly barricaded the door so no one else could enter.

When I attempted to squeeze my way in, a policeman grabbed me and shoved me to the ground in front of the parked, empty truck and left me there. I tore the newspaper off of the front license plate and took a picture of what was on it. The license plate looked strange and was fastened on with new bolts. I crawled to the back of the truck and unwrapped the rear license plate, and then realized that they were two different plates, indicating that one or both of them were fakes.

By nightfall, when seated at my computer uploading the remaining images from my camera onto various activism sites, I realized that other people had similar images and footage from all over the country. The parliamentary elections were but a façade, and it was all published online, yet no one could do anything about it.

I saw videos of NDP members with knives manning the entrances of voting stations. I saw images of dead bodies a few feet away from police stations right after the elections came to a close. There were election casualties everywhere, ten here and seven there—as if this was a normal part of the electoral process. I remember thinking that the government was getting brazenly sloppy, and our acceptance of this was a crying shame.

The next morning the government announced the NDP's smashing victory with a majority of the votes. The message was plain: *We* rigged it and *you* will accept it. We don't even have to make the numbers pretty, like we did in the past.

That was their stand. Not a single non-NDP candidate won the first round. Unbelievable! Literally, unbelievable. I started calling my Brotherhood connections and ranting. We needed to boycott future elections and call for investigations.

Opposition parties went wild over the results in the papers, but the government nonchalantly moved forward to the second round, which pitted individuals with the highest votes in their areas in the first round against each other. In the past, when corruption was still motivated to don sheep's clothing, a good number of Brotherhood candidates would win in the very first round.

The Brotherhood boycotted the second phase of the election, deeming it a useless charade. Other opposition parties followed suit and were widely absent from the process to prove their solidarity and lack of faith in the system. On the other hand, NDP candidates saw this as an opportunity to seek personal gain for themselves by running against each other and seeing who could get a piece of the abandoned pie.

I remember thinking that was the perfect time for a short break for me and my family, since the elections were solely NDP candidates against NDP candidates, there was no need for me to be engaged. I headed home for dinner, unaware that right across from my apartment building there was a voting station that was collecting votes for two strong, opposing NDP candidates.

I had no way of knowing that the post-dinner nap would be my last as a free man for close to a month. I had no way of knowing that my most challenging experience of incarceration would be the result of me *not participating*, as opposed to all of those other times I got away with the riskiest of moves.

I woke up to the sound of gunfire in the street. Molotov bombs were being thrown in the vicinity of the voting station. Apparently, the two NDP rivals were accusing each other of cheating. (How ironic.) The scene was unusually chaotic and violent, even by Egypt's standards.

Gangs from the neighboring Basateen area came and participated in the street fight. Police were running around with no apparent control over the situation. I figured I would grab my camera and document events on the street. My wife, who at times advises against these endeavors, looked out the window at the excitement and acknowledged that it was worth capturing.

I ran out into the street and started snapping away. When a few officers yelled at me and asked me what I was doing, I said, "I'm a reporter, this is my right!" The officers asked for my journalism permit card, and I explained that I had left my home in a hurry without it. They had their hands full at that point and let me be without too much of a hassle.

After dodging a thrown stone that almost took out my camera lens, I decided to enter a cyber café right in front of my building's entrance to upload the material I had just captured. Within minutes of starting that process, police forces flooded the café and started grabbing and beating up everyone in it.

There were a number of children in the café between ten and fourteen years old, and even they were being indiscriminately beaten and thrown into police holding trucks. This was the punitive standard police procedure against the Egyptian people: When provoked, the police would arrest anyone regardless of age, gender, or level of involvement.

I watched the chaos and violence around me in a daze. The cruelty to the children struck fear in my heart. I could not defend them though they had done nothing wrong. Children like my son a few years from now. If they were doing that to the children, what would the policeman running toward me with a stick, in what felt like slow motion, do when he finally reached me?

෬ ෬

"I am a Sixth of April activist and reporter! Do not attack me or there will be repercussions!" I yelled at the first officer who grabbed hold of me. "You don't know who you are messing with here! Stop this madness at once!"

There wasn't much of a thought process behind this plan to announce my identity and hope that it would invoke some kind of caution on the police's end. On a whim, I felt that it might protect me from the violence directed at me and the other cyber café customers who just happened to be at the wrong place at the wrong time. It also deflected any suspicion of me being a Brotherhood activist, which was infinitely worse than anything else that I could possibly be.

The officers in the café temporarily paused to mull over the implications of my claims. I took a few steps forward and no one tried to stop me, though one of the officers had a sneer on his face. I inched my way past the people and crying children, and still no one made any move to grab me. I started to quicken my pace as my heart thumped in my chest. I could see the door to the café ahead of me, and through it the door to my own apartment building. A quick image of my wife and son upstairs flashed through my mind. I was so close. For a split second I actually believed I was exiting the nightmare.

As I stepped though the café doors, I was struck on the head with a thick club. In my initial adrenalin-filled reaction, I turned around and yelled, "Who struck me? I am a Sixth..." but before I could continue the club forcefully descended on me one more time.

I yelled out in blinding pain, "Animals!" and that was the last phrase to leave my lips for the following ten minutes or so. More than twenty men started punching, clubbing, and kicking me into the ground. The blows were so fierce, I barely had the chance to take a breath and passed in and out of consciousness many times.

The whole time two thoughts kept racing through my head: First, I was amazed at what the human body could withstand in terms of pain. Second, could my wife and son see me from the apartment windows?

My wife and child.

My wife, whom I sheltered and catered to so much that I would barely even ask her to leave the apartment to get milk for my son. I made sure she had everything she needed without having to face public transportation or the hassles of the street. She left the apartment only when she wanted to or out of necessity. We would leave hand in hand, and I would carry my son.

My wife, I thought to myself as the blows came down. What was she doing this second?

Would I make it to the house with all the blood that was flowing out of me? Were they going to let me reach the apartment building's door, or would I die right here? At that point, for some reason, it didn't cross my mind that I would be arrested. I had stood in the streets in the past and called for the removal of the president and didn't get into any major trouble. Yet here I was getting the life beaten out of me for uploading images of events that were taking place on the street? How could this be?

In my attempt to halt the blows to my face, I grabbed at the person right in front of me who was punching me and pulled myself into a standing position. I couldn't see anything. I was blindly grasping at whatever I could in the darkness of my swollen-shut eyes. All I could do was say, "Who are you? What's your name? Why are you doing this?"

I was met with silence and violent blows to my arms, which were holding on to the officer. "If you are a real man, let me know your name. I will commit it to my memory. You cowardly animals! You cowardly animals!" I said between deep, panting breaths.

I had taken the second round of beating on my feet for what seemed to be ten minutes, but finally fell to the ground when they started beating my legs. I still had the officer in my grasp, so as I fell to the ground I punched at him wildly. It turns out my panicked fight combined with lack of flight response had been directed toward the highest-ranking officer of the police station just around the corner.

Above the screams of the children still being beaten around me, I heard him whisper into my ear, "Sixth of April movement won't save you. Nothing can save you now."

CHAPTER THREE

MOEZ MASOUD, 32,
RELIGIOUS SCHOLAR AND
TELEVISION PROGRAM HOST

3.

It was Saturday night, February 5, 2011, at Liberation Square, and the atmosphere was festive but structured. It was no coincidence that I was there. This is where a religious lecturer *should* be in an uprising. I had no doubts about that.

At this point, there was method behind the masses gathered in the square, and every individual there had a role to play. I just happened to be categorized as a "man of God" in addition to my role as "protester."

The religious makeup of the square reflected Cairo's population, with Muslims as the majority. Still, had it been otherwise, I could have fit in just as well. I had never excluded people of other faiths from my programs or lectures. In fact I had always hoped for a multi-faith audience and had selected my topics and materials accordingly.

My assigned role during the protests appeared to be to maintain spiritual strength in the ranks. I attempted to reinforce the momentum of the movement by connecting protesters to a higher goal behind this show of civil disobedience. People needed to know if it was OK to risk their lives for this cause.

At this hour, well into the night, to walk through Tahrir resembled walking through an old neighborhood. Protestors lived here. This had become home to "resident" demonstrators. Together, we protected conquered territory won in daylight and risked being here past sunset.

I was no stranger to this neighborhood—my university, the American University in Cairo (AUC), is literally right around the corner—but the square now felt timeless, like it was from another, more majestic era.

By now, I was a regular among the "locals" of Tahrir Square, among activists and opposition parties who had lived and dreamed of this day, and I had dreamed of it with them. We had quickly become the population that *couldn't* go home. With our identities known and our records on file, our homes had become traps. We all knew that if a concrete victory was *not* achieved, we would be arrested immediately upon an attempted return to our families.

The crowd broke into cheers as I was recognized approaching one of the assigned stages. The square had several of these small stages with small stereo speakers. Each stage could address only thirty thousand protesters or so at a time, a fraction of Tahrir's current population.

Drums and music played on the speakers and the crowd chanted *"Al Masriyeen ahoma"* ("Behold the Egyptians") in jubilation. I shook people's hands as I approached the steps of the stage and felt an intense sense of gratitude for this chance to play a role in such a historic moment. I had initially been reluctant to speak. The responsibility of affecting the ebb and flow of such a massive human ocean trapped the words in my throat.

This was me finally giving in to the fifth or sixth request to address the crowd and to say I was apprehensive would be an understatement. Yet my course was clear. I would speak of the "traditional" Islam in which I believed. The Islam that my parents and Al Azhar Islamic University preached and followed. The inclusive interpretation of the faith that has made me a relatively popular and respected Islamic figure at the young age of thirty-two and cemented my career in television and the media.

People have a tendency to call the Islamic message I spread "moderate." I do not believe in that description. I don't believe there exists a "moderate" Islam and a "violent" Islam. What does exist, however, are moderate individuals and violent individuals, and it is wrong for us to blame God's holy books for our misinterpretations of their teachings.

As I began to speak, a protester shouted out a profanity against Hosni Mubarak, and I immediately objected. I explained to him that though I shared his anger and his insistence on the president's departure, I would not forsake our culture of common decency by falling into the "hate" trap and incorporating a vocabulary of violence.

I spoke of the spirituality behind the journey upon which we were currently embarking. I spoke of purifying our hearts and minds during this journey. God was freeing us, so we must free ourselves internally by becoming loving to and inclusive of persons of all faiths and schools of thought and experiences. We should despise the "sin," but *never* should we hate the "sinner," for hate takes down its owner along with the enemy it targets.

There were frequent claps and expressed agreement to my words from about 90 percent of the crowd. The remaining 10 percent became restless and shifty, and one of them finally shouted out, *"Yasqut yasqut Hosni Mubarak!"* ("Down, down Hosni Mubarak!"). Again, the words I agreed with, but the wildness of the anger scared me, and the sense of responsibility rose into my chest and passed my lips as a prayer: *"Allahum wally alayna man howa khayron lana minho"* ("Please God, remove him and bless Egypt with a better leader").

I was not after revenge as a means of transformation for this great nation. I was after a better future and a land of peace. Ten years of my beliefs and teaching stopped me from changing my tune to fit a minority of the crowd's sentiments, and I resolved to stand my ground.

The same protester shouted out again, "*No!* Say it the way I said it!" I calmly repeated the same prayer: *"Alahum wally alayna man how khayron lana minho."* At that point whoever was handling the stage abruptly disconnected my microphone and played music instead.

My sense of calm started to leave me, and a sense of insult crept in where the prayer had formed. I struggled to remind myself that this was not about me but about God's will for his people during these turbulent times. With my hands, I gestured to the crowd, asking them if I should leave. The overwhelming majority responded, *"Kamil, kamil, kamil"* ("Continue, continue, continue").

The microphone crackled to life again, and I realized that this was the first show of democracy I had witnessed in this infant Egypt we were all stroking. I looked toward the man who had turned off the microphone and said, "Even before the twenty-fifth of January, I did not fear saying the truth though I knew it may anger the government. Now, I will not change my message for fear of angering the people. I have a way of speaking and I turn to God to help us, and *this* is how I will say I want the president to be removed..." I repeated my prayer for the third time to an accepting crowd.

I continued with a message of peace, love, and reconciliation. "We can win this," I told the crowd. "We can win this without losing our serenity and inner peace". I reminded them of God's words in the Quran to Prophet Mohamed: *"Inna fatahna laka fathan mobeenan"* ("We granted you a blessed entry and path") upon his peaceful, almost bloodless conquest of Mecca. History recorded that the period that closely preceded the Mecca victory was a time of peace, self-reflection, and deep faith despite the battles that were raging before it.

I pointed out parallels between that victory and the one on our horizon, and urged the crowd to follow in the Prophet's path toward peace. "Let us not be angry or selfish in our approach,"

I said, "for we will prevail as God told us, and oppression will sink to the depths of the darkest areas of hell on judgment day. This regime will end. There is no doubt about that. But in the meantime let us wear the robes of patience with solid and calm perseverance."

I prayed for their peace and safety and descended off the stage. I was relieved to see people quickly gather around to tell me that they supported my stance. They explained that the vast majority in Tahrir was against rampant rage, anger, and profanity, and that they were proud of my message, as it echoed their own.

I felt reassured that most of these protesters had retained their spirituality amid all the heartache and kept God close to their hearts.

Both sentiments I came across that day reflect the gamut of approaches available in Egypt before as well as during and after the revolution. I was no stranger to the human ego and its undertakings upon the human soul. I was no stranger to the misuse of religion to fit our emotional journeys on this earth. It was why I began studying philosophy and religion in my early twenties in the first place. Eventually I started sharing what I learned with the world through the media. Looking back now, I can certainly say that my "career" was hugely accidental and unintended.

You see, I had felt a strong demand grow around me for a *contemporary* understanding of Islamic faith by young Egyptians. What was widely available appeared to be a rigid, ritual-based format that focused on the "outward" elements of Islam as opposed to what happened internally upon embracing this multifaceted and multilayered faith.

It was after a personal near-death experience and the loss of a dear friend that I had turned to the Quran for comfort. I ended up wanting to learn so much more about this holy book than I had ever thought I would. I sought out traditional Islamic scholars all over the world and pursued them relentlessly in hope that any of them would be generous enough to tutor me.

I was not the typical candidate. I was a graduate of the American University in Cairo, which meant my English was stronger than my Arabic. I came from an affluent background and had a rebellious past, which was not uncommon among young men of my financial status and age group. With a bachelor's degree in economics and theology as a listed hobby, I began to diligently pursue Muslim sheikhs who preached the Islam I was accustomed to and wanted to gain a deeper understanding of.

The mentors I pursued were Azhari graduates, and their curriculum was contemporary and considered highly *adaptable* to modern everyday life. My mentors and I formed a "Daniel and Mister Miyagi" sort of relationship, as they treated me with aloofness and gave me what appeared to be impossible assignments until they believed my commitment was genuine.

Having a Western background strengthened my bridging abilities and I began to hone my technique in unraveling the Quran's message to people from all around the world.

In 2002 I was approached to create an Islamic television program in English for English-speaking Muslims in America, Europe, and Asia. The show was a big hit and the ratings were solid. In 2007, based upon the popularity of my English Islamic show, I was offered the host position in a high-budget production of an Arabic version of my show.

The Arabic version had a very modern feel to it, with me dressed casually and all episodes taking place outside the studio in venues abroad and across the globe. I covered issues controversial in the Middle East, such as premarital relations and homosexuality. I spoke of careers, love, marriage, and enjoying a life full of satisfaction through faith.

The show built a solid audience that I began to utilize as a channel through which I could come closer to my budding vision. My goal was to bring Islam's message to Muslim youth, as well as to reach out to the Christian Egyptian population and non-Muslims around the world, to come together in peace for our creator and the prosperity of our planet.

In 2009 I added the Egyptian talk show *90 Minutes* to my television engagements, and I began to expand my teachings. Episodes would call for self-improvement and striving toward the greater good for one's community.

My career was inching closer to what raised flags with Mubarak's government.

You see, the more influential you became, the more you appeared a threat to the status quo. The more positive your message, the more likely phone calls from Amn El-Dawla would come in. A voice would introduce himself on the phone, mention that he had seen a particular episode of *90 Minutes* and say nothing specific to me other than indicate that Big Brother was watching, so I should be very careful.

❧ ❧

January 2011—a few weeks before I stood on the stage in February—had found me at University of Cambridge working on my thesis on "Violent Religious Radicalization". This dissertation became my shield against my deep sorrows for the Alexandria church bombing that shattered Egypt on New Year's Eve—sorrows that sought to weaken my resolve and defeat my spirit.

True opposition for the system was solidifying in my chest at that point. It had all become too personal. Mubarak's regime appeared to have torn down everything I was working for. Many Egyptians had theorized that the president and his men had been carefully weaving a feud between Egypt's two key religions to keep us all busy in our own petty battles. I did not know that to be true or false but had slowly begun to feel the feud materialize.

As some Islamic groups grew too rigid and openly opposed the system, the system cracked down on them and often made a public spectacle of it. This saga scared people away from religion in general, and made Islam appear dangerous.

This sentiment of fear was carried into the international repertoire as well as part of the President's survival strategy. The "boogie man" of radical Islam would be kept in check as long as they helped keep him in his seat.

And there I was, a young, "modern" spiritual figure in 2011's Egypt fighting to keep myself on the path that our Prophet would have taken. Any well-read religious leader could also see the resemblance to stories from the Torah, Bible, and Quran. It was the "people" against the "Pharaoh," and the "people" were winning. We had lost so much but were so close and had little else to lose.

In stripping us of our lives, rights, spirituality, and happiness, the regime inadvertently equipped us with enough frustration to bring it down. Quite a fumble for such a seasoned dictatorship—or so we were lead to believe. The days would later prove to us that it was one thing to remove a president, but an entirely different thing to truly dismantle a regime.

My friend Mohamed Diab had found guidance in a Nobel Peace Prize winner and fellow Egyptian Mohamed El Baradei. El Baradei was openly campaigning for "change"—a surprisingly bold approach for someone who had chosen a career that kept him abroad for the better portion of his adult life.

While I was away from Egypt, many of my long-distance phone calls with Diab focused on filling me in on the Politics 101 sessions he had attended with this new Egyptian "change" salesman. I was interested in the political education aspect of these meetings, but my public persona prevented me from attending El Baradei's sessions in person, because of the responsibility the suggested advocacy a move like that would entail.

In essence, I stuck to the tools I was allowed to have, lest I lose the right to spread my teachings. That was my policy before Tunisia's revolution. However, shortly after it, when rumors of Egyptians plans to protest started circulating, my stance to openly become an "oppositional" preacher began in an episode of my live show on January 17.

A question had come up on my show to which I candidly responded. I openly stated that the chances of an outburst happening soon were significantly high. There was, of course, a limit to how blunt I could have been on television, or else I would get the phone call from Amn El-Dawla—or if I was unlucky enough, a visit.

Nevertheless, seeing the wave of self-immolation beginning to spread in my country, I exercised less caution than usual, and stated, referring to Mubarak and his regime—and in a religious tone that befitted the region's beliefs and culture—"The wealth of the Egyptian people is being routinely stolen by a bunch of criminal elites, yet God is not unaware of what the oppressors are doing."

That night I did get a phone call, but it didn't faze me. I half expected to be stopped in the airport on my way back to Cambridge after doing that episode. But the regime's police force did nothing of the sort, and my oppositional stance was finalized with my return-ticket booking to Cairo on the twenty-sixth of January.

My destination was Tahrir Square, but my first day in the midan, as planned by the almighty, would not be until Friday the twenty-eighth (now popularly known as the "Friday of Anger") with Mohamed Diab.

On the night of the twenty-seventh, I worked with Diab on a media tool that we felt would be of assistance to the protests. To announce my decision to be an official, public supporter of the budding revolution, I recorded a video along with another young religious leader, Mostafa Hosny, urging Egyptians to protest peacefully and in a responsible manner.

I explicitly requested that we adhere to the morals and values of the blessed Prophet and our culture. Consequently, no one should take upon himself/herself the task to destroy, burn, or deface Egypt in any way. This was a peaceful protest that would most likely be met by violence, but it should not launch itself as a violent protest that the government needs to contain. This was a balancing act that only the heroism of self-control could achieve.

The initial plan was to upload the video online to my page, and we did. However, because we already knew that we would lose the Internet before the prayers on the twenty-eighth, I began making phone calls to TV stations to have them air my video. I gave it to Dream and El Mehwar, both Egyptian channels that I had a lot of dealings with in the past.

At that point neither of these channels had taken part in the media "fiasco" orchestrated by the government, which entailed the two joining forces with the state-run media to perpetuate anti-revolution lies. Their future fabrications would stink up the airways over the two weeks of protests.

As the revolution unfolded, we would watch in disbelief as various TV channels took varying degrees of moral detours in regards to the truth and their responsibility toward reporting it.

∾ ∾

On the twenty-eighth of January, I met up with Mohamed Diab and headed for Tahrir right away. It was my first physical encounter with the amazing atmosphere of Liberation Square. How fitting was the name. How noble was the cause.

It immediately took me back to the twenty-fifth, when I was still in Cambridge. Upon seeing the news of what was happening, I had closed my eyes and dreamed of the square. The whole day had gone by with me glued to my computer, logged onto Facebook and constantly pressing the "refresh" button. I found that Facebook was giving a much more up-to-date and dynamic version of events than anything that was being reported on international news channels. Protestors were uploading statements, images, and videos to Facebook minutes after they occurred on the ground.

Friends tweeted their locations and the events taking place around them. Later that night they would use the Internet to cry for help when the police turned brutal. It was an amazing time of technology marrying the human spirit. Not only could you follow events at an almost live rate, but also read the thoughts and fears of those reporting them.

Now I was actually standing where they had been, but even the initial peacefulness witnessed on the twenty-fifth was already absent. The square was a battlefield from the get-go. Protestors who recognized me hurriedly told me how tear gas and rubber bullets started almost immediately when the first protesters had arrived in the square—even before the first chants were fully completed.

Diab had a video camera and started filming my conversations with people between tear gas bombs and rubber bullet raids. I traveled across fighting zones in the square, witnessing the bravery and fortitude of the protesters and barely containing my shock and disappointment at the actions of the government.

In initial segments of the video, I appear excited, thanking God, and in awe that I caught the peaceful protests in their angelic beauty and civility. But my demeanor quickly changed as the government's aggression toward us increased. I became as angry as everyone else, making the day's name, the Friday of Anger, truly fitting.

I was angry that our positive, peaceful approach was being met with unabashed disregard and attempts to thwart it. I was angry that we had to run, scatter, and take cover from the very entity that was supposed to be there to protect us. I was angry that communications were purposefully cut off to endanger us. But mostly I was angry as a man and as a father whose right to speak his mind was being revoked.

"Mankind was brought to this earth in dignity," I said to Diab's camera. "These people are, as you can see, peaceful and asking for very basic human rights. We are not children who are misbehaving. We are human beings asking for the right to maintain the dignity that the almighty bestowed upon us. And we will, God willing, achieve that."

Phone calls to our families from small shops in the surrounding area worried us, as the situation in Egypt beyond the square became fraught with looting and threats of violence. If felt like the end of the world as we knew it. We tried to speak to as many reporters as we could in an attempt to use our fame to be of some added value to the crowds.

Gunfire had initially halted our exit from the square, but we managed to reach my home to see the president's reaction on air. We were heavily disappointed. Mubarak painted the picture of a democratic Egypt plagued by demonic, anti-"stability" protesters with personal goals that benefitted none but themselves. He spoke of his dismay at the loss of lives of protesters and police alike, but bore no responsibility for them. He appeared tired but detached, as if he was watching us from another country.

He defended the actions of his security forces and spent the remainder of the speech reminding us of his "days of service" to the Egyptian nation, which were being forgotten and trampled on by a faction of rogue protesters. The speech was the ultimate slap on the face to every Egyptian who knew the truth. Still, this was the tip of the iceberg of the kind of perplexity the regime would create during this battle.

Diab and I were automatically signed up for the continued protests on the twenty-ninth. We vowed to stay in the square until some form of a tangible, positive result was obtained.

SHAHINAZ MESHAAL, 50,
MOTHER/ SIXTH OF APRIL ACTIVIST

4.

t is a beautiful thing to be the mother of three boys. I often watch them in awe, though I hide it from their egos. If one man can change the world, wouldn't three be able to at least make a dent?

My eldest is studying to be a lawyer, my middle son is a senior in high school, and my youngest is a freshman in high school. In Egypt, our children do not move out of the house until they have a woman to share their life with. So my four men (my husband included) and I share a home in Maadi, minutes away from central Cairo.

I have dedicated my life to these men. I was not a working mother. I spent what seemed like the entirety of my adult life taking my boys to and from school, sports, and friends' houses. I looked forward to our dinners together every evening, when they would tell tales of the hours they spent away from me and outside of this home.

Every time I walked with one of my boys to his room I would learn a new piece of information about the world to which I was too busy to personally attend. I never had regrets about the time I spent with them. I was building the infrastructure of three individuals that would inhabit Egypt for a long time, and I wanted them to be worthy of the health and strength they had been given by God.

That is why it really hurt that none of them wanted to stay in Egypt. I had noticed that dinner conversations were slowly beginning to focus on the "great escape." My three men were preparing to flee the world I had brought them into and had tried so hard to equip them for.

It had started with my eldest, and went airborne to the two others like a virus. They had it all down: which countries were possibilities, what the Visa processes of different countries were like, which countries were more tolerant of Muslims, and so on.

This had not been my intention for my men. This had not been my intention as an Egyptian woman.

I was not blind. Nor was I selfish. I knew the drill. I knew that careers here were limited and corruption was rampant. I could see the trash in the streets and the time lost in traffic. I understood they had better opportunities and would most likely flourish abroad.

No, I was not blind, but the pain of these facts had made me lose my vision about what needed to be done. Every mother feels that if she dedicates herself to her children, all will fall into place. Every father thinks that if he just feeds, clothes, and educates his children, all will be OK.

But it was not. It was not all OK in Egypt and it hadn't been for a while.

I tried to explain to them that it had not always been like this.

I explained that *they* were privileged with their private schools, clean homes, fancy summer resorts, and able bodies. What would Egypt do without its men?

Then it dawned on me that maybe I was asking the wrong question. What would Egypt do without *me*? What had I done to change things? Did I really think that parenthood meant that I had given *tawkeel* (power of attorney) to these children with respect to all that needed to be done in this world?

What an unfair assumption that was. I started to notice parallels to this argument in all my social circles. We would sit in our social club and complain and lament the lack of channels through which we could impact things.

These conversations had a cycle: complain, complain, complain some more, admit that nothing can be done, then delegate the struggle to our children. Our children were not buying it, though. They would not stick around to clean up the mess.

When my family's dinner conversations began to resemble a conversation by inmates setting up a prison break, I figured that if I did nothing to change what I was selling these children, they had no reason to subscribe to my idea of how and where they should spend their lives. So in 2008, like a good mommy, I decided I would try to fix things for my kids.

I announced this to my family.

"I am going to try to fix this," I said with determination.

I do not believe that at that time, these four men who had watched me for twenty-plus years took me seriously.

෬ ෬

My 2008 resolution was clear in my head. I would find my way to be part of an effort to turn things around. I have specifically noticed that life waits for you to make these decisions before it opens doors for you.

Haven't you ever felt that when you decided the time is right for a specific change, how oddly relevant things start to happen?

That is how it all started with me. I was reading the paper, and I read that on April 6 there would be a strike to protest the awful conditions in Mahala, and the government's blatant disregard of the poverty, high mortality, and low quality of life of the city's five hundred thousand-plus residents.

I decided to join them. But how could I strike if I had no job to strike from? I walked into my children's rooms as they were getting ready for school and I announced that there would be no school today. We, as a family, were on strike in solidarity with the people of Mahala, a place we had never been to, but was nonetheless part of Egypt. My kids thought I was losing my mind, but welcomed the day off nonetheless.

I decided to extend the rebellion to our apartment building and called the doorman up to our apartment. I told him that it was his civic duty not to do errands or any work for the apartment residents today. He was to announce to everyone that for today, he was on strike. I never found out for sure if the doorman heeded my suggestion because he was convinced of its merits or because a resident had given him the license to take a day off.

The end result was that I had participated in the strike and extended it to my small immediate circle. I began to draw energy from my mini-experience in civil disobedience.

It felt good.

Naturally, because of the insignificance of my strike, that feeling was short-lived. I began feeling trapped in the design of my own life. Was my career choice as a mother confining me to a limited scope of participation? Well, my children were older now, and I vowed to find my way into the more active elements of Egyptian society. I was sure there was someone out there doing something by now. I discussed this with my husband often. He supportively told me that if I found a way to participate that made me feel of use, I shouldn't hesitate for his or the children's sake.

So when I read in the *Destour* newspaper that Dr. El Baradei was visiting Egypt, I decided to welcome him at the airport. My husband had a work engagement that day, so I asked a sixty-five-year-old friend from our sports club to go with me, and he accepted. He said he respected El Baradei and thought the trek to the airport through vicious traffic was worth it.

An officer at the airport door asked me why I was there, and I confidently responded that I was welcoming a friend who was arriving on Austrian Airways. I could feel my companion fidget nervously. I whispered to him, "We are not doing anything wrong. El Baradei *is* our friend."

A friend is someone who offers you help. He was offering us much more than that. He was offering us a way out.

I paid the five Egyptian pounds required to enter the airport—an odd tariff I never understood—and happily entered through the glass doors. We went into the airport's welcoming area and stood there with the families of loved ones eagerly waiting for their reunions. The flight was delayed three hours, and I became concerned with my friend's stamina. But upon closer examination of the crowd around us, we began to identify a number of Egyptian writers and celebrities.

This could not be a coincidence. My friend and I began to feel that we were in the right place at the right time, and that our effort bore pertinence. Here we were with Dr. Hamdy Kandil, Dr. Alaa El Aswany, Dr. Hussein Nafaa, and so on—Cairo's educated elite, so to speak. We must have been onto something if these people felt it important to wait for El Baradei as well.

I decided to walk around to get a more accurate picture of who was there for El Baradei and who wasn't. I excitedly noticed that there was a group forming outside of the airport. Young men in modest clothing were gathering at the airport doors. Apparently the five-pound entry fee proved too expensive for them, so they waited outside. There must have been five hundred of them standing out there, some carrying signs that read, "The Youth of the Sixth of April Movement Welcomes Dr. El Baradei."

There were riot police surrounding them.

By the time El Baradei arrived, airport security refused to let him out to the main welcome area for fear of causing mayhem within the airport, and instead hurriedly exited him out of the VIP lounge exit. This meant that he went directly out of the airport straight to the crowds outside the doors. His fans and admirers clapped and cheered for him as he got into the car that awaited him. I briefly caught the look on his face. He was a very humble man. He appeared visibly touched, but moved with the speed of one uncomfortable with all the attention.

I was happy that the young men outside got the best seats in the house regardless of their inability to pay. My friend and I deemed the visit a worthy experience, and we headed home with a third party named "hope."

☙ ❧

Later that year, I had heard from friends at the club that El Baradei had published seven demands for governmental reform that he directed toward Mubarak himself. He was looking for brave, forthright citizens to sign a petition that outlined these reforms and expressed that they were popular demands desired by the Egyptian population.

My new career as a brave and forthright mom meant that I needed to sign that petition. The petition was published online, and you could log on to access and sign it. I would need more bravery to learn how to use the Internet and the computer as a weapon in my new arsenal.

My men (my children) assisted me in the process. I signed the petition and defiantly typed in my national ID (now the government had my address and everything). I set up an e-mail and a Facebook account. I was all set.

Google was a miracle to me, a library I could access without leaving my house. My first research topic was the "Sixth of April Youth Opposition Movement." I found out who these people were and what they had done so far. I joined their Facebook group and found that they had a phone number listed. I called them immediately and signed up to attend their next meeting.

I dressed for the meeting with the excitement of someone preparing for a date. What would it be like? Would my age surprise them? Finally, I thought to myself, I would have a conversation about the country that would break the "complain, complain, delegate" cycle I was so sick of.

The meeting was in a humble coffee shop in a modest area. Sixth of April had no budget and no meeting place. Members came from different income levels, so even moderately pricey locations were not an option.

Only a few members were present when I first arrived. Though they joked about my age, as they appeared to be in their early twenties, they welcomed me so warmly that it touched me deeply. I could tell that these were young men and women who had a much more difficult life than my children had been exposed to. As our table filled with about thirty more members, my heart was bursting with pride for them.

"I knew it!" I thought to myself.

I knew people were doing something about the situation in our country and now I could be part of it.

As I began to regularly attend their meetings, my children started to complain about the places I was frequenting. They expressed concern for my safety and felt my efforts inappropriate for my age. "Why can't you just donate money to the movement or something?" my eldest son asked one day.

"Then I wouldn't feel that I participated fully," I said calmly, "and they don't really need money right now. They need large numbers of people to join in the struggle. I am one person, but I count."

My husband would give me my purse at the door and say, "Don't listen to the boy. Good luck dear."

I had become a sort of godmother to the group because of my age. I became *Tante Shahinaz* ("Auntie") to the members, and I cherished my motherly role with them as if they were my own children.

Then I finally got the chance to join in an actual protest. It was April 6, 2010, and we were gathered at Maglis El Shoora (Consultative Council) to commemorate Mahala's struggle, which was not yet over, as well as every injustice in Egypt combined. There were no more than three hundred of us gathered. At the time, that was considered a decent number.

My excitement quickly turned into fear and claustrophobia as police formed a human cordon around us.

For the unseasoned protestor, allow me to give you a glimpse of this experience.

A police "cordon" in Egypt at the time, was constituted of four rows of riot police in full gear creating an impenetrable, thick, human circle around protesters. Once their circle closed around a group of protestors, they began to push against it with their shields, making the circle smaller and smaller. When this happens, there is no place to escape, and you feel the space you inhabit shrink until it becomes nonexistent. Suddenly your body and those of the people to your front, back, and both sides, become mashed together in one big human mass that connects to everyone else.

That day, they kept pushing until I thought my bones would break.

With us closely packed together, police would send four trained plain-clothes officers in to violently drag a random protester out. The officers would beat, drag, and insult him/her all the way to the holding truck parked nearby. Every time this happened, with my heart beating wildly in my fifty-year old, unfit chest, I would try (along with the others) to keep them from taking one of us. Every time we failed at saving the unlucky one. Despite our best efforts, they must have taken at least ninety to one hundred of us that April day.

To that point, that experience constituted the greatest level of terror and physical pain inflicted upon me by another human being that I had ever endured in my life. The proximity of the other protesters, their smell, their chants, and their screams when they were attempting to resist arrest would become a recurring nightmare.

It made me feel that we were hopelessly outnumbered. We were fighting a beast with no conscience or shame and no eyes for the truth. The zombie monster of a gluttonous government that never had a moral compass to begin with.

One of the last people to be arrested that day was an old man who had not been participating in the protest at all. I heard him yell out that he was a respected doctor as they dragged him away. His crime was to shout out to an officer beating a female protester from the group, "What you are doing is *haram* [against God's wishes]! Let her go!" In an act of defiance, he extended his arm with his cell phone to take a picture as evidence.

The image of him being repeatedly slapped across the face would become my driving force. Right then and there, I vowed to never let this scenario be part of my children's reality.

Not like this.

It could never be like this.

∽   ∽

Dr. El Baradei's seven reforms became a unifying flag for national opposition movements across the country regardless of their religious, political, or ideological affiliation.

The church backed him. The Muslim Brotherhood took to the streets to gather signatures for his petition. The educated elite concurred with the demands and the masses understood the validity of this basic and simple stance for the human prerogative of self-governance.

The demands were as follows:

1. The immediate lifting of the emergency law that enabled the government to arrest and hold whomever it wanted indefinitely without charge.
2. Reinstating judicial oversight of elections and election monitoring by local and international NGOs.
3. Guaranteeing equal media coverage and television time allotted to all candidates running for the presidency in 2011.
4. Ensuring the right of Egyptians abroad to vote at their embassies and consulates worldwide.
5. Removing all obstacles to anyone wishing to run for president, thus enshrining the right of every citizen to run.
6. Amending the Egyptian constitution, especially Articles 76, 77, and 88, which govern the eligibility of presidential candidates and the role of the judiciary in monitoring the elections.
7. Instituting a two-term limit on any president who governs Egypt (as opposed to the current lunacy of having no

restrictions on the number of terms a president can hold, with incumbent Hosni Mubarak in his fifth term).

I took to the streets as a prophet for this message. I believed that if people truly understood what these seven demands represented, a real sense of awareness might be born.

I had a plan and was given a geographic map of the areas that needed grassroots campaigning. My age and gender made me nonthreatening and easy to listen to. I went all over Cairo, including some of its most impoverished and humble areas.

It was such a complete change from my previous life, which had been lived through the eyes and tales of my children over hot, comforting meals. This was raw reality, witnessed firsthand. Nothing you could study could teach you what you learned when you delved into the country like this. I went to areas like Fayda Kamel, Dar El Salam, Hassanein El Desouky, and El Basateen, places where women from my sports club in Maadi wouldn't be caught dead.

The stories of poverty and hardship overwhelmed me. It became difficult to go home to my privileged life without a boulder of guilt on my shoulders. The responsiveness of the people from these areas was my inspiration. People welcomed me into their homes or grabbed a chair from a nearby coffee shop so I could sit and tell them more over sweet, sugary tea.

These were my "Arthur of Camelot" days and my roundtable was set up every time I said, "Excuse me, may I have a minute of your time?" to someone on the street. They all had their own grudges to bear, I began to build a roster of "knights" for future Sixth of April meetings.

One of these new knights, who became quite popular in our meetings, was a passionate young man in his twenties who bonded with me immediately. Mohamed Shawky was a live wire who carried on like he was high on positive energy. He was confident that we were exactly where we should be, and that God's victory was around the corner. He was a Brotherhood member which initially made me uneasy, but his charm would make you like everything he represented.

To sit with him would completely energize you. I quickly added him to my list of adopted Sixth of April children. We talked regularly. He looked me in the eyes and earnestly told me how youth his age were constantly waiting for people of my generation to give the signal to proceed. He said that seeing me there made him feel like a victory was approaching.

He made me feel important.

Despite his loyalty to the Brotherhood, of which I did not always approve, he came across as encouraging and inclusive.

I really liked Mohamed Shawky. We all did. I honestly don't think that a single person who met him and sat with him walked away with a bad feeling.

Our relationship began to extend a little beyond the Sixth of April meetings, as he began to call me out of social courtesy on religious holidays or when I was sick and missed a few meetings. He told me about his wife and two-year-old son, about whom he was so passionate. I grew accustomed to our talks; they kept me informed, focused, and energized.

I could not believe it when I heard that the government had captured him. He had always been like a cat with nine lives. I could not stop myself from imagining what the police were doing to him and what he was enduring at this very moment. I was frantic, as if the police had taken one of my children.

His wife would call, broken down and in shambles. Shawky had instructed her that in the event of his arrest, she should keep the news from his parents for as long as possible. She adhered to his wishes, and so had the added burden of trying to keep a stiff upper lip with them when they contacted her to speak to their grandchild and inquire about their son. They did not read opposition newspapers, so it was not easy for them to find out on their own.

News of his arrest would rock the Maadi branch of the Sixth of April movement, and push the youth to fight like they never had before. He was the movement's pride and joy. An activist, a father, and our dear friend, we would not rest until he was freed. Sixth of April was *not* losing this one.

MOEZ MASOUD, 32, RELIGIOUS SCHOLAR AND TELEVISION PROGRAM HOST

5.

On Saturday the twenty-ninth, Mohamed Diab and I arrived at the square right before noon. We kept our cars parked near our homes and headed out by taxi and any other form of transportation we could find. We were a little nervous about the lack of police presence on the streets on our way to the square. It was like walking through a hospital with no doctors. It was just us, the patients. It would take great strength to step out of our figurative casts and wheelchairs and check ourselves out of our tyrannical hospitalization.

In Egypt, very few traffic lights work independently. Instead, there are traffic policemen at traffic lights, operating the lights and directing the flow of cars. On this day, they were completely nonexistent and the cars were stopping and going at whim.

By the twenty-ninth, the army presence was widespread. I believe they appeared close to midnight on the twenty-eighth, or at latest around sunrise. They did not shoot at protesters. The tanks sauntered in and placed themselves around Tahrir Square and all over Cairo like silent referees.

The soldiers on the tanks had their rifles in their arms and looked at us with a gaze that was difficult to read. Their presence cemented in our brains that we were now at war, and our enemy was quite possibly our own police force. We were fighting Mubarak's men, but we did not know exactly to whom that definition applied. Not all policemen were his men. And not all soldiers were our protectors.

As we joined the protests, people began to recognize us and smile. You could see in their eyes that our presence was comforting. When you are publicly opposing an entire system, and getting killed in the process, seeing familiar faces you see on television makes you feel that you are not alone.

We filmed some more videos in hopes of sharing them on television or the Internet when it was up and running again. We wanted to show the reality in the square. We showed that there were no foreign agents among us, and that we were not engaged in any kind of violence. More importantly, the videos showed we were a mixed group that spanned class and income levels, religious orientation, gender, and age. In short, we were Egypt, and Egypt was announcing that she would take it no longer.

We started to film conversations with other protesters as well. They got excited at the prospect of live documentation and started to crowd around us, eagerly telling their stories. I watched their faces as they gave us their accounts, and I began to silently pray. This documentation was their proof, and you could hear the sense of faith they had that *this time*, it would be different. *This time* the world would take notice.

For their sakes, I prayed that this was true. I prayed that we could be of help, even though we did not know if our careers would still be there when this storm was over and a winner declared.

I prayed for God's blessings and protection for those who were being filmed and their identities going on record. Were we creating evidence that could be held against the protesters if our cameras were seized, or was the regime indeed in its final, dying stages?

The El Arabia television channel's main office was coincidentally on Tahrir Street. Diab wanted to go to the channel representative with whom he dealt regularly, share our tapes, and touch base on the issues taking place in the square. I waited for him at the building's entrance. He mentioned that I was with him, and the representative told him to invite me up for live comment.

Diab had to physically come down to get me, since cell phone communication was still cut off. We went up to the floor that held El Arabia's reception area. As I waited for the studio to be prepped, I thought of what I wanted to tell people. It was still early in the afternoon, and we had no definite numbers on the death toll for the day or the escalations outside of Cairo. The worst thing you could be at times like this is inaccurate. Rumors were common and highly damaging when the truth was so critical. I decided I would speak of what I had seen, of what I knew for sure.

I had seen firsthand the lack of police security in the streets and the shamble that was now our traffic system. I had seen chaos and tear gas and the sounds of gunshots all around. I had seen dead bodies in the street, and I had felt the tense existence of the army.

I decided I would focus on four messages that I believed in dearly. The host asked me my opinion on what was happening that afternoon, and I told him that I was calling on the Egyptian people to take to the streets and support the local security committees, formed by brave concerned citizens, and protect themselves and their property. The government would not render us weak through this chaos tactic, for we were more than capable of protecting ourselves. The ticker on the screen read, "Religious scholar Moez Masoud calls on Egyptians to form committees and protect themselves".

Secondly, I had a message to Egyptian police forces. "Where the heck are you? Do not listen to whatever powers are controlling you, and come out and protect your people."

Thirdly, to the Egyptian army: "Thank you for being present and being a source of comfort. May your guns be solely designated for Egypt's defense and never be used against the people of this proud nation."

The fourth message was a true risk at this early stage. My conviction and faith in the power of the people I had witnessed on the street prodded me. "To the president of Egypt, Mohamed Hosni Mubarak," I said calmly, feeling the host's resolve falter a little. "With all due respect, all the actions you have taken so far, including reshuffling the government and promising reform, are of little value to the people in the protests. It seems you are not in touch with what is going on on Egypt's streets currently. Please remember that God will ask you about these days. The almighty will ask you if you cared more for your people or for your position as head of state during these historical protests. Think about it. Do you care more for your worldly position or for the everlasting hereafter?"

My uncle (my mother's brother), who was an ambassador at the time, would later tell me how shocked and concerned he was that I decided to voice such a dangerous statement. He was mildly comforted when, a few hours after the interview, news that the president had appointed a vice president was announced on local television stations. The news reflected that the government was playing it safe and was not on the offensive.

We walked out of the El Arabia building and were overwhelmed by our own actions. The past forty-eight hours were surreal in every respect. Now we were returning to the field to protest.

Protest.

What a strange thing to be doing in our thirties in Egypt. What a strange world we had awoken to in 2011. We walked for distances that we had previously deemed only travelable by car. We participated in protests and later shook hands and talked to people. We heard updates of what had taken place while I was giving my interview. It felt like we were campaigning for the unknown to replace the status quo.

Once again, phone calls to family at home worried us. Nightfall was approaching and stories of thugs attacking apartments and houses, looting, and kidnapping began to violently circulate. Our wives clearly needed our support. We decided to go to our families for a few hours. There were no taxis any more, as the situation got more dangerous in the square and in residential areas around the country.

We tried to go through Zamalek, a residential area neighboring Tahrir, but there was sporadic gunfire coming from unknown locations. We would walk a little and run a little, seemingly in circles, not succeeding in our attempts to get closer to our homes. Fleeing from danger in Egypt's streets, known for their safety, felt surreal, and I often became isolated in my mind and experienced a strange survival-mode detachment.

Since their retreat on the twenty-eighth, riot police and other uniformed police were nonexistent. What we were dealing with now were snipers, plainclothes policemen, and "thugs," men who would attack you for what appeared to be no reason. The message to us was, you have angered Mubarak and without him you are defenseless. Quickly repent and he will swoop in and save you.

In response, we witnessed—as did everyone around Egypt—local security committees, led and operated by volunteer citizens, flooding the streets to protect everything and everyone. There was a lot of not knowing who to trust going around among both regular people and those within the committees themselves. It was becoming increasingly difficult to differentiate the good guys from the bad guys. The committee members carried sticks, makeshift swords, guns, and any other kind of protection they could find. But so did the bad guys.

The committees came up with a code, a system of wearing different-colored bands on their arms and alternating the arm that held the band so they could catch any imposters. All this added to the surrealism of the situation. It was surreal that we were at war with our own police, but it was also surreal how active and organized we appeared to be. Who were these people taking control of their own destinies? I often asked myself. Where had they been locked away for the past thirty years? It was truly a pleasure to meet them.

We all stood in awe of each other, in amazement at the dormant nationalism that was crawling out of the woodwork, fearless.

I would pray while I watched my fellow Egyptians. . Pray while I listened to the gunfire in the distance. Pray when I thought of my wife and three children.

∾   ∾

Diab and I came across a friend of ours on the street who lived in Zamalek. He took us through side streets to his house. We were grateful for the chance to enter a home. We held glasses of hot tea in our hands and I tried to comfort Diab, who was becoming increasingly distressed about the safety of his pregnant wife in all this madness. She had told him in their last phone call that prisoners across Egypt were being set free and were appearing around homes and residential areas, still clad in their prison garb.

I comforted him and told him, "Whatever you decide to do, or wherever you want to attempt to go, I will go with you. If you want to try again to get to her, let's do it."

We gave it one more try. Once again, we were shocked by how hard it was to get out of Zamalek in one piece. Frustrated, we stopped at another gas station that had a phone and called our families. Upon describing to them what was happening to us, our wives feared for our safety and started to deter us from attempts to get to them, lest it lead to us coming home for our funerals.

At that point we were all equally worried about one other, but there was no way to effectively protect our loved ones when we were not physically together. The division of labor at that point was clear. Protestors protected fellow protesters and the cause in the streets, while families at home protected the women, children, property, and each other. This policy extended beyond one's own network, and therefore you could feel the sense of love and neighborly responsibility creating a sort of task force that protected millions of Egyptians very effectively.

Part of my role was to report on it all, so we made the decision to head back to El Arabia's building again and give another interview about the precarious situation. The nature of our relationship with the channel implied that since we agreed to do interviews with them when they needed it, they would give us airtime when we requested it.

So we went up there and I asked to speak on air again. It was already becoming very dark outside and the highly dangerous hours were creeping in.

The news host turned to me on air and said, "We have with us here religious scholar Moez Masoud, who just came to us from the square and its surrounding areas. Tell us, Moez, what is the situation like currently?"

Obviously upset, I replied, "Well, my friend Mohamed Diab and I have failed in our attempts to get home for the past three hours to see our families. There is gunfire on the streets. Egyptians are being shot at randomly for no reason other than the fact that we are physically present in the street."

The host urged me to continue. "What is your analysis of the situation? What position do you think the protesters are in now?"

I decided to step out on a limb again in hopes of contributing in any way to ending the nerve-racking situation we had just been through. "Well, to be honest with you, I believe that the president is very late in responding to popular demands. Not only is he not responding, but also the situation on the ground is becoming increasingly dangerous for civilians. Our basic human rights and needs, in addition to the political demands, are being trampled upon. For me personally, if he is any later in his response than he has already been, he places himself in a position where his only acceptable action would be to resign."

At home, my mother sat up in her chair and went into a panic about my public declaration. I had not shared with her my goals for this uprising. I did not wish to worry her or exhaust her in arguing with me over something I would never go back on. She was hearing it on air for the first time. She would later tell me that it scared her to the bone. It was as if I was in the lion's den and she was watching.

The host tried to steer the conversation away from my last comment, asking, "Do you think the thefts and the looting are reflective of Egyptian society?"

I responded, "The thefts and the looting are clearly part of a well-thought-out plan. The government is attempting to force us away from the square and into the arms of our wives and children, but we will not be deterred. Do you think it is a coincidence that all these prisoners have been simultaneously let loose in the streets? Could we, the people, have done that at such a scale on our own? I believe that the Egyptian people are good people. Any evil and destruction that we see today is not from among us citizens. Furthermore, it should not distract us from our primary goal, which is to change Egypt permanently and for the better."

On instinct, the first person I called from the station was my mother. She worriedly (and perhaps angrily) said, "Oh my God, what are you doing? You know what, I am not even sure I want to talk to you right now. You really scared me. I am not sure *what* you are thinking."

I just told her, *"Kheir ya Mama insha Allah"*—"It will all be OK, Mother, God willing." Her disapproval did not extend any further than her deep concern for my safety. She did not attempt to stop me. She only urged me to exercise more caution. The very fact that she was not pulling the "mother card" and attempting to *forbid* me from continuing down this path cemented my resolve. I felt I was onto something, as we all were. Even my own mother could not say with any kind of true resolve that she wanted me to step away from the fight.

My second call was to my sister-in-law Kismet. She is the Business Development Director of a very vocal newspaper called "El Masry El Yowm (The Egyptian Today)" and I knew that she was stationed in the Semeramis Hotel in Tahrir for reporting purposes.

I called her and asked if we could come and stay at the hotel as it was possible that the State Security would be looking for us. She said she would do her best to get us in. Hotels had actually evacuated all occupants and only reporters with special passes were allowed to use the facilities.

We nervously started our attempt to safely reach the area that had the hotel. It was no leisurely stroll given the circumstances.

It was shocking to see the popular, five-star hotel in the state it was in. The usually fully occupied massive building appeared completely dark and deserted. Reception and entrance lights were all off, and there were bars and chains on most entrances.

We kept circling the building looking for a way in. We met a foreign journalist, and he banged on the doors with us in hope that someone would respond. We could still hear gunshots in the near distance and, though I am unsure of how long we stood there, suddenly I felt exhausted, cold and hungry, all at once.

It seemed like an eternity before someone finally came to the door.

Kismet herself appeared with the hotel receptionist. We gratefully rushed in to the deserted and dark reception area. It reminded me of the eerily empty hotel scenes you see in horror movies. It was strangely devoid of life.

The receptionist recognized me, smiled, and said, "Mr. Moez, we just watched you on El Arabia. It is a pleasant surprise to see you so soon."

A few other employees gathered around in what appeared to be excitement that they were sharing this experience with Diab and I. Again, I found it interesting how people found comfort in well-known individuals being among them even in a life -or-death situation. One would think they would be too overwhelmed to care.

We pooled the money in our pockets because the ATM machines were not working, but the hotel employees indicated that we could pay whenever it was possible. They seemed oddly concerned that I did not have my ID on me. I quickly told them that it would be better to have the room in Diab's name, anyway, for security purposes, and they quickly agreed.

Then they told us with an almost childish pride and excitement, "We have good news. We have Internet here and it is working!"

We hadn't been online since the twenty-seventh, and we were thrilled to check our e-mail and see what our friends and contacts abroad were saying. I thought about my friends and acquaintances from Cambridge, and wondered what they could possibly be thinking now.

We contemplated what would be the most useful messages to send the world at the moment. The connection was slow, but I managed to upload one video that I had filmed on the twenty-eighth for the world outside of Egypt to see. I sent some quick e-mail accounts of what had occurred earlier and read international news websites. Even *that* practice felt exciting and daring, like eating fruit from a forbidden tree.

Housekeeping staff was, of course, long gone by the twenty-ninth, so the room we were given was disheveled and had obviously been previously occupied by a reporter. His/her notes were strewn all over the place and it appeared that he/she had left in a hurry.

There was little food in the hotel, so the hotel employees gave us some bread, and it took a while for them to find some hamburger patties they could cook to go with the bread. The hot meat was comforting but difficult to finish with all the adrenalin running wild in our systems. Food and sleep would prove to be a luxury for the duration of the protests to come.

I lay in the hotel bed, too wired to doze, as a thousand thoughts raced through my head. Would I be able to walk the streets tomorrow or would I be arrested? I had heard so many tales about what Amn El-Dawla could do to one upon arrest and Wael Ghonim was already mysteriously missing. I remembered the authoritative tone of the phone calls I had received in the past and began to panic a little.

I tried to comfort myself by thinking that Amn El-Dawla had its hands full at the moment with all the NDP buildings and police stations being attacked. Its officers did not have the time they'd had before to sit and scan television channels.

I coached myself back on track and reminded myself that there was nothing to fear when you were dealing with God's people and plans. Whatever He brought about would be for the best. Painful or painless, my position had been taken and I would stand by it.

I got lost in My thoughts only to be interrupted by a rise in the television's volume. Diab had insisted that it be left on so we would know if the electricity got cut off, a sign that police may be ambushing the hotel.

I turned off the television, thinking he wouldn't notice since he was asleep. But the minute the room fell silent, he jumped out of bed and shouted, "I told you this would happen, I told you!"

I quickly stepped close to him and asked, "Told me what?"

"I told you that the lights would go out and we would be trapped in this high-rise helpless!"

"The lights did not go out," I said gently. "I turned off the TV because I couldn't sleep. Please go back to bed."

We both caught a few hours of uneasy sleep that night. It was more than any Egyptian, even those who had stayed at home, could hope for during this strange and transformational time.

CHAPTER SIX

MOHAMED SHAWKY, 26, MUSLIM BROTHERHOOD/ SIXTH OF APRIL ACTIVIST AND SHAHINAZ MESHAAL, 50, MOTHER/ SIXTH OF APRIL ACTIVIST

6.

(Mohamed Shawky)

5 December 2010

It was midnight when I was finally loaded into the back of a police truck. The backs of these trucks are fully enclosed metal chambers with two miniscule windows at the very top. I'd endured at least an hour of continuous beating from at least twenty different individuals before reaching this stifling enclosure.

The truck chamber in and of itself is a well-known part of the torture experience. It is designed to be dark and unventilated and the police pack it with people to the gills, purposefully, to suffocate and create mass panic among the detainees.

An arrest in Egypt is set up to break you as a human being. It is a truly dehumanizing journey that tests the limits of individual endurance. Many, in fact, die in the process because they can't take it mentally.

Police officers jam-packed the truck with everyone they could get a hold of in the cyber café and the surrounding area. The more than four thousand actual perpetrators of the street fights and electoral station's assaults were long gone by then. So instead, the truck was loaded with innocent adults and children. They loaded it until I could swear that there were at least one hundred of us detained in that truck. I felt as if I would suffocate at any second. The children, who were just ten to thirteen years old, screamed, cried, and called out to their mothers.

After what seemed like half an hour of us all being stuck in the truck as it was parked, they opened up the back, removed half of us, and shoved them into another truck. In the process of this relocation, everyone left behind in the first truck, as well as everyone being moved to the next, received a beating with thick sticks.

By then, a strange feeling of being almost bored with the beatings had come over me. It wasn't that I was tough and this was all nothing to me, as that was clearly not the case at all. It was simply that I was beaten for so long that I was emotionally and physically numb. My desire to know what was going to happen to me next was greater than whatever antics they were pulling on us now.

Furthermore, I believed that if we reached the station, I would be released, as they had released me before after past arrests. I wanted to get to that part as quickly as possible.

Young activists like myself typically weren't considered "hard core" and worth holding onto or the effort it would take to torture us.

During the drive itself, I managed to pull out my cell phone, crouch into a corner, and make a number of muffled calls. I called my wife first and was relieved that she had not seen me get beaten up or arrested. It was normal for me and men in general in Egypt, to stay out late, so she had thought I was still uploading pictures and blogging at the cyber café. I told her I went to a coffee shop with my friends and would be staying out late to discuss what happened and its implications.

I then called my father-in-law in Mansoura and told him the truth. We agreed that he wouldn't tell his daughter over the phone because she would have no one in Cairo to share this with and would be in terror alone through the night. He said he would catch the first bus to Cairo and be at our apartment at dawn.

I then called a friend from the Brotherhood and another from the Sixth of April movement and gave them a synopsis of what happened and asked them to get me a lawyer. My friend from the Brotherhood told me not to worry, and said that he knew someone from the Internal Investigative Unit (Egypt's equivalent to the CIA) who knows someone on the inside who could possibly get me out.

When we finally arrived, it was 1:00 a.m., but the station was full of officers who appeared to have known we were due to arrive this very second. They stood in two rows lining the back entrance of the truck. This was what seasoned detainees call a *tashreefa* (an honorary reception committee), a sarcastic term used to describe the "beat-upon-arrival" team.

I watched in horror as everyone around me received a second helping of kicks and blows on their heavily bruised faces and bodies as they exited the truck. My mind was preoccupied by one thought: If I could just find one reasonable person to talk to, I could explain that I was not participating, in any shape or form, in the electoral ruckus that had been taking place when I was arrested. If I could do that, maybe I could get myself out of this.

As I scanned the faces of those in charge beyond the *tashreefa*, I quickly realized how everything was more intrinsically violent than anything I had seen before. Even the curse words they used were dirtier and more graphic than anything my days as a streetwise Egyptian had prepared me for.

The detainees emerging from the *tashreefa line* were dragged to a kneeling position on the floor in front of one of the officers seated at the entrance of the building. From that position, one by one, they were slapped across the face and hit on the head. The officer would then take the detainee's name and occupation and curse him off of the floor into the hands of another officer, who would lead him away.

At least half of this miserable truckload of detainees was children, and they were sobbing uncontrollably. When it was my turn, I was the only composed individual, despite the cuts and bruises across my face and body. I quickly said with as much courage as I could muster, "Without cursing or hitting, please." The officer looked at me suspiciously but did not strike me, so I continued. "My name is Mohamed Shawky, and I work in sales and marketing for a coffee house."

A second officer, the one responsible for taking the detainees into the building, yanked me up and pushed me toward the entrance, where I discovered that we were expected to go up three flights of stairs, all lined with *tashreefa* officers, who would assault detainees as they were pushed and shoved up the flights of stairs to their designated holding room.

I broke away from the officer and quickly approached another, higher-ranking officer and said, "Excuse me, sir, could I just say something…" But before I could continue, he slapped me hard across the face. At that moment, I realized that that had been the most humiliating thing that had happened to me so far that night.

In a panic and with what little resolve I had left, I started again, "I work in sales and marketing and I was just trying to tell you that I…" I was interrupted by another hard slap across my face. At that point I realized that this officer was simply not human. Like something from a science fiction movie, he was devoid of emotion, a conscience, or any other quality that could possibly equip him with enough compassion to actually care.

I ran from him and quickly climbed across the three flights of stairs with barely enough speed to avoid some of the delivered blows and kicks. It was easy to find the holding rooms, since all you had to do was follow the cries of the children who had arrived with me on the truck.

I looked around the room and confirmed that not a single perpetrator that I had left my home to photograph during the Basateen electoral NDP conflict was in that holding room. The police, failing to catch the thugs who were causing the street riot, had taken in every innocent person they could find within a ten-meter radius.

It became painfully obvious that I was not the only person here who had nothing to do with the street riots. *Everyone* here had nothing to do with it. This was intentional. We were here because authorities could not come out empty-handed after what had occurred so publicly on the streets. We were a collective patsy group, and we were being processed to solve the problem of where to set the blame.

It was 2:00 a.m. when they started to group us into categories before presenting us to the district attorney, who was mysteriously present at this ungodly hour. Someone shouted out at us, "Which of you bastards have IDs that state that you do *not* live in Basateen?" Those who had such IDs would put the lie to this frame-job, so the police wanted them gone as quickly as possible.

"My ID states that I do not live in Basateen!" I called out, but they ignored me, seemingly intentionally. They skipped me, took everyone else who fit that category, processed them with a charge similar to disorderly conduct, and released them. They knew it would have been far-fetched to claim that these people were involved in a street fight over an election for a Basateen representative for whom they couldn't even vote.

Ultimately, our truckload of detainees was split up into three groups: those whose IDs had an address in Basateen, which, to the police, meant it was fair to stick them with the false charge of causing the mayhem; those whose IDs said they lived elsewhere, and who were released; and then there was a third category, those whose injuries were substantial and difficult to wash away, ice, or hide.

I began to realize that they were leaving me until the end. Was there a separate category just for me? A strong foreboding flooded my system.

My camera was still hanging on my arm when the officer finally walked up to me. "Aren't you the Sixth of April guy? Come with me." My face was busted up, but not as badly as the members of the third group, the mangled group, that the officer was now taking me to stand with.

Group 3 was comprised of people with broken bones and slashed eyes. If these people went to court for insubstantial charges, their wounds and injuries would not be "justifiable" by Egyptian police standards. So they got slammed with the heaviest charges the police could drum up before they were taken into the district attorney's office.

As the officer moved away from me he took the camera off of my shoulder. He went straight for the memory card and stopped dead in his tracks when he realized it was not in the camera. He walked back to me quickly and started to rummage through my pockets. I was wearing jeans, and the front pockets had miniature pockets on top of the main ones, which were designated for carrying small items or change. The officer searched one small pocket, found the memory card, and slapped me across the face with such force I stumbled a couple of steps back. He pulled me back toward him and proceeded to look through everything I had on me.

In my wallet was a flash-memory stick; he confiscated it. In another pocket was a small USB connecting cord that one uses to connect a digital camera to a computer; he confiscated it. In my back pocket was a small Bluetooth device; he confiscated it. And of course he found my phone and confiscated *it* as well.

I stood there defenseless, realizing that the phone calls I made in the truck were the last I would make for a while.

We were charged with assaulting officers on duty, vandalizing public and private property, and engaging in civic violence. They wrote up our injuries as having been caused by fighting with other gang members. If convicted, any one of us could face anywhere from four to ten years in prison.

I was charged with destroying eight vehicles parked in the street, assaulting and injuring four police officers, resisting arrest, vandalism, and arson. When I stood in front of the district attorney, I told him that I was innocent of my charges, that I worked in sales and marketing and was originally from Mansoura but had recently gotten a job in Cairo. I told him I was married and had a two-year-old son, and that all I was guilty of was taking pictures—if that was a crime, they should charge me with it, but not the other listed accusations.

The district attorney looked at me sympathetically and said, "I believe you, but this thing is bigger than me. There appears to be orders from the highest-ranking officer in this station to hold onto the Sixth of April guy, and that, unfortunately, is you."

～　～

For the next twenty-four hours, the twenty-six of us were kept awake in an interrogation room. We were ordered to sit in a stressful, quasi-seated position with our heels flat on the ground and hugging our knees, and forced to keep this position for hours. The officers would alternate between yelling the dirtiest curses at us while ordering us to stand for a few hours and ordering us back into the uncomfortable, quasi-seated position again.

This was the routine through the night. Along with a number of the young children still with us, we were allowed no sleep or physical rest of any sort. We were denied access to the bathroom and many urinated and defecated, fully clothed, right there where they stood.

Occasionally they would enter the room, single me out, and say, "You, Sixth of April guy! Aren't you the one who cursed the head officer's mother?" I would reply that I never use profanity with anyone. They would then beat me up, shouting between the blows, "Are you calling us liars, you son of a bitch?"

After the full twenty-four hours of terror, in our dirty, soiled clothes, they again brought us before the district attorney, who announced that we would be held for four days, pending further notice.

We were taken down into a dark, dirty cell with no windows. The minute they left us, we all collapsed onto the ground almost simultaneously. Most of us had horrific injuries and could barely bend our bodies. Yet still, we fell asleep.

After only about twenty minutes of rest, the terror antics resumed. Every half hour, an officer would come in, demand that we all stand up, hurl insults at us, and then demand a bribe so he wouldn't beat us up. Detainees would pool their cash to pay officer after officer until they had nothing left.

At one point an officer came in with a bucket of dirty water and ordered us to clean the holding cell with it. The water smelled, and there was nothing with which to mop it up, so we could no longer sit or lie on the floor, and we were again forced to stand.

The beatings continued despite the bribes that were initially collected. An officer would rush in, single out one person, and basically beat the crap out of him. If the detainee had a broken arm or leg, the officer would focus his blows on the injury—over and over and over again.

They seemed to direct the especially humiliating beatings at one detainee who appeared to be older, probably in his early fifties. Because of his age, they would repeatedly slap him across the face and kick his behind just to disgrace him in front of everyone else.

The screams were deafening, continuous, and as painful as receiving the injuries firsthand. There were no breaks or down time over the entirety of the four days. Indeed, it is amazing what the human body can endure.

At times the officers would aggressively rush in, cursing and yelling at us to face the wall. Terrified, we did as they said, and they would leave us there in trepidation but do nothing for what seemed to be hours. They would then order us all to lie face down on the ground side by side, and they would walk across our bodies and heads with their shoes as they laughed and cursed at us.

We had not eaten for close to two days, and began to fear that they intended to kill all or at least some of us. Martyr Khaled Saeed's story was fresh in all of our minds, and we knew that the police force had become brazen in what it allowed its officers to do to citizens on a whim.

In the early hours of the third day, an officer came in and threw chunks of old, stale bread on the ground for us to eat, then placed a few buckets of water on the ground next to them. We all ate what we could manage and drank as much as we could.

We were then visited by the NDP candidate who'd lost the Basateen election. He came in with his clean clothes and relaxed look and told us not to worry. He claimed that he personally was working on getting us out. I barely cared about, let alone believed, anything he was saying. I was just grateful that his presence was giving us a break from the officers and their terror routines.

The minute he walked out, an officer came in and ordered us take our clothes off. We were told to lie on top of each other in a heap on the floor. Images from the Abu Ghraib prison scandal in Iraq flashed through my head. I remembered how shocked and saddened I was by those pictures and now here I was in this sad, smelly, bloody pile of human pain and sorrow. I prayed for God to save us and not let them get away with their actions.

I started to cry. It was gradual at first, but then turned into full-fledged weeping. I was not weeping from the pain, hunger, or insults. I was weeping from the discovery that life could offer such a horrific situation completely devoid of justice. How could God allow this to happen?

Was I questioning God?

I quickly backtracked in my head and begged for his forgiveness. I would not doubt his plans. I knew this situation had a purpose in my life. I was not forgotten, I was going through an experience and I would go through it willingly and emerge from it, *insha Allah* ("God willing").

We had another visit, this time from the NDP candidate that *won* the election that caused the street fights. In clean garb, looking annoyingly well-rested and fed, he lectured us on how he would stand by us regardless of the fact that we had been so obviously protesting against his win.

It was all a game. Neither of the two NDP men had any intention of participating in any effort to set us free. Still, they let the families waiting outside the station kiss their hands and feet and beg them to help free their children.

At some point on the third day, they allowed our families to send in food. Police charged one hundred Egyptian pounds to each family who wished to see their son for three minutes and give him a bag of food.

Families would send in huge quantities of food so that it could be shared with other inmates—as well as with police officers, who demanded their share. It was an odd thing to be fed and then receive beatings nonetheless. We were basically continuing the same torture routine, but now on a full stomach. There was one instance in which an officer grabbed a Pepsi bottle from me as I passed by him in the hallway, twisted open the cap, spat in it, and gave it back with a smile.

After the torturous four days, all twenty-six of us were finally escorted into a courtroom where we would see our lawyer for the first time. The lawyer was not representing any particular individual. He was appointed to represent the whole group. He spoke of how we all knew that these arrests were a charade and that the judges should not partake in this sham.

In Egypt there are three appointed judges instead of a jury. These three individuals listen to a hundred cases a week and their decisions are often quick and based on their own judgment of the law and the situation at hand. The lawyer spoke strongly to the judges about the importance of evidence and the apparent signs of abuse that we were exhibiting.

The judges were indifferent. They sentenced us to be held without bail for another fifteen days pending further investigation. The nineteen adults in the group were to be transported to the prison Torah, and the remaining seven children would be held in a juvenile detention facility. I wondered how their poor families felt.

Personally, I was crushed. I had instructed my father-in-law to keep my arrest a secret from my family for as long as he possibly could. This sentence would mean that they would inevitably find out. My wife had already completely broken down in the courtroom; I did not want to witness my father and mother in the same predicament.

I saw Shahinaz, the movement's *tante*, standing with my family with her arms around my wife, literally holding her up. I was so grateful to her at that moment. My father-in-law's gaze was serious and somber but oddly reassuring. He had seen all of this before and had experienced it firsthand more than once. It obviously pained him to see me go through it, yet he believed it was an activist's rite of passage.

I smiled at my wife as they led me away, and it took every ounce of strength I had left. I mouthed the words "I will be OK" to her, and I hoped that it comforted her in some shape or form.

∽ ∽

(Shahinaz Meshaal)

You often hear people describe moments of great stress by saying, "It felt like it was happening to someone else," as you feel less of an emotional impact. Well this *was* happening to someone else. To another mother, to someone else's husband. Yet, when the judge announced that Shawky would be held an additional fifteen days, I could feel his wife's heart literally drop inside my own body.

I didn't need to face her to see what had become of the features of her face. I didn't want to face her, lest I lose my own resolve. Shawky looked terrible. The poor kid had "torture" written all over him. He had a slight limp and looked unclean and physically ill.

Mona, Shawky's wife, lasted just a few minutes after the judge announced the sentence and Shawky was led out of the room with the other detainees, and then sobs began to rise out of her chest. The crying was not particularly loud, but heaving and constricted, and she began to lose her ability to stand. Her father and I accompanied her out of the courtroom into the bright sun outside of the courthouse.

Her father turned to me and said, "Madame Shahinaz, do you think there is any point in us hanging around?" He pointed toward the Sixth of April members gathered with signs and pictures of Shawky in protest outside the courthouse.

"Oh, no, I honestly think it is important that she leaves. I will stay with the group," I told him. They had already been camping out in front of the district attorney's office for forty-eight hours and intended to continue their vigil at the courthouse for Shawky's freedom.

Mona wanted me to oversee the defense lawyer that the Brotherhood and the Sixth of April movement had recently hired in his work on Shawky's case in collaboration with the attorney representing the whole group. The new defense lawyer had attended today's hearing and was already working on a plan to get Shawky in front of a judge again as soon as possible.

A Sixth of April member handed me a large stack of fliers with pictures of Shawky and his two-year-old all over them, summarizing the details of his unjust arrest, false charges, and detainment. I knew the fliers would be too much for Mona to see at the moment, and was glad she was going home with her parents.

I wished there was a way I could have somehow let Shawky know about all that was being done for him. He passed by us so quickly and was at such a distance that it didn't occur to me to shout it out.

I wanted to tell him that the seventy thousand online members of the Sixth of April Facebook page had changed their profile pictures to his picture—the same one on the flier—in solidarity. I wanted to tell him that every night close to one hundred Sixth of April members camped out in front of the district attorney's office in protest. It would have helped him endure whatever it was that he had just come from—and was returning to.

Beneath his smile to us, there seemed to be so much hidden horror. I believe that any communication with him at that point, had it been possible, would have shattered his own resolve to be strong for us. Maybe things were all they could be. He would have to go on without our help, in the isolation of the depth of the trouble he was in.

No, it was not happening to me, but as a mother I wished it were me, not this beautiful boy that I considered my fourth son.

The next morning, opposition papers' headlines read, "The Free Bird of the Sixth of April Movement, Mohamed Shawky, has Been Caged." These papers were read not just by activists, but also by dissatisfied citizens who felt the need to stay informed. The public was slowly becoming aware that there were youth who were now actively part of an actual modern-day movement against the system. In a way, Shawky's bad luck would immortalize him in the history of Sixth of April pre-revolution efforts. He became one of the many scars the movement bore to join the battle for change.

∾ ∾

(Mohamed Shawky)

I was still in a daze when I was handed the Torah inmate garments, which included government-issued underwear of the worst material and fit, and admitted into prison. I was unaware of the magnitude of the campaign being launched to liberate me. Knowing that would have helped when prison guards were shaving my head and strip-searching me. Sadly I wouldn't be informed of any news from beyond the prison for another eleven days, when I was finally allowed visitation.

They forced us into a large sleeping ward called the *eerat*, which housed all incoming inmates for the first eleven days of their stay. This ward grouped together people who were behind bars for a variety of charges, including murder, drugs, and theft in the same medium-sized room for the initial period of confinement. It was situated at basement level and had no windows. Inmates were not allowed out for eleven days. It proved quite difficult to endure the lack of light. Being confined to the same walls for hours upon hours takes a toll on one's psychological coping mechanisms.

We were also not allowed any food from our families during the initiation period. The prison offered generally inedible food, except for the beans and white cheese that came packaged. There were no beds or chairs in the *eerat*. You slept on a blanket and covered up with a blanket, and that was about the extent of the shelter you got from the cold, cockroach-infested floors.

It was December and I found that to be cold was akin to being in constant pain. It was amazing how the number of the people in the room did not make it any warmer. Being below ground kept the sun away, so we were exiled from its warmth. We were temporarily buried here, and the eerat was our casket. When brought to the surface again, we'd be officially "broken-in" and less troublesome.

You could hear the other inmates snore through the night, and you were conscious of the various sounds they made during the day. Their smells and voices became part of your own personal space. It was as if we all shared one caged, un-bathed body.

The inner dialogues in my head would eventually lift me above the eerat's confinement. I had faith that God's choices for me were far better than my own. I vowed to embrace his choices.

I really meant that.

I was thankful that Torah prison did not have the terror/beat-up sessions. The living conditions were on the subhuman side, but at least the beatings were not a regular part of the day.

I began to understand the inmate community and get a feel for the routine. I started preaching the Brotherhood's awareness curriculum, of one's rights to a dignified life, of how we were born free and were to obey God and to fear and worship Him only, to whoever would listen. Initially, the others would get really nervous and tell me to be careful. I would say, "Look around, we are already arrested! This is the very most they can do to us. Apart from torturing us and killing us, there is nothing more they can do. Even if they kill us we become martyrs and go straight to heaven."

I started to develop a following and many now chose to sit and listen to me speak about freedom, choices, and dedicating your life to the betterment of those around you. A group of Saeedi Egyptians (from northern Egypt) who were in for rural revenge killings, not unusual in that area, took a liking to me. They had access to extra blankets and food. They told me that I would be officially in their care for the duration of my stay in Torah prison. I enjoyed my new jailhouse popularity. Most of all, I think I enjoyed having human contact again and being treated with respect.

It distracted me from thinking of my son and my wife. It helped me embrace God's decision and kept me close to him.

Then a small miracle happened. For some reason, the prison warden decided that my group of new inmates should stay in the eerat for only eight days. We joined the general population, in which inmates were housed according to their crimes in groups.

We were allowed to move around the facility to do chores and gather for prayers. It was odd how prayers were strictly observed by the inmates in prison. Even the murderers woke up and gathered for the dawn prayer at 4:00 a.m.

We were all equally and regularly seeking God's mercy five times a day.

We followed the rules that the warden explained to us when we were admitted into the general population. "From now on you do as you are told and you stay out of trouble," he said. "If you are obedient you will do your time in peace. If you disobey us, we have our own disciplinary procedure and believe me, you don't want to end up there."

The "disciplinary procedure" to which he was referring was the prison's sewage system. If you crossed the prison warden, you were placed into the sewage system, in the fecal matter and urine produced by the entire prison. You were there without food, drink, or access to anything but human remains. For two full days, regardless of obvious health and hygiene issues, you were left in the sewage. If you survived, you were most definitely rehabilitated of whatever infraction you had dared to attempt.

Oddly enough, this made Egyptian prisons unusually safe. You would rarely get jumped by other inmates. Your greatest fear would be from the guards, but the other inmates were neutralized by all the insane measures that were devised for inmate control.

Outside of the eerat, your family was allowed to send in food once a week. We valued that food dearly, as once again families would send in portions for more than one person, and we all shared the treats.

We were housed in what was called Anbar 3, a political crimes and business fraud ward. This meant that most of the people I bunked with were college graduates. The majority claimed to be framed or taking the fall for a bigger fish in exchange for compensation for their families. I made it a point to listen to every story and to regularly share mine.

I found myself in a constant state of chatter. Even when I prayed, I made sure I voiced the words to fill the space around me. Silence was my worst enemy. It reminded me that these were alien hours that had abducted my life and mutated what once was the regular schedule of a young man in his twenties. The guards let us out of the cell for an hour a day, and during that hour we played soccer as if our life depended on it. When you see the sun and open space only once a day all you want to do is run, even if it is in circles chasing a ball.

Before my first visitation by my wife and son, I had blocked them from my mind because I could not handle not knowing when I would see them. I had resorted to pathetically pretending I was at some odd convention somewhere. When I finally got to see them, I filled the room with jokes and chatter. I'd had hours upon hours of training in Torah on how to use denial as a strategy. I told my son, "Look at how fashionable your dad has become. They make us all wear uniforms so we are all part of a special club!"

My wife strained to maintain a steady demeanor as she filled me in about everything that was taking place outside and the freedom campaign that had been ongoing since my arrest. As she spoke, I could hear my own prayers confirmed. *This* was what God had meant for me. I knew that it was part of a greater plan—I just knew it! To go through this and represent a story of triumph and survival would be an honor I wasn't even sure I deserved as an individual. It appeared I was destined not be a Khaled Saeed story; I would get out and live to talk about it.

Mona spoke of the lawyers and their efforts with hesitation, but my faith in what was about to happen started to strengthen. I could already see in my head how I would use this experience when it came to helping the Sixth of April movement.

At that point I think I got so positive that I actually succeeded in lifting Mona's spirits. She became upbeat, and believed my assurances that the whole experience wasn't that bad.

When visitation was over and she picked up Eiad as they came in to get me, I could see that she had renewed her strength. I have never loved anyone like I love this woman or the child she carried in her arms. I had so much respect for the effort she put in to maintain her stance and tone of voice with my son. I was at peace with where I was going because it led to a better road for them.

Asmaa Mahfouz, the woman in the YouTube videos that had made me a Sixth of April member to begin with, had been waiting to join in at the end of the visit as a representative of the movement. She was quite the celebrity in the world of activism at this point, and though I was honored by her presence I made some quick calculations in my head when she asked me how I was and how they were treating me. I knew the extent of the movement's influence on the outside and knew that there was only so much she could do for me. The more negative aspects of my incarceration would perhaps motivate her to work harder to get me out, but they would also demolish my wife, and she was standing right there next to her.

"Mohamed, please tell me if they did anything to you on the inside and if you need anything at all from the movement. You know we are working hard on getting you out of here, "Asmaa said earnestly. Mona had Eiad on her hip and wore the smile I had just helped put on her face. It wasn't worth it.

"Everything is fine," I replied. "This is really not the end of the world. I appreciate you being here and all the effort that is being undertaken on my behalf."

She told me to hang in there and exited with my wife. I went back to my shackles. There would be plenty of time to share my story when I got out of here, I told myself as I held on tight to my heart, which was trying to follow my son out of the room.

৽৽   ৽৽

When I stood in front of the judge the second time I was hopeful. Ten of those arrested with me had already been released on a three-thousand-pound bond. I heard the lawyer tell the judge that I was not a flight risk, and that he was asking for my release on a two-thousand-pound bond. Court trials took forever in Egypt so to be released on bail was akin to getting off altogether. You could live your whole life on trial and actually pass away before there's a verdict.

I could see my father, Mona, my father-in-law, and Tante Shahinaz seated faithfully in the courtroom. I could see their lips murmuring prayers as the judge examined the documents submitted by the lawyer. This was it for me, I could feel it.

I closed my eyes and heard him say the words.

"The accused is to be released on bond under his lawyer's responsibility."

My eyes flew open and I looked out to my wife, her image was blurred by my tears and as they dropped onto my cheeks I could see that she was crying all over her smiling lips as well. My dad was sobbing uncontrollably. I gave him a big smile and kept mouthing the words, "It's OK, it's OK."

It had only been twenty days but they were the longest of my life. I was in a cage, but I expected to be out of it any minute and run into my family's arms. However, the judge announced—curiously—that I was to be processed in Mooderiya Amn El Qahira, Cairo's police and district attorney headquarters. My eyes met Mona's again, and I could see her panic as the guards took me away, I saw Tante Shahinaz and my father-in-law quickly envelop her from both sides. I lost sight of her, and with two stern guards at my side I was shoved into a truck similar to the one that I had embarked upon in the beginning of this horrific journey.

I felt nauseous as the sounds of the street came in through the small, barred window atop the truck. I willed myself to hold it in, as I had no idea how much time I would be in the truck and did not wish to have vomit as my companion for the duration of the trip. (The skills you learn in Egypt...)

We reached the station in what I think was about an hour and fifteen minutes or so. The aggression that was characteristic of police stations returned, and it was a shock to my system after the relative lull that Torah had presented. At every juncture, to move me from truck to street and from the street to the stairwell and from there to a room, I got pulled by the scruff of my neck or shoved or kicked as if I could not propel myself forward on my own. There were so many in the truck with me, and so many in the room where I was lead to wait. I wondered where Mona was. What had they told her? When would I be allowed to join her? How was she feeling? The thoughts tortured me.

After a long wait, an officer came in and shoved me into a holding cell. Memories of my arrest and the four-day terror experience came flooding back, and I could feel my heart beating in my chest. In the cell another inmate was hunched over something on the ground.

At first I thought he was nursing a wound on his face, but then I realized he was snorting cocaine. Where had he gotten that? Wasn't he afraid of the officers? I looked around the cell to see if anyone else could see this and noticed that several men in the cell looked obviously stoned as well. How was this possible?

That question didn't linger long, as a prison guard's arm came in through the bars holding what appeared to be a cocaine packet, and the inmates rushed to place money in the hand and grab the packet. This was the station's "captive demand" population. Here the guards sold the drugs they picked up on the street to the men getting ready to be released back onto the street. No marketing needed.

The fact that the inmates had money worried me. Where had they gotten it? Did their families send it? How long had they been in here to have the time to request that? I turned to the man next to me, who looked fairly coherent, and asked, "Why are we in here? Do you have a court order to be released as well?"

He turned to me slowly. "We are here so they can check our paperwork and determine that there are no other pending cases or reasons they should continue holding us."

"What? I asked in an obvious panic. "They don't have that cleared at the hearing? How long have you been in here?" The druggie who had been hunched over his drugs sat up at the sound of my voice.

The man looked at me, and for a brief instant I believe I had caught some sympathy in his eyes. "I've only been in here a few days," he said. "Don't worry about it." He patted my shoulder and looked away.

A guard came to the cell door and yelled, "Mohammed Shawky!" and motioned to me to follow him. We entered into a large room with several booth windows like the ones you would find at the automobile licensing department. I went to the first window and the government employee asked, "What's your name?"

"Mohamed Shawky."

"Do you have any money on you to share with us here?"

"I just came out of Torah prison. I don't have anything on me."

"That's OK," he said, smiling sarcastically. "You can just spend a few nights with us here until you raise the money."

"Honestly, I don't have a *maleem*"—the equivalent of a penny— "on me and I have not been allowed to contact my family. How am I supposed to have money?"

"That's OK. We love having dirt bags like you keep us company," he sneered. "Go on to the next window and see what they can come up with there."

I reluctantly went to the next window, and I could tell what he would say without him even uttering the words.

"Listen, asshole," he said, with a serious look on his face. "If you don't pay I will transfer you to the police headquarters of Mansoura where you came from and they can dig up every little incident on your record since you were born and reexamine it. You will be tied up in paperwork there forever."

"You can do whatever you wish with me," I said in a matter-of-fact tone. "It will not change the fact that I have no money now and cannot access any more until I have contact with my family." I felt an immense sense of despair settling onto my shoulders, the heavy sadness of one who had seen too much to be surprised by this particular injustice.

He stared at me for what seemed like ten minutes and then pointed toward a third window, where I was asked the same thing and gave the same answer. At that point the man in the third window told the officer that I needed to be transferred to the Basateen police station for a further review of my paperwork.

So I spent the night in the holding cell and then boarded the squalid truck once more to go to Basateen, where they told me I was to meet with Ra'ees El Mabaheth (the head of undercover investigations), who would decide what was to become of me. Unfortunately he was a "late riser" and was not expected to come in to his office before 2:00 p.m.

Once again, I was shoved into a holding cell in the Basateen station with a few other individuals who were lying about in desolation. I recognized one of them as a fellow detainee who had been arrested with me. He had shared the same ward as me as well, and I had thought that he had been released.

He looked at me sadly and said, "Oh Shawky, you are here. I heard that everyone would get out but you."

"What?" I asked. "Who told you that?"

"Don't worry, Shawky, it is just something I heard. Seems the officer you pissed off when you were arrested has been trying to pull some strings to keep you in. It is not necessarily true, just grapevine talk"

His words found their way into my head and swelled up like a rotting infection. I could not believe that the nightmare had just been set on replay. All of a sudden it seemed as if my resolve was completely depleted, and that I could not go through it all again.

And then, suddenly, I felt like a coward. So many other men had been in here much longer and had endured much worse. I had not even been extensively tortured, at least compared to the average activist's experience in Egyptian prisons that often included burning with cigarettes, hot irons, electrocution and worse.

This delay should not be getting to me…but it was, and I could feel myself coming close to tears, which was a dangerous thing to do in this environment.

∽ ∽

(Shahinaz Meshaal)

I sat with Amr Ezz, the impressive twenty-seven-year-old Sixth of April attorney who was handling Shawky's case, and a group of Sixth of April members in Shawky's home. His wife, Mona, listened anxiously as we discussed what happened in the courthouse. We had expected that Shawky would be among us by now. It seems that there were still some strings to be pulled.

One of the young activists looked at me intently and said, "Tante Shahinaz, I believe I can push things along from here. I know someone who is a close friend of the Ra'ees El Mabaheth in Basateen. If I have Om Eiad's permission," he continued, referring to Mona as "the mother of Eiad," a more formal way of addressing a married woman in Egyptian middle-class society, "I could call him and he will ask that Shawky be released in a timely manner in accordance with his sentence. He will expect a favor in return at some point, but Sixth of April will pay him back, if necessary, should he ask for something."

Mona eagerly gave him her blessings to do whatever it took. As he called his friend from his cell phone, Amr and I told Mona that we should all head to the Basateen police station anyway and await Shawky's release. I was confident at this point that a happy ending was in sight. The media was aware of Shawky now, and there was little wiggle room for the police after the judge had ordered his release.

The past few weeks had been a roller coaster ride for me. I could not remember the last time I had sat down and had dinner with my husband and sons. In addition to all the work for Shawky's campaign, we were also diligently preparing for the *Quila Mondassa* ("Infiltrating Few") conference, which was set to take place in the morning.

We had booked inspirational speakers such as Hamdy El Fakharany of the infamous Madeenaty court case, in which he sued the government for corruption and won, despite the fact that the ruling was later buried in paperwork and nothing became of it. We also managed to book Mohamed El Beltagy of the Muslim Brotherhood, as well as Karima El Hefnawy of the Kefaya ("Enough") movement, a brazenly brave woman who had inspired me to join the efforts for change very early on.

The Quila Mondassa, which started in 2008, had become a yearly tradition, with speeches, songs, and live discussions. Its name was meant as a sarcastic jab at the system. The term "Quila Mondassa" ("Infiltrating Few") was coined by the government itself to refer to opposition groups in Egypt. The regime used such terminology to semantically reduce any and all opposition movements to petty hell-raisers that supposedly did not reflect public opinion.

However, what had become evident in these conferences, year after year, was that there were definitely more than just a few

Egyptians unhappy with the system, and every day they were getting more vocal in their discontent.

This year, the conference would take place at the headquarters of Hizb El Gabha ("The Coalition Party"). We were always holding our events in "donated" spaces, as Sixth of April never had enough funding for any kind of formal presence. We had no cards, no office space, no money, and pretty much no hope. We had nothing but a relentless resolve to hold on to our end of the rope until the last of us fell.

The vast majority of Sixth of April members took public transportation to go to opposition meetings and arrived disheveled and out of breath, but we wore our commitment to the cause with an elegance that won us the respect of other opposition parties that consequently offered us their help and facilities whenever possible.

I fully believed I would attend the conference with Shawky by my side, so I headed out with his family to the Basateen station to get him. We sat on the steps outside of the building, taking turns going in and asking the indifferent officers for news. We started out as a group of one hundred members, but only about fifty of us were left by 1:00 a.m., when an officer finally told us that Shawky was coming out. We all rushed into the entrance of the building with our hearts in our hands.

◦～　～◦

(Mohamed Shawky)

I cannot take another day in prison. I cannot take another day in prison.

The thought kept running from one end of my brain to the other like a caged animal. I could not shake it or keep it from pounding against my skull. So when they called my name and the names of four other inmates who had been arrested around the same time and informed us that we were to be released, I could not stop shaking. I did not say a word. I remained quiet through the whole discharge procedure, fearing that any wrong word or gesture may land me back behind bars.

I wondered who was waiting for me at this insane hour of the night. The first person I saw was Amr Ezz, the attorney. His demeanor was serious, but he was smiling and he took me by the arm and quickly led me out to my family.

Mona could not contain her emotions; she hugged me strongly but quickly. Public displays of affection, especially among young Muslim couples, are not very popular among conservative members of society. Under normal circumstances, she wouldn't have even attempted the quick hug at all.

My embrace with my father lingered and was followed by hugs from my father-in-law and about fifty Sixth of April members who were there, looking haggard but excited. They all had posters with a picture of me on them. The picture showed my son and I on a family outing. I had a big smile on my face and was kneeling next to Eiad, hugging him. Who would have thought that that image would be part of a campaign to get me out of jail?

Ahmed Gomaa, a well-known activist of the Horreya opposition group, handed me a cell phone and said, "Shawky, Dr. Ayman Nour"—the former Egyptian presidential candidate who was sent to jail for daring to run against Hosni Mubarak—"wants to speak to you."

I took the phone from him in a daze. It was already starting. My incarceration had made me worthy of communicating with the most well-known activists in Egypt. In my heart, I felt that I had not endured enough to deserve any kind of special treatment. It was an honor that I would constantly strive to live up to.

Being me, I resorted to joking with Nour. "Hello, Dr. Nour! Had I known that I would get to speak to you in person I would have gotten myself arrested a long time ago!" Mona shook her head and smiled. I think she was relieved that I was still the same person and I wasn't exhibiting any signs of obvious trauma. That is what I wanted for her. I wanted her to feel that she had nothing to worry about. I wanted to make it all up to her and Eiad.

Nour's voice came across as strong, confident, and welcoming. His prison experience had been a horrifically public ordeal that included the government targeting his wife and family for the duration of his incarceration. The government even resorted to releasing a tape of him in bed with his wife onto the Internet to further terrorize and shame them as a family. He congratulated me and told me that I would forever grow from this experience, as had he.

"Listen, Mohamed," Dr. Nour said, "are you free tonight?"

I laughed and said, "I was in prison until five minutes ago, so my schedule is wide open."

"Well, then, how about I take you out for a celebratory dinner?"

I looked at Mona and thought of Eiad, who was being cared for by family, and all I wanted to do was go home. I longed for my bed and my apartment so badly it physically hurt.

"Dr. Nour, I am so honored by your invitation," I said. "But I need to be with my family tonight. I will definitely take you up on that offer soon if you still have the time for me."

"Of course I will," he said warmly. "I can see that you will play an active role in Egypt's future, Mohamed, God willing. You take care of yourself."

The amazing phone calls continued throughout the night, including one with Mohammed Abd El Kodous, a prominent leader of the Muslim Brotherhood. He invited me to attend an event in my honor the following week. I was to be presented with an award for bravery for my role in attempting to document government corruption.

Leading activists from all over the country congratulated me on my release and welcomed me into the ranks of those who fought and bore the scars of their bravery. Apart from the night my son was born, I cannot remember when I had ever been happier or prouder of being who I am. There were millions who had been incarcerated by the oppressive regime and were released in utter silence. The fact that I was a member of Sixth of April and that the movement had done its homework and carried out a widely successful campaign was the only reason anyone knew my name.

Tante Shahinaz told me that, even though it was now 2:00 a.m., I was expected to give a speech the next day at the Quila Mondassa conference. On that note, I parted with my parents and headed home with Mona.

At home, as I ate eggs and cheese that now seemed insanely delicious, I stuck to the stories that wouldn't depress Mona. I told her nothing of the humiliation and pain that were integral parts of my experience. I did not want that to be the theme of the night.

Instead I spoke of being popular and respected by the inmates in Torah. I told her of soccer matches and of us inmates eating all the delicious food she sent us. She and I took turns kissing Eiad as he slept and crying in each other's arms. *Insha Allah*, this situation was behind me and only positive things would result from it in the future.

MOHAMED DIAB, 33, SCREENWRITER AND FILM DIRECTOR AND MOEZ MASOUD, 32, RELIGIOUS SCHOLAR AND TELEVISION PROGRAM HOST

7.

(Mohamed Diab)

Moez and I woke up on January 30 in the Semeramis Hotel after about four hours of sleep. The first thought that came to mind was my wife. I picked up the phone and called her. She'd had a tough night. She was concerned about sporadic uterine cramping she'd been having and wanted to check on the baby, but her gynecologist had not yet reopened his office and the hospitals were mostly devoid of staff. I tried to reassure her though I was worried sick, and in turn she reminded me to get some food into my system. She was relieved I was safe, but we both knew that our worries were far from over.

The whole interaction made me think of Wael Ghonim's wife and the fact that she and his family, who were our dear friends, had had no contact with or news about him for five days now. What could be happening to him? Was he strung up from some hook in the wall being electrocuted—or worse? Or was he in a hospital morgue lying cold and unidentified? I wish I had a true grasp of how much or how little he was involved. I knew he was as committed as any of us to the cause, and I was truly impressed that he had taken leave of his Google job to participate. I was always bothered by the question of why the government would arrest him. Were we next? Would we ever find out what truly happened to him? His disappearance made international headlines, which added to the surreal feeling of everything taking place around me. He had children—what would become of them now?

He would have been amazed at the turnout and the ensuing courage of the twenty-eighth. The numbers Moez and I had seen were beyond anything I had dreamed about with Wael. His cell phone had been eerily out of reach since Thursday. Just like that, he had fallen off the radar—another lost ship in the now-tumultuous sea of opposition.

As Moez was getting ready, I went to the balcony and saw that already the square had newcomers coming in. Those who had spent the night were cleaning up around their makeshift tents and clearing blankets and leftover trash. The pavement still showed signs of blood and battle, and one could smell the smoke from the smoldering NDP building and the handful of cars that had been burned on the street.

We had a quick breakfast of bread and tea and thanked Moez's sister-in-law, Kismet, for helping us get a room in the mostly abandoned hotel as we headed out to join those in the streets. We passed through the hotel lobby, where journalists were hunched over their notes and taking turns reporting over the phone in the reception area.

We started speaking to other protesters the minute we joined the crowds. Some recognized me and others gathered around

Moez. There appeared to be two kinds of protesters there: The overnighters, who were showing visible signs of stress, hunger, and sleep deprivation (most of them had not seen their homes or families since the Friday of Anger), and the newcomers, or returning protesters, who had a fresher look and brought with them whatever medicine or supplies they could manage.

Once again the diversity of the square's population amazed me. The men and women were from all walks of life. Women in tight shirts stood nonchalantly next to men in traditional Egyptian garb. Men in T-shirts with Tommy Hilfiger written in bold across their chests were brandishing bloodied bruises on their previously sheltered faces. They walked next to those whose shoes bore obvious holes and whose faces told the story of a more long-term struggle than the one in Tahrir.

I had spent months and months researching sexual harassment for the movie *6, 7, 8,* my directorial debut. Its characters were women from different class levels who suffered from severe sexual harassment in Cairo and decided to take matters into their own hands and exact their revenge on men by stabbing them in the groin. How different was the reality now before me. The women of the square were proud and fearless. Their voices were audacious and steady in the face of the police, the army, and more importantly, in dealing with other men in the square. For once, they seemed oblivious to the role their gender played in interactions and in turn, they were met with respect and attentiveness. Women were revolutionary peers during this wondrous time.

I believe that this is the first time in my thirty-two years of life that I had seen such different kinds of Egyptians sitting on the floor, eating and conversing with each other. All the class, educational, gender, moral, and financial barriers were on hiatus, and people looked at each other with clarity for the first time. The plans they made to stay or go, chant or rest, and form new committees or strengthen the ones that already existed were impressively organized and stunningly effective.

Protestors would inform us that this "neighborhood" was consistently at risk of shrinking in the night. Army tanks would tighten the circle they had formed around the square slowly, inch by inch, while protesters slept. Protestors had become aware of this and were sleeping in front of the tanks to inhibit this process.

Moez had found himself in these conversations in the square. I watched and filmed him animated and energized. The fears and panic that had plagued us just last night seemed to have been forced out of his head by the contagious will of those around him. He was so *into* connecting and conversing with the people one by one. It was clear that this is what he, too, had hoped for in all his shows and lectures, this sense of unity and mutual love and respect.

We were not aware of how difficult it would later be, just a few months down the road, to get the same group of amazing people in the square at the same time or to recreate even a fraction of this "peace train" of change.

A group of protesters attempted to convince Moez to address the crowd through one of the multiple bullhorns situated throughout the square. Protestors took turns chanting into the horns and reiterating the goals and demands of the revolt. The horn-bearers were Tahrir's conscience, out loud, the voice inside protesters' heads that kept them steady and focused.

Moez seemed reluctant to assume a leading role. His sense of responsibility was a deterrent. I had known him to be both precise and calculating. He seldom made spontaneous moves when it came to his mission, function, image, and career. His very participation was probably the most impromptu act of his adult life. He stuck to addressing small groups of four or five, and I filmed the interactions for our records.

The protest chants were creatively contagious and summarized the trials and tribulations of the last thirty years in short, singsong bursts. If, for any reason, you happened to be there and lose track of the goal of the protest, the chants would prod you on: *"Itisam, Itisam hata yasqot el nezam"* ("We are steadfast in our strike here, until the current regime is cleared"), or *"Thawra, thawra wi gheerha mafeesh, lehad mansheel hokam tarabeesh"*("Revolution, revolution, and nothing but, get rid of our leaders stuck in a rut"). But the dearest to everyone's heart was the simple Tunisian-inspired refrain, *"El Shaab yoreed isqat el nezam"* ("The people demand the fall of the regime"). This chant would sear itself into common Egyptian vernacular, and its spark would set up more fires across the Arab world.

The "sign-bearers" were a culture of their own; though they carried their sentences across their chests and at times on their faces, they did not shout the words out. Instead they stood, and in some cases, walked about in silence. In a country in which oppression had ruled for so long, the mere right to bear a controversial message in public seemed a spiritual experience. The expressions on their faces were bold but calm, like they had exerted all their chanting energy, and now was the time to silently present their argument.

The messages on the signs varied in content, ranging from political jokes mocking the president and the regime to images of protesters who had been killed a mere few days ago. The defiance of the jokes was just as moving as the more sorrowful posts. The unifying elements were that they were as concise and to the point as the chants, and they painted a collective picture of the prevailing mood, which often changed from hour to hour.

This was the most powerful drama I had ever experienced. I filmed and filmed and filmed some more, not truly knowing why I was doing it or what purpose the footage would serve. Still, it seemed like I needed to capture it on film in case it went away fast, like a child's adorable nuances that will soon be outgrown.

❧ ❧

(Moez Masoud)

Rumi's poem, "One Who Wraps Himself," so eloquently says:

> God called the upon Prophet Muhammad, naming
> him the Muzzammil
> ["the One Who Wraps Himself"], and said,
> "Come out from under your cloak, you so fond
> of hiding and running away.

"Don't cover your face.
The world is a reeling, drunken body, and you
are its intelligent head.

"Don't hide the candle of your clarity.
Stand up and burn
through the night, my prince.

"Without your light
a great lion is held captive by a rabbit!"

I had seen the great people of Egypt held captive by what they feared, and I was privileged to have seen them come to the realization that their enemy was a rabbit in the face of their refusal. I was humbled that God had allowed me to refuse this system alongside them during my lifetime. I, too, had been guilty of not being aware of how swiftly our collective Lion would bring about change.

There was so much that religion could add to this equation. It was a delicate argument because it removed fear by implying that there was an afterlife beyond the current realities of pain and danger that your enemy may be wielding before you. It implied that even if you perish for your cause, there is an existence with God beyond this that will reward you. If this sentiment is abused, it is an invitation to many to expire for myriad reasons, selfishly assuming that they will get to paradise with ease as a result. However, if it is understood correctly within the context of love and humanity and the struggle for freedom, it becomes a force that is inexorable.

This force engulfed me as we prepared to line up for our prayers. The great Abrahamic Egyptian Lion materialized before our eyes, as young Christians prepared to protect Muslims in prayer, bravely pausing to meet with the almighty amidst a battle so obviously far from over. They linked their hands together and formed a circle around the Muslims, their faces serious and their demeanor that of respect.

This became an honorable ritual that Egyptian Christians took numerous times during the initial protests. There was an intense drive to bring religious unity to the forefront to fuse together the forces of Egypt's two faiths.

At this point there was a noticeable presence of the Muslim Brotherhood in the square as well. To a great extent, its members had attempted to participate as individuals and not as a collective. However, their tendencies to lead and their pull and scope could be felt in Tahrir. I was definitely becoming more and more aware of them.

I bowed my head in prayer and marveled at the calm that appeared to wrap itself around us. For a brief moment, it appeased my fears that had plagued me when I spoke to protesters a few minutes earlier. I had feared that they would lose their focus and succumb to the emotional runaway train that often comes with posttraumatic stress.

On the other hand, oddly enough, I had an equally strong fear that protesters may give up the fight prematurely. I had urged whomever I spoke with to stay in the square, though I had feared the reprisal of the regime. Would these individuals hold me responsible if the regime struck and they experienced casualties? How many of those I had spoken to today would lose their lives in the next few weeks?

As I tried to conquer my thoughts and focus on the prayer that was beginning, they were driven out of my head by a searingly loud noise that exploded into the square. I lifted my head and lost my place in the prayer. To our shared shock, we witnessed F-16 planes swooping down onto Tahrir. They flew so low they invoked pain not only in our ears but also in waves across our bodies.

As I covered my ears with my hands and ran, the consecutive prayer lines broke apart. Men who had been gathered in a calm line a mere seconds ago were running wildly with their mouths open, apparently yelling to each other to take cover, but no one would hear a thing above the thundering blare of the plane's engines flying over us. The scene moved around me in what felt like slow motion.

I could see a young woman in tears a few feet away from me look around frantically, as if in search of someone. I hoped it was not a child she had brought with her. Some men and women believed that it was important to show the children the struggle up close, to ensure that new generations would never fall into the paralyzing trap of silence that their parents had. Then, in an instant, she was removed from my line of vision by others running in her direction.

I was separated from Diab as we scattered about. Groups of people churned in different directions with no obvious route. It occurred to me that the planes were a typical dictatorship move. It was perhaps a marvel that they had not been sent in sooner.

It was all painfully predictable. Logically, what else was left to try? The regime had tear-gassed and shot at us, it had released the criminals from their jail cells, pulled out the police force and sent in thugs…it was no wonder that these fighter planes were its next move. The obvious question was, who was flying them? I searched the faces of the soldiers on the tanks for signs that that they had known of the attack, but they appeared as bewildered by it as we were.

In the end, the planes never fired at the crowds, but managed to create a sense of panic, and quite a number of injuries resulted from the sporadic stampedes that occurred as protesters tried to take cover.

Diab and I had agreed upon a meeting point should we be separated, and it was a comfort to see him standing there disheveled but unharmed. We hugged each other and expressed our amazement at the dramatic thirty-minute performance the government had just presented on Tahrir's stage. At that point, we felt that the regime was pushing its luck with every wrong move it made. Once again, Diab and I believed we had a role to play beyond the square—through the media. We wanted to connect with those in their living rooms again and bring them closer to what we had just experienced. We wanted to reach out to those in the square as well, and rebuild the positivity that we was in jeopardy.

We left shortly after the F-16 incident, along with a sizeable number of participants who expressed the need to exit and regroup. They vowed to plan a *millioniya* ("million-man march") protest for the upcoming Tuesday. That would be the response to this cowardly attack. The collective feeling was, when you scatter us, we multiply. We were not retreating anymore than a wave retreats when it pulls back into the ocean. When it comes back, it does so with a higher, more forceful gush deeper into the shore.

That Sunday afternoon, I carefully considered what my next moves would be. There were a multitude of feelings going through my heart and into my head, but one thing I knew for sure: I was utterly convinced that Tuesday had to be an unprecedented show of unified strength. We had to drive the message across that the only right way to end this escalating situation was to make the changes demanded by the Egyptian voices on the streets.

"Could Mubarak really shift his thinking at this age?," I asked myself. "Could he end the law of emergency that came into effect the moment that Sadat's bullet-ridden body hit the ground next to him 30 years back. Could he do that? Could his mind be brought about to digest that now is the time, to act in a polar opposite manner to everything he was accustom to?"

I kept these thoughts in my head as I wrote my upcoming statement to the media. I tried to think of the president as a mere man with feelings and actions and reactions that we could influence by both our words and our stances. I liked to believe that at his core he was an Egyptian like us. I liked to believe that it was possible to sway him toward a course of action that could reconcile him with his people. No one was beyond God's grace or mercy, not a soul on this sad earth.

I had several interviews lined up for Monday, and my goal was to thicken the ranks for Tuesday with whatever power God chose to place behind my words on air.

On Monday evening, Moataz El Demerdash, the host of Mehwar channel's *90 Minutes* show, which I had been a part of for the past two years, went over what we were going to discuss. We had had no time to prepare beforehand because of my preoccupation with the protests on the ground. In the fifteen minutes we had, we discussed the possibilities of our on-air conversation affecting his job and invoking the anger of his bosses. I told him the many themes I would tackle and the many venues through which I would be understood—and misunderstood—and he bravely committed to maintain the integrity of our conversation on air.

This would be different from the interviews I gave to El Arabiya and similar news-oriented, eyewitness-report formats I had engaged in over the last four days. This gave me more of a chance to comment on the various, ever-changing angles with which this iconic situation had been presenting us. Although the program was filmed live without editing, its pace was slower than most and would allow me to integrate an in-depth analysis from my perspective into the discussion.

∾ ∾

(Moez Masoud)

I listened to El Demerdash, the *90 Minutes* host, explain to viewers why he believed my thoughts on the recent events unfolding in the square were worth listening to. We did not assume that the viewers had seen my appearances on EL Arabiya or had any knowledge at all that I had been participating.

Accordingly, I believed it was important to first state clearly that I was not speaking on behalf of any political party, or religious group. My appearance on this program was simply a way to tie in my research, lectures, and television work to what was going on and come up with a proposed course of action for likeminded citizens.

I began by explaining how my involvement began after following my friends on Facebook and several news websites online on the 25th of January, and how those extraordinary events led me to quickly book a ticket and join in. I explained why the only reason I was not physically in the square at the moment was to appear on this program and evoke a dialogue with viewers at home that would perhaps convince them to join in on Tuesday's march.

At this point, I was still going in and out of a strange state of shock on the very subject matter we were discussing and the fact that so early in my adult life I was witnessing (and a part of) a radical historical turn of events in Egypt. At times it felt like an out-of-body experience or a strange dream. It had been that way in Zamalek (a neighborhood near Tahrir), a mere forty-eight hours ago when Diab and I attempted to head closer to our homes with great difficulty, and it was like that now as I sat on set and attempted to mobilize fellow citizens in this leap forward, which I couldn't believe was available to us to begin with.

Fifteen minutes into it, I took a deep breath and said, "You know, Moataz, there is nothing and no power that is pushing me to say what I am about to say to you now. I seek no personal benefit from it, and am driven only by the belief that what I am proposing is for the betterment of our country. And because this is a personal perception, I have no doubt that it will possibly anger the regime and/or even segments of society that are either for or against the revolution. I urge you and the viewers to remember that this is my humble opinion, and therefore it will not necessarily always be what they want to hear."

Moataz insisted that I continue.

"First, let me begin by praying that God and his Prophet approve of my endeavors. I talk to you without restraint under the very umbrella of the freedom of speech that President Mubarak had mentioned in his latest address to the people on the twenty-eighth of January. I believe that we need, from here onward, to operate with the needs of our children morally, financially, and physically at the forefront of our planning process. It is critical that we not let the current actions of the regime distract us from the fact that for the first time, the true will of the people has materialized before us and is present on Egypt's streets. This deliberate sabotage of the nation was nothing but a red herring to distract us from the reality that it was the regime itself that is truly destroying Egypt."

I was looking toward the host, but I was addressing the viewers when I said, "If you feel the need to argue the point that the true will of Egyptians is making a seismic shift even as we speak, I advise you to reconsider that action for several reasons. The first being for God and his Prophet, but the second is of tactical benefit to you on a personal level. Whoever speaks out against the revolution now will not be forgotten or forgiven when all the chips fall in the right places, which I am confident they inevitably will. So I urge you to either offer your help or say something positive now. If not, then, for the time being at least, hold your peace and reflect upon everything that is taking place around you. There is no going back for Egypt now. This fight, God willing, has already been won."

"At the heart of the spark that led to the explosion we are witnessing is the accumulated lack of trust between the Egyptian people and the current regime. This is what I am delivering to you on behalf of those I spoke to in Tahrir. This is their opinion and I will tell you mine shortly. The vast majority of Egyptians have lost their trust in our president, Mohamed Hosni Mubarak."

I paused for a second to let these words, which were seldom said this bluntly on television in Egypt or any other Arab country, sink in.

"I believe that the very lining of Mubarak's system is rotten and corrupt. This element has stolen from the Egyptian people. It has pillaged Egypt's land and it has tortured and murdered and put its own prosperity above the entire Egyptian population without shame or regard."

"There were those around Mubarak that may have led him to believe that certain decisions were for the greater good of the country when they weren't. They could have pushed him toward certain actions, promising the containment of the situation while not being clear of either the methodologies or the possible outcomes. I have no doubt in my heart that roles were abused and actions were taken without research or strategic considerations. No president rules in isolation, like an autonomous king. "

"On the other hand, the way the government ordered the mass killing of a predominately peaceful group of citizens who were out to call for a much-needed change toward a true democracy has rendered it unworthy of negotiations. We are left with only two options here. If President Mubarak wishes to stay until the end of this presidential term, he can save the situation by responding to each and every one of the seven demands of the revolution as soon as tomorrow morning. In addition, he must begin bringing all those responsible for the bloodbaths of the past few days to justice immediately. Sadly, if these aforementioned actions are not done, the president will have to resign, and with great speed."

I had stated my positions and fears, and all that was left was to call on people to support the mass marches in Tahrir on Tuesday and join together as a peaceful and unified body of Egyptians.

"I am honored to announce that tomorrow I will be one among the million who will march in Tahrir for the sake of this country."

I did not go home after the interview. Instead, I headed for the hotel nearest to the TV station. I did not believe that Amn El-Dawla was as strong at this point as it once was, but I wanted to eliminate any possibility of something or someone preventing me from participating in what was set to be one of the biggest protests Egypt had ever seen. I took off my suit and carefully folded it since I had nothing else to wear for the next day.

I had a brief phone call with my family and my mother, who was literally worried sick. She was physically unable to keep the conversation going for more than a few minutes, despite the fact that she did not know when we would be able to speak to each other again.

My wife and I discussed some rumors that were circulating about the "thugs" that were present in past demonstrations and how they were allegedly planning to infiltrate protesters and shoot at the army to get the protesters caught in the crossfire. She had received texts urging her to convince me to avoid the protests, as they would be a "bloodbath."

I told her that we should not fall into the trap of buying into the old regime's scare tactics, and that we should believe in ourselves and our ability to handle this situation, regardless of the volatility it presented. We made a joint decision to remain steadfast in our convictions and be positive of the outcome of the next day's undertaking.

MOHAMED SHAWKY, 26, MUSLIM BROTHERHOOD/ SIXTH OF APRIL ACTIVIST AND SHAHINAZ MESHAAL, 50, MOTHER/ SIXTH OF APRIL ACTIVIST

8.

(Mohamed Shawky)

27 December 2010

When the sun came up and seeped through the shutters on my bedroom window, I opened my eyes and looked around me at the walls of my modest home. I had so many dreams and plans for my little family. So many times I had looked around this apartment and hoped for more for my son.

But at this moment it all seemed like such a luxury. It did not bother me that the case against me was still open; the whole experience felt like it was being held at bay by a secret force. When I was in jail I was exactly where God wanted me to be. Now, that was true as well. I would remain in my home as a free man for as long as God plans for me to be so. There was no point thinking or worrying about any other realities or possibilities. There is a thin but impenetrable line between faith and denial.

I got up and got ready for the Quila Mondassa conference. Mona and I would catch the microbus — a miniature bus and popular mode of public transportation in Egypt – to get there, so I had to factor in the traffic and walking distances. If that had felt like an effort before, it did not now.

Mona's mood was absolutely celebratory and Eiad was excited and active. I imagine that he was disappointed that we had arrangements for family to stay with him while we attended the conference. Mona felt bad for him but did not let it put a damper on the fact that she and I were together *and* going on an outing. We talked and talked all the way to the unassuming headquarters of Hizb El Gabha ("The Coalition Party"), where the conference was held.

Bear in mind that this is not a conference like those held in five-star hotels, or even in those held in small motel conference rooms, for that matter. Hizb El Gabha's headquarters is basically an apartment with medium-sized rooms, originally designated for offices, set up with chairs and a desk and podium in front of them. However, for Sixth of April it was exciting just to have walls—and avoid arrest.

Eagerly committed Sixth of April participants filmed the talks in the various rooms so they could later be uploaded to YouTube. The speakers were opposition celebrities, which probably meant that they were only known to about 5 percent of the entire Egyptian population. Still their presence was a big deal to us.

Dr. Mostafa El Naggar, a thirty-two-year-old dentist, accomplished activist, and El Baradei's campaign manager, was among the attendees. I saw him being filmed in a room on his own. He was giving a one-minute commentary on the events of the day from his perspective. He had a quiet, calm demeanor that seemed unfitting, considering the frequent arrests and beatings he had been subjected to since his early twenties.

I looked at him now through the eyes of one who had been there too—and may go there again. In fact the thing he and I had in common was our willingness to go there again and again, until we were physically incapable of doing it any more. We were both very young, which means there were many years ahead of us, and therefore a lot to endure still.

When it was time for my speech, members crowded around and cameras snapped as I spoke. This would be the first time I'd go into detail about my ordeal in front of Mona, and I was very conscious of her presence. Accordingly, I went into joke mode and danced my way across the painful incidents like a magician on hot coals. I made the crowds laugh when I said that the beatings were so frequent that you longed for the insults. I quipped that prison police must have undergone a regimented training so detailed that it also covered the sequential build-up of curse words to be hurled at inmates. They always seemed to follow the same sequence of insults, as they first cursed your mother, then father, and then your religion (it didn't matter that they shared the same faith)—all of them, always in that same order.

I treaded lightly on the sad parts and focused heavily on the lessons behind the experience—and how I could grow from it.

I met Tante Shahinaz several times during the conference; she was upbeat and excited and completely at home in the Hizb El Gabha headquarters. She was so proud to be in the company of those who had fought the battle for so long when she was still, comparatively speaking, a newcomer despite her age. She shook my hand, patted my shoulder warmly, and hugged Mona in a congratulatory embrace.

"Did you see Dr. Kareema El Hefnawy's speech?" she asked us elatedly.

"I think we only caught the end part of it," Mona said apologetically.

"Well, she confirmed what all of us are feeling. The end is near for this regime, Mohamed. What you and so many like you

endured was not in vain, and we are close to seeing our supporters reach a critical mass. The tone is different this year, change
is in the wind. I will see you in our next meeting—a very crucial
meeting, as we will be discussing how the movement will celebrate
Police Day in January." Her eyes sparkled. It was contagious.

Mona and I were on a high for the rest of the day. When we
were finally alone, she prodded a little more about what happened
to me in prison. I deflected and made light of the facts that were
irking her.

However, a few weeks later, when I attended the small ceremony
in one of the modest Muslim Brotherhood conference rooms that
had been set up to celebrate my release, I began to experience
posttraumatic feelings that would hit and recede in emotional
waves. Memories of the beatings and hunger of the first few days
of my incarceration were showing up in my dreams. It would take
me a few weeks to get them under control.

I had the honor of having Mohammed Abd El Kodous, a leading Muslim Brotherhood member and the head of the Egyptian
Journalists Syndicate's Freedom Committee, introduce me and
present me with a certificate of appreciation on behalf of the
Brotherhood. He himself had been kidnapped, arrested, and tortured numerous times, and had achieved so much for so many freedom movements in Egypt. His very presence next to me invoked
all kinds of emotions in my chest, and I struggled to overcome
them before it was my turn to speak. I attempted to keep my hands
and heart busy by jotting down notes with the pen and paper in
front of me.

His introduction was moving, powerful, and to the point. It
summarized how a successful revolution could take shape very
quickly. There were four necessary elements, he explained: The
unity of the people behind the cause, regardless of their differences; a clear vision of what the goal of the revolution is; revolutionaries who are success stories and have impeccable reputations;
and finally, a mission that clearly reflects the desires of the bulk of
the population, and especially its poor.

"Do you know how Tunisia's revolution started?" he asked.
"It started with one poor and unemployed man who set fire to

himself. He set fire to himself because that was the last thing left in his power for him as an individual. His burden was then transferred to the youth of Tunisia. They had the choice to either watch the tragedy with no reaction or identify and adopt the tragedy of what he resorted to and take action to ensure that this would never happen to another Tunisian again. Thankfully and impressively, that is what they did, and that is what we will do, too, *Insha Allah*. One expects no less from a country like Egypt."

He followed the short introduction by making some announcements about upcoming events and then added, "And now it is time to present this brave young man with a much deserved certificate of appreciation," he said as he stood up and forcefully shook my hand.

I held up the certificate with shaking hands as the cameras snapped a few pictures. My demeanor was very different from the jokester persona I had adopted during the Quila Mondassa conference. I was tired and overwhelmed all of a sudden.

I gave a short and serious five-minute talk. I sped through what happened to me for the benefit of those who did not know the details, but the whole thing was too heavy for me to carry out in detail right then. Instead, I wanted to share with them two points. First, I did not regret a single thing that led to my arrest, and therefore, I did not regret the arrest.

"It would take me forever to list the benefits of such an experience that the almighty chose for me to go through," I said. "The reason I mention this point is to drive home the message that for every cause there is a great tax to be paid. I would be willing to get arrested over and over again if it means that this country will one day be free.

"The second point that arises from the pain of this experience is that I used to believe that if one became fairly known as an activist in this country and his or her cause was known to be just, the law of the country would prevail and you couldn't get into too much trouble. Well, I was wrong." I paused and looked at them sadly. "I was really, really wrong. There is no law that protects true efforts for change in this country. In fact, there are forces out there designed specifically to prevent change from happening by any means necessary. This deterrent should no longer deter us. The knowledge that the fight is unfair should motivate us all to reject the status quo, with all the pain it has to offer. This country cannot change without us. There is no other heroic population that will come in and do the dirty work for us. We will have to do the bleeding ourselves."

I took a deep breath and attempted to keep my voice leveled. "I have learned to play the regime's game and to be smart. But no matter how smart or careful you are, you must be prepared to go through the absolutely horrific parts to get out on the other end of this."

I swallowed hard, forcing down what felt like a giant urge to cry welling up in my chest.

"The unfairness that I witnessed last month," I said slowly, as my eyes watered, "the torture that I saw inflicted upon innocent children as young as ten years old...it's unspeakable. I listened to them weep through the night and saw their parents weep during the day as they kissed the hands and feet of the officers and prison guards begging them to let their innocent children go. There was another young man I will never forget, who told me through tears that he had approached an officer on the street in Abdeen amid all the fighting. He told the officer that he was scared to pass through the area where the heaviest street fighting was taking place, and asked for help finding a way for him to safely return to his wife and children. The officer took him by the hand, seemingly to take him to safety, but then shoved him into an arrest truck parked nearby. They had a quota of detainees for the day, and that gentleman seemed to have literally walked right into it."

The faces of those who had come to see me honored were veterans of our cause. My stories were probably familiar to them, and there was not much that truly surprised them, yet their eyes seemed tired and sad as I told my stories.

"Though I am honored that people did so much to get me out after I was arrested, and though I vow to help anyone who is innocent and falls into the same trap," I continued, "the real help we can give anyone—and all of us—is to not give up the fight. We should never lose the hope that things can be different for our children. We should do the work now that will make their reality different later. Our revolution is in our ability to stick with the preventive measures we can take now to end this mass Egyptian impotence, which is becoming pandemic."

The speech exhausted us all, and we all mentally limped away as we struggled to find our motivation amid the ugliness we had just shared. The enemy was powerful, resourceful, and scary as hell. And the activists were…well, they were people like me who had to catch a bus to get home. I looked at the attendees scatter out into the hustle and bustle of Egypt's overcrowded streets. They would each go home to their own problems, sad stories, and challenges, and find the strength to find time for this again tomorrow. I had nothing but respect for them. Actually, that's inaccurate. I also had an immense feeling of love for them. Love and respect. That is where I found *my* strength.

⇛ ⇝

January began with the church explosion in Alexandria, and we were all emotionally maimed as a result. Our enthusiasm took the biggest hit as we searched among ourselves for an enemy we could not define. Events like these were as shocking as they were divisive. Young Egyptians spent massive amounts of time online attempting to ensure that the ugliness of the assault did not achieve its goal of making Christian Egyptians feel targeted and isolated.

Profile pictures on Facebook proudly bore images of the Crescent embracing the cross, which initially went over positively, but unfortunately, spurred a slew of subsidiary religious debates. Online, the religious tensions began to brew, as citizens' feelings made their way across the Web. Articles from both faiths were shared, and comments were analyzed to death.

We spent so much of our time online consumed by this that we became suspicious that the timing of it seemed all too convenient. Khaled Saeed's brutal and public murder at the hands of Alexandrian police on June 6, 2010, a mere six months earlier, and the drama surrounding the unfairness of the trial against the perpetrators, had been fresh on everyone's mind before the bombing knocked it out of the spotlight. The explosion was the perfect distraction for Alexandrian youth specifically, and Egyptian youth in general.

It wasn't long before most activists began to speculate that the Alexandrian police were behind the explosion. Witnesses came forward with accounts that the police had appeared miraculously quickly, which is very uncharacteristic of Egyptian police, and began to disrupt what was a massive crime scene. Police had also hurriedly identified suspects who obviously had little of the required knowledge or IQ to pull off the bombing.

Shortly after all the dust began to settle, Sixth of April held a meeting to finalize its plans for Police Day protests on the twenty-fifth. Since 2007, we had "celebrated" Police Day, a national holiday designating to honoring the police, Sixth of April-style, with protests, sit-ins, or whatever civil disobedience we could muster. We would often joke about how we looked forward to our yearly beatings. I am sure the police did, too.

This year, for all intents and purposes, was set to be a rerun of past "celebrations." As usual, we held our hope as high as our arms would be when the blows rained down on us, and believed that this time it *would* be bigger and it *would* make a difference. We adopted the same positivity every year and willed ourselves to accept it as a truth every time, regardless of the number of times it wasn't.

Ahmed Maher was an active member of our movement who managed our coordination with the "We Are All Khaled Saeed" Facebook page, which had drawn more than forty thousand members since Khaled's murder. At the time, none of us knew that Wael Ghonim was the page's administrator. In fact, we weren't familiar with his name at all.

Prior to Khaled Saeed, Sixth of April's Facebook page had the largest oppositional online presence, with over seventy thousand members. We had learned of more than twenty events online that were promoting protests or other similar shows of resistance on Police Day. However, we quickly discovered that nothing rivaled the extraordinary number of "We Are All Khaled Saeed" followers who'd indicated they were attending the Khaled Saeed Police Day event. When you clicked on the event itself, the numbers showed a staggering eighty-nine thousand confirmed attendees, one hundred thousand "maybe" responses, and an additional one hundred thousand responses pending.

"OK, so I talked to representatives from the 'Khaled Saeed' webpage about Sixth of April attending their planned event," Maher told us, "and they said that we were welcome. *Everyone* was welcome. They said they did not know how accurately the numbers tallied online would actually translate into concrete street attendance, but that we were welcome to do our grassroots campaign to support the same event. Their exact words were, 'Sixth of April can work on face-to-face campaigning and the Khaled Saeed page will do what it does best, which is keyboard campaigning.'

"They haven't been around long enough to have any documented consistency of attendance to their events. They are not really a political party or anything like that. In the past, all their public events have been designated to the fight for justice for Khaled and his family. Their first attempt to participate in a political stance that was not related to Khaled, was to gather in mourning for the church bombing, and that did not translate into the expected numbers they had noted online."

"Yes, but what we are seeing online for Police Day on their Facebook page surpasses any kind of response we have ever seen online, or anywhere else in Egypt, for that matter," Tante Shahinaz interjected. "It cannot be taken lightly. I think it is a no-brainer that we should join forces with them."

"I think it is all coming together because of Tunisia," I said. "This one will be different. I can feel it in my bones... This will not be like the meager gathering in 2005, after Mubarak rigged the presidential elections, or the twenty-first of September this year"— the anniversary of Egyptian hero Ahmed Orabi's death—"when we failed to create the massive protest we had hoped for, or the twelfth of December when you gathered in front of the prison, or April sixth in 2007, 2008, or 2010...*This* one ...we will have our revolution. It can really happen."

What I said that night I posted to my Facebook page as well. In fact, I repeated it to just about anyone who would listen. I believed it in my heart and just thinking about the possibilities would get me so worked up I couldn't sleep.

On the twenty-fourth of January, I took a screen shot of the Khaled Saeed Police Day event page and posted it to my status on Facebook. The comments beneath it were endless, as people marveled at the numbers attending and their apparent fearlessness of having that attendance documented online. Others doubted that the supposed attendees will ever show up. I would answer these doubters with what I thought then was *crazy* optimism, writing, "I am confident that we will be seeing numbers close to twenty thousand on the streets."

Sixth of April created its own online banner that linked to the now joint event, and I proudly made it my profile picture. In a simple, rectangular format it had our trademark fist and a small calendar with the number "25" on it and simply said, "I am going." It was bringing in attendees by the minute. Every time I refreshed the event page, I would see that at least ten more people had responded.

The Muslim Brotherhood had announced that it would not be attending the event as a group or political party, but that it supported the demands that the protests were out to achieve and any Brotherhood members who believed in attending as individuals. I believe that, tactically speaking, this was a brilliant move, though a faction of Egyptians misunderstood it.

These people did not understand that if the Brotherhood went all-in, the government would have claimed that the (largely banned) political party was planning a coup, and that would have given the police the excuse to use all means necessary to control what they would have deemed a group of "radical Muslims" fighting the regime. By allowing the members of the Brotherhood to attend but not in the Brotherhood's name, the Brotherhood both participated in and protected the revolution.

My friend Yehia was spending the night with me so that we could head out together in the morning. He was sleeping peacefully in my bed. I had taken Mona to Mansoura earlier in the day to ensure that she was with family on the twenty-fifth so she would have their support if anything happened to me.

As Yehia slept, I tiptoed around the room readying myself for this epic day. Even though I had just been voted the movement's leader for the Maadi area where I lived, we had collectively decided that Tante Shahinaz (who had been the leader for the previous two years) would be a better coordinator for the day, since she had all the contacts and the strongest relationships with the various members of our group. So thankfully, I had nothing to prepare related to the movement.

This gave me a lot of time to focus on myself and what it was I was willingly stepping into. I knew well it had only been one short, happy month since my release, and I was already risking going to jail again. However, there was not a single cell of hesitation in my heart. In fact, as a gesture to myself, I pulled out my prison garb, with which I had been released, and decided that this would be my outfit for the protest. Perhaps by doing this, I would at least skip one humiliating step of the arrest—being forced to strip and wear prison-issued garments. Luckily, it was cold enough to slip my jeans over the thin, white prison pants without it being uncomfortable.

I sat down and wrote out what I would say in a video of me that Yehia and I were planning to film in the morning before we headed out. In the video, I would say that if people were watching this video, I had already been arrested or gone missing, but that we hopefully had succeeded in making some form of a notable protest. The purpose of the video was to tell every person watching it to not leave us alone and unassisted in our efforts. We wanted viewers to join in and continue whatever we managed to start on the twenty-fifth, and not to stop until we achieved what Tunisia had.

I felt that people needed to know that we went to jail for them and for us, our children, and our country, and that they must continue for us or Egypt will go nowhere. We would leave the video in my apartment with instructions to friends on how and where to upload it to. I knew now that being imprisoned usually motivated and at times shamed those on the outside to do the best they possibly could. Sacrifice was contagious. Once others saw that you were willing to do it, most reacted by reshuffling their daily priorities.

When morning came, Yehia and I filmed the video and departed for the square. We had butterflies in our stomachs and the reality of our probable arrest made our steps heavier. We felt there wasn't much of a chance that we would make it back home with the public claims we made online—that we were out to have our own revolution. The regime had probably set up the torture tables in advance.

∽ ∽

(Shahinaz Meshaal)

On the morning of the 25th of January, I got up early for the dawn prayers. I sat on the prayer mat for at least twenty or thirty minutes asking God for his blessings and assistance. I put on one of my designated protest outfits, a top and a skirt complete with a matching but durable veil. The ensemble was characteristically dark and comfortable—dark to withstand sitting on the ground and at times falling into it, and comfortable so the clothes did not work against me during the long hours of the fight. We were lucky that all this was taking place in the winter. A revolution in the blazing heat of an Egyptian summer would have been an easy fire to put out.

All of my men, my husband and three sons, were preparing to go to protest as well. This was an unprecedented development that both surprised and delighted me to the core. I had been so busy with the movement's preparations for this day that I did not even consider spending my time at home convincing the boys that they should go. However, about ten days before the event, my youngest informed me that he and his brothers had been following the "We Are All Khaled Saeed" page and had signed themselves up online as attendees.

My husband was on a business trip to Germany at the time, and as the date drew near, I started to fear his disapproval of the boys participating in such an unpredictable undertaking. I smiled to myself as I remembered all the arguments for and against them going that I had tossed about in my head in an effort to find the perfect way to present it to him. I fretted all night, only to hear him say as soon as he walked through the door, fresh from the airport, "I am joining the protests of the twenty-fifth, and I think we should go as a family."

Initially, they had wanted me to leave the house and head out to Tahrir with them. But I had to decline. I was the head coordinator for the Maadi Sixth of April branch, and we had agreed upon a secret meeting point in the impoverished Nahia area, where we were to group together and head out as a unit.

I couldn't even share this information with my family, so they were letting me head out first without them, not knowing exactly where I was going, but they would wait for me in the relatively affluent Mostafa Mahmoud area near downtown Cairo—where a famous mosque was a very popular Friday prayer location—at the entrance of a highly visible building there.

We said our goodbyes at the apartment door without much drama. We were determined to be positive and cheerful and to not let our fears take over. Once or twice, I had to chase away thoughts that I was too old for what I was getting into or that I could be leading the whole Sixth of April Maadi group—not to mention my family and me—to their arrests and torture. I got myself through it by focusing on the logistical details, trying to flag down a taxi to take me to the underground metro station, trying to make sure I had all the phone numbers I needed on my phone and my money tucked away securely, adjusting my veil so it was fastened in a way that would withstand some action yet remain comfortable throughout the long stressful day.

I met the first group at the metro station, and I was supposed to meet up with the rest at a fruit juice shop in Nahia. Shawky had taken a Google Earth picture of the shop and sent it to movement's members. We had purposefully picked these locations that were at least a few kilometers away and entirely different in theme from those announced on the Khaled Saeed pages—Mostafa Mahmoud and Tahrir Square. Our point was to build up as big of a crowd as possible on the outskirts before getting to designated protest locations in case the police had established presences there to prevent a large gathering from taking place.

As Shawky and I and a few other members of the movement approached the Nahia area, we began to notice the overwhelming presence of police cars and arrest trucks, the ones most commonly known to Egyptians as *arabyiat el box* ("the arresting box cars"). The trucks were parked in a row, each one about twenty feet from the next, on both sides of the street that had the fruit juice shop.

"Someone must have leaked the meeting point," I whispered to Shawky, as I noticed that plain-clothes policemen were everywhere.

"I think we should split up into pairs until we figure out what is going on," Shawky replied, as he took Yehia sharply to the left and I moved across the street with another young movement member.

Things got really tense, and I could tell that there was a lot of hesitation to go through with the plan. We were supposed to form a group of at least fifty of us and start the chant inviting others to join in. When I looked around, the entire Maadi group was here. We were all standing around aimlessly up and down the street in pairs, not knowing exactly what to do. We were definitely outnumbered by the police, and it seemed that everyone was afraid we would get attacked the minute we grouped together.

My phone began to ring in my pocket. I pulled it out and could see it was Shawky. I looked back to where he was standing but he was looking in an opposite direction, obviously trying to appear like he was calling someone else.

"Yes, Mohamed," I said in a low voice.

"Listen, Tante Shahinaz, I think we should change the plan a little. We should head toward Mostafa Mahmoud and try to support whatever is taking place there. If we all start in unison here, we risk getting taken before we even get the chance to begin." His voice was serious but unshaken, and I thanked God for that.

"If all of us head out now, they will try to grab us. How about you take a group of people and move on to there?" I asked.

He started to argue with me that he would stay and I should move on, but I said firmly, "No, Mohamed. I am going to stay and start the chanting here. You move forward with about twenty members if you can signal them to come with you. I think we shouldn't abandon the plan altogether, as more members and their contacts are supposed to be coming in to this area. You go and you go now. I will go over to the members I see here and see how we can get this thing started. We will meet you there, God willing, and we will meet you there with a big group of people. God help me, I promise you that."

I said it with as steady a tone as I could muster.

My heart was pounding and my thoughts were racing. I could risk getting immediately arrested here (something to which I had never been subjected to before) and causing enormous pain to my family, who were waiting in Mostafa Mahmoud for me. But I was the group leader and we were following the plan. We had not selected Nahia randomly. We knew a few activists from the area and they had told us how the people here, though they were poor, they were brave as hell and there was no love lost between them and the government. I had faith that people here had heard of what was happening all over Egypt today, and they wouldn't let us down.

∽ ∽

(Mohamed Shawky)

I ended the phone call with Tante Shahinaz and filled Yehia in on what the orders were. We had little time to consider it, as she was already walking toward four members who were standing together. When the rest of the group saw her make a move, they began to head in her direction.

I made eye contact with a number of those initially going toward her and motioned for them to come with me instead. Soon, about eight of them were at my side. The police started heading in Tante Shahinaz's direction and her group immediately began to chant, *"Wahed itneen, el shaab el Masry feen"* ("One, two, where are the Egyptian people?"). I did not look back to see what happened to them, but I was sure that they were as good as gone, and I did not want us to lose this early as well, so I tried to block everything out and continue with quick and steady steps out of the area. We could not lose sight of the goal of the day, to achieve what Tunisia had and to have our own revolution.

Yehia and I explained the plan and our destination to those with us. We made some phone calls to friends we knew were already there and they informed us that there were about one thousand protesters in front of the Mostafa Mahmoud mosque, but that the police had formed a thick cordon around them and were squeezing in, preparing for arrests. We quickly discussed our options and decided we would approach the cordon from the outside, as we chanted and try to create a parallel crowd outside the cordon to distract and confuse the police and disrupt the arrest process.

With our hearts already in our throats, we quickened our steps as we finally had the cordoned protesters in our sights. We started to chant *"Wahed itneen el shaab el masry feen"* and *"Ya ahaleena doomoo aleena"* ("We are calling to our Egyptian family to come and join us!") We were used to these chants only attracting a handful here or there, but this was our first brush with the miraculous atmosphere of the twenty-fifth, and what we were about to witness was historic in every sense of the word.

We quickly noticed that we weren't the only ones chanting, and our group wasn't the only one growing. In what seemed like minutes, several groups of twenty here and thirty there and more and more in every direction amassed until there were at least two or three thousand people outside the police cordon.

The police cordon broke open as protesters surrounded it from the outside. It flailed about with no apparent direction. The protesters were nonviolent but their voices were strong and fierce. The police cordon had become disconnected from its officers and arrest trucks, and to attempt to apprehend someone in this ocean of humanity was an absolutely futile exercise.

About fifteen minutes into this marvelous occurrence, there was a hustle and bustle and the chants trailed off. Protestors appeared to be talking among themselves and pointing in the direction of the Nahia area that we had just come from forty minutes before. Sure enough, a group of what appeared to be over two thousand protesters was headed our way. The Nahia people had joined in and were propelling the small group we had left behind at their forefront with unified chants and no police in sight.

When it had become clear that there were at least six thousand of us in the Mostafa Mahmoud area alone, and we began to receive phone calls from friends and family reporting that this was also taking place all around Egypt—in Dakahlia, Alexandra, Qalyoubiya, El Suez, El Mansoura, and more—Sixth of April members began to hug each other and cry.

No one on this street understood more than we did how miraculous all this really was. In 2010 alone, we had three planned protests that were huge disappointments, with dozens of arrests, an unnoticeable turnout of protesters and thankless media coverage. The juxtaposition of the six thousand around us (at that point, we had not yet been to Tahrir or experienced anything of greater magnitude) against our memories of meager protests past was creating a rising sense of euphoria in our ranks.

Thoughts of my son hit me out of nowhere and I couldn't contain my tears: It would happen for him in his lifetime, he would know something different than I had, and I had helped it happen. I never gave up on the alternatives to our harsh reality. I could not think of anything else that I could have done with my life that would amount to an achievement that rivaled this one in significance.

෴ ෴

(Shahinaz Meshaal)

When we approached Mostafa Mahmoud, I so wanted my family to see me. This was my cap-and-gown moment, my graduation march, after all the hours of work I had put in. I had traveled on foot for hours upon end, all over Cairo, handing out fliers for the twenty-fifth and all the other protests that had been planned before it. I had walked Egypt's polluted streets and ingested the disinterest of its pedestrians. I attached fliers to parked cars that probably went from windshield to the ground without ever managing to get read. I had missed meals with my family and took years off of my life with all the stress I subjected myself to, and I had thought that I would have nothing to show for it.

I was on the frontlines of the massive Nahia crowd that descended upon Mostafa Mahmoud, and I was prouder and more excited than I had ever been before. I was sure that it was close to impossible to find my family in all this. My husband had called earlier in the day, when I had not yet reached Nahia, and had told me that it appeared that there weren't enough people in the Mostafa Mahmoud area to make a dent protest-wise. I bet he'd changed his mind by now. I wondered if they were worried about me. I did take a little longer than expected to arrive.

Oddly enough, I could see my husband and the three boys very easily as I came closer to the mosque. On their faces was not a bit of worry or any other negative emotion. They were bursting with pride and elation.

We hugged and kissed and got choked up, all within the matter of five minutes. There was not much time to talk or to mull about. My phone was constantly vibrating and we were all preparing for the walk to Tahrir. At this point, all fears of the police and arrests had been laid aside. Most people believed that the police wouldn't dare disturb this crowd. And for the most part, they were right. The police didn't stand a chance in Nahia earlier, and we were grossly outnumbered when we started. The thing was that within minutes, people literally came out in droves from their homes and joined us. It all happened with such speed and synchronicity that the police had no other option but to fall back. Like a pack of elephants, there was no risk to the pack as long as no one was left lingering behind.

Word traveled among the crowd like a bush fire in a dry field. It was now time to head to Tahrir. There was no real attempt to completely coordinate Sixth of April members at this point. Because of the sheer numbers, an attempt to congregate and make group decisions now would be highly disruptive. We had not discussed this specific scenario in meetings because we had never imagined such numbers in our wildest dream, but we had always touched upon the fact that when one was in the field, it was very important to be intuitive and to go with the flow of events.

It was not considered prudent to attempt to control the situation. Alternatively, every individual was responsible for his/her performance and effort to maximize the collective benefit of any given situation. Accordingly, I did not try to ensure that all movement members were doing the same thing. They had all received a lot of training through the years, and it was expected that they were already doing the best they could. Given that the collective destination was Tahrir, I believed it went without saying that everyone was to head there.

I moved forward as soon as my family and the large group that I had been standing with started to head out. We walked until the Galaa bridge, where we could see a police blockade set up to keep people from going toward Tahrir. We moved forward at a steady pace chanting, *"Inzil! Inzil!"* ("Come down and join! "Come down and join!") as we passed apartment buildings and homes.

Our group was getting larger by the minute as we approached the blockade. We would see the police officers conversing with each other as we inched closer. In what appeared to be an unrehearsed decision, the police opened its blockade before we arrived. We went straight through without pause. I walked hand in hand with my husband, my three children at our side.

We arrived at Tahrir Square without being harassed by a single policeman. What a distance we covered on foot, and what a distance that was for the movement! We passed the square itself and took a left to join a large grouping of people who were organizing themselves to begin a massive *asr* ("evening") prayer.

For a few minutes I was caught up, marveling at the beauty of the scene before me, but unfortunately that was short lived. Like a bad memory, it all came rushing in. The police decided to pull out the old protest-suppression routine. It followed the steps in a painfully predictable sequence.

First, the police brought out armored cars with the water cannons, and started spraying at the crowds to disperse them; in fact, they started with those who were praying and most likely to be caught off guard. The prayer lines broke apart and the mass of people would open up, let the armored car pass through, but then it would close up again. It was apparent that the numbers were too great to be dispersed in that manner.

So they moved to the next level, and shot out sporadic tear gas canisters. The canisters would fly up into the air and land around and onto protesters before bouncing onto the ground to spew their gasses. Again, protesters would disperse, cough their lungs out, locate the canisters, and throw them as far away as possible, then return to their positions.

The cowards then adopted their next lowly move, which I did not recognize from protests of the past. Actually, it seemed like quite a desperate maneuver, but one that showed that they actually had to send for supplies to carry it out. Well-shaped rocks, which were obviously not from this urban area, began raining down on protesters from the direction of the police cars and trucks, bashing these citizens in their heads and faces and bruising their bodies.

I ran toward the officers before anyone from my family could stop me, and approached one of them angrily. "Officer, look at these people!" I said. "They are unarmed. Look at me! I do not have as much as a nail clipper on me, let alone a stone or any other weapon that would cause damage to your forces or the public property surrounding us. You must order this to stop!"

He looked me up and down, as if to select his response according to how much trouble I could possibly be to him. My husband and sons ran to catch up with me and stood by my side.

"We do not have stones. The stone throwing is not coming from our end," he said with an expression that was closer to disinterest then it was to any kind of effort to exonerate himself or his men.

I took a few steps away from him, found a stone, and rushed back. "Do these look like stones that came from the midan? Do you know how long these people walked to get here? Do think we could have walked all these kilometers with our pockets laden with heavy stones like these?" I raised the stone closer to his face, but his eyes did not acknowledge it.

"You see how many people are out here, lady? It could be anyone," he responded, looking away. "We have ordered our troops to not use any methods beyond those in our crowd-control manuals."

The stones continued to rain down on people and members of the movement were getting hurt.

Young doctors set up make-shift first-aid points on the side-walks, and I stood next to a twenty-one-year-old member of the movement as he got two stitches above his eye with no anesthesia.

Most Egyptians did not know of the violence of the twenty-fifth. Most of the people who participated on the twenty-fifth were those who were following the activists and were readers of opposition papers. They were also aware of the planned efforts to emulate Tunisia on Police Day. Therefore, those who were relatively detached, namely the majority of Egyptians, knew only of what they saw, read, and heard online, and viewed on international news channels, which focused on the achievements of the day and not the setbacks.

Local media attempted to dismiss the day as nothing of significance, claiming that only about two thousand protesters were in the square. Luckily, in this day and age, news of the outstanding show of discontent reached almost all Egyptians in their home in some version or another.

The police remained engaged in tactical maneuvers from the asr prayers to the *maghrib* ("sundown") prayers, and then they took a break. By 10:00 p.m., I was wiped out. We had all been out of the house since 10:00 a.m., and I was finding it difficult to remain in an upright position.

For the majority of protesters as well, they seemed to have interpreted the break in violence as a victory on their end. There was a lot of sporadic hugging and celebration, and a lot of breaking out into song, especially *"Belady Belady,"* the national anthem.

At that point, many protesters began to declare victory and head home, while some elected to stay and considered spending the night and remaining in the square until some show of a response to their actions had taken place. My husband and I told the boys that we should go home and regroup.

The boys refused. They said that if they were not going to spend the night with the protesters, the least they could do was buy them food and water for the night. A committee was already in place looking for volunteers to help bring supplies to those who were setting up to stay.

To be honest with you, I was proud of them. I was too old to stay longer without becoming a liability. In a sense, I felt that the very fact that I willingly left my children behind to continue the fight for as long as they could bought me the right to rest a little at home. So, though I left my heart with them, I took my nerves and my worries for them with me home to attempt to recharge what I could for the days of struggle yet to come.

Indeed, there was no turning back now. There were miles to go before anyone in his right mind would allow this country to go into a slumber again.

⁊ ⁊

(Mohamed Shawky)

Yehia and I stood and looked at Tahrir in awe. Night had fallen, and it had turned into what resembled an outdoor concert. It was as romantic as it was festive. We were experiencing a level of euphoria that we had not known was even attainable in this context. All of the adrenalin of the day had turned into pure, continuous endorphins.

The culture of the square was akin to a college campus, except there was no corner for the rich kids on one end and the poor on the other. There was no "cool" zone or "nerdy" zone; everyone— and I mean *everyone*—was connecting with everyone else.

No matter where you walked, people were engaged in passionate conversations about change. Should they stay until their demands were met? What were their demands? Were they valid? Were they attainable?

The highly educated were taking the time to exchange ideas with the working class. There was a sudden, spontaneous eruption of revolutionary awareness and sense of ownership of the country and the cause. All of a sudden, we were in this endless waterfall of people who *got it*. This was a grassroots activist's dreamland: a

136

massive sea of people you didn't need to talk up because they were already there.

If the struggle for change was akin to courting a hard-to-get woman, this was the part of the story where she finally says yes, and now the lovers were sitting down to discuss the logistics of the relationship, where they would live, a big or small wedding, how many kids they'd have, and so on. Despite it all, I had an underlying, nagging feeling that we should be searching for that other shoe that was due to drop at any minute. Instead, Yehia was suggesting that we go buy blankets for ourselves as well as the others spending the night.

"I don't trust this setup, Yehia," I said. "What if everyone leaves to do something and the regime feels it is a good time to strike while the numbers are low? They have not used rubber bullets or live ammunition yet. Do you think they would fold this easily without pulling out all the stops first?"

Yehia looked around with childlike glee and said, "Look at this, Shawky. We won. They're not going to do anything now. They have seen what we were capable of today. They are in retreat mode, believe me."

In my head I could see it happening, the regime moving in with sticks, spontaneous arrests, the beatings…The monster that had attacked me a month ago was still out there. But everyone around me disagreed, and when I relived what I had experienced earlier in the day, I tended to agree that we seemed to be in a position of strength.

It had all been too beautiful. I could barely control my brain from constantly replaying scenes from the day. Tante Shahinaz told me that her group had a straightforward walk to Tahrir, but we had a different experience. For us, it was much more of a struggle to get here, but the triumphs we experienced almost made me feel bad for her, that she missed the beauty of witnessing the subjugation of the police.

I had had the awesome privilege of being introduced to the Egypt and Egyptians of my dreams firsthand. When we approached the Dokki area, which was between Mostafa Mahmoud and Tahrir, the police had called out special forces officers from El Dakhlia (the internal police force) to stop the flow of protesters to the square.

A group of maybe five hundred troops armed with sticks began to shove their way into the crowds, attempting to push them away from the route to Tahrir. A number of the protesters began to fight back and a few blows were exchanged. We then witnessed the wondrous unanimity of the crowd demanding that the protests remain peaceful. Those who had lost their tempers and were striking the police were not only subdued by those around them, but also appeared to be quickly reprogrammed to move forward in peace without inflicting any aggression. The chants *"Silmia, Silmia"* ("We are peaceful, peaceful") would rise up from the crowds in a beautiful song that appeared to lull even the police themselves.

While everyone looked forward, I couldn't help but study the faces of those around me, as my mind would not cease asking the question, "Who are you people? Who taught you to act like this? Where were you hiding all these years? How did you achieve such simultaneous beauty and perfection?"

We had spent hours upon hours in the movement studying peaceful protest and researching methods of mobilization. We studied Serbia's revolution and Gandhi's methodologies and every nonviolent technique we could find, but nothing we had read could explain what we were seeing.

Who taught these masses *"Silmia, Silmia,"* and who told them to say it now and in unison? There was no dialogue about this online. These faces were never present in any meetings or past activities.

Social scientists had long predicted that populations that endured the severity of the injustices that Egyptians had, once allowed to speak out, would erupt in a violent show of force that demolished everything in its path. Instead, protesters chained themselves together, hand in hand in a protester cordon of safety around officers who appeared at risk of getting assaulted.

I even surprised myself when I protected an officer who looked no different than the ones that made me lie down on a floor of human urine and feces as they stepped over us. My heart was suddenly full of a calm and intrinsic knowledge that my war was not with him, but with the system that created him.

Officers were Egyptians like us. This guy could be my brother, my friend, or a member of my family. If this particular officer had tortured helpless people, God would take up the people's revenge with him another day. But today, the goal was to stand up peacefully for change, and that is what I intended to do.

With this shared feeling of peaceful determination, we pushed forward and the internal police fell back. We broke through them like a hot knife through butter, with minimal resistance. The protester body moved forward like a piston. A group would spearhead and move quickly while a smaller group fell back and moved slower. The slower group would then swell up into a bigger group, and then move forward quickly, leaving another small group behind to swell and catch up. The relay movement propelled thousands and thousands in Tahrir's direction in a continuum that lasted several hours.

At one point in the road, a swanky BMW pulled up next to me and lowered its window. The driver, an obviously wealthy man in his early thirties, asked me, "I want to join in, should I just park anywhere?" I gave him some tips on where to park and how to catch up with us with a big, goofy excited smile on my face.

By the time we reached the Kasr El Neel bridge, the protest had turned into a thick, never-ending snake. There were protesters ahead as far as the eye could see. I left my position for a second and ran along the massive snake in an attempt to reach its head and gauge how far it reached, but I couldn't get to the front without going so far forward that I would risk losing touch with my Sixth of April companions. Not that we had any organizational power at this point. The sea of people was moving forward on its own accord, like a massive puppet without strings.

The snake had a mind of its own, but the movement didn't mind one bit, since it was doing such a remarkable job on autopilot. There was no need to direct it. It was following the proper protest protocols to a T.

Our studies told us that, for a successful revolution to take place, you needed a large mass of people to protest. The protest should be followed by a mass sit-in, the sit-in followed by a mass strike, and the strike followed by widespread civil disobedience.

The hardest part was always to gather the large mass of people to begin this process, people who agreed that the aforementioned steps were necessary and worth risking their personal safety. This target mass, which had eluded us for the past three years, had materialized seemingly out of thin air and appeared to be headed in the right direction.

In our meetings, we had always fantasized that if this day ever came, we would focus on three ambitious demands: first, removing Habib El Adly (the Minister of Interior Affairs believed to be the designer of the current Egyptian torture curriculum); second, a fair minimum wage; and third, free and fair elections. But these people aspired far beyond that. They were boldly singing Tunisia's refrain, seen on satellite television channels and news broadcasts: *"El shaab yoreed isqat el nizam"* ("The people demand the complete fall of the regime"). This was not a crowd you could fool by raising some salaries or faking your way through some governmental concessions. They were out for the jugular.

When we finally reached Tahrir, it reminded me of a scene from the movie *Braveheart*. We were welcomed as a reinforcement battalion with glee and celebration. We then became the welcoming committee as we ushered in reinforcements from Shoubra, the pyramids area, Nasser City, and more. It seemed endless.

At that point, the regime must have felt the last vestiges of control slipping through its fingers, and hence sent in the water cannon vehicles. But these crowds were a feisty bunch, and they were pulling stunts I had never seen before. Brave young men would jump on the cars while they were in motion, Hollywood-style, locate the water valve, and empty the water tank, disabling the car.

I got a little caught up in this one, and thought that it was my duty to do my part in what looked quite frankly like an exciting endeavor. I quickly changed my mind after I managed to jump on one of the vehicles. The ground was speeding by so fast. I could not jump or move or do anything that was of specific use to anyone. So I clung there in a panic. In fact, I began to think that I could lose my life in the next few minutes.

The vehicle itself veered left and right in its menacing attempt to disperse protesters. It actually ran over a few in the process, with me attached to its side. Eventually it slowed down while taking a turn and I managed to throw myself onto the pavement in a painful roll. I skinned my arms and tore through my pants at the knees, but I was fine for the most part.

I said a prayer for those that I had seen get hit by the vehicle and said a prayer against those inside it.

Even when we were within the borders of Tahrir Square, we witnessed about ten more of these cars pass by over the course of two hours, accompanied by some tear gas canisters here and there. But by Egyptian standards, the police were actually holding back. Maybe they had orders to do so.

Maybe Yehia was right and it *was* safe to go get the blankets. It was getting pretty cold and the night would be unbearable without something to place on the ground under us and something to cover our bodies with. So we headed out and planned to be back in about two hours.

∾ ∾

(Shahinaz Meshaal)

We had only been in the house for twenty minutes when my eldest son called. His cell phone didn't have much battery power left, but he wanted to let us know that the police had begun coming at them with sticks around midnight, and they were launching tear gas at protestors. The phone call then ended abruptly because they were being chased.

I sat up in bed with the phone in my hand, unable to come to terms with how I felt. I was in a panic, but disappointed that I wasn't stronger. Wasn't this what I'd always wanted for them? I wanted my sons to be involved and to adopt the fight as their own. This is how they must have felt when I was out there all the time.

I ran out of the room and told my husband and we discussed the option of going back out there. He believed that the three of them were probably getting around quicker without us, and the chances of finding them in the middle of the fight now were not high. He felt it was probably wiser for us to stay put and follow the developments online. We logged onto my Facebook page and saw that, surely enough, all the Sixth of April members who were still protesting were posting messages and images of the ongoing assault from both the official crowd control forces and the plain-clothes police. The tear gas had intensified, and people were being beaten and arrested.

The story that we could piece together from Facebook was that hundreds of men armed with sticks and knives were chasing protesters along the Nile Promenade in the direction of the Nile Hilton and the NDP headquarters. The square was being cleared by force. There was to be no spending the night as planned. The government wanted all evidence of the protests obliterated before daybreak.

I found Shawky online. He tried to go back in with Yehia after receiving phone calls from friends about what was taking place. The police had the entrances to the square heavily blockaded, and with only the two of them it was nearly impossible to get in without being arrested. Instead, they rushed home to get online and follow the situation from there.

The boys called again from someone else's phone, as their cell batteries had all run out. An old store owner had opened up his storage area and let some of the fleeing protesters hide there. The police then launched tear gas into that storage area, forcing everyone to flee; the police waited, caught who they could, and threw them in the box trucks.

The boys had managed to get away and run onto the Sixth of October Bridge nearby. They told me it would be very risky for them to head back home, since they'd have to go in the direction of the police. I told them I would wake up my sister and tell her that they'd be going to her. She lived in the Dokki area, about a forty-five-minute-walk from where they were.

We fell asleep shortly after hearing that they arrived at my sister's house safely. You would think we wouldn't be able to, but the sheer exhaustion coupled with the relief that the boys had made it out was a powerful sedative.

The next morning the heads of the Sixth of April groups began phoning members to gather for a meeting in lawyer Khaled Ali's *El Markaz El Masry* ("The Egyptian Center") activist group headquarters. Shawky phoned me and told me of the names of all those who were arrested and in custody since last night. A close friend of ours, Mohamed Adel, had been taken, and witnesses had told us that he was already beaten up pretty badly before he even reached the arrest trucks. Wherever the detained members were at the moment, we knew for sure that they were being tortured.

That added a sense of urgency and determination to our plans that made our proposed moves bigger and more dramatic than anything we had thought of before.

"Two or three Sixth of April groups are already protesting at the district attorney's office and the lawyers' union headquarters, and there are reports that they are being beaten as badly as last night," Shawky said, "Therefore, many of us are feeling that we should focus our efforts for the next two days on gathering as many people as possible for next Friday, which the 'Khaled Saeed' page is dubbing the 'Friday of Anger.' It is a day off and easier to get everyone out there."

We created an operations center right then and there. We posted a phone number for people calling in for information. We updated the movement's page to focus on postings and banners that called on people to fulfill their nationalistic duties by joining the march. In addition, all members were instructed to remain online as long as possible and go into other pages and chat groups and talk to as many Egyptians as they could. They would post the pictures of members who were still in custody and explain what happened to them. They cited examples from the Tunisian struggle. They spread awareness about protesting and civil disobedience, what to expect and how to maintain the unity and spirit of the struggle. It was an intense forty-eight hours, and everyone was committed entirely.

I watched my boys completely consumed by what was going on. They were not even thinking of their studies and for the first time in their lives, their father and I didn't say a word.

However, later in the day, we held a family meeting and in it we announced that their father and I had decided that our youngest should not participate. He argued and pleaded with us, but we insisted that he was too young to face the possible repercussions. He would not be able to withstand an arrest or worse.

Initially, my husband wanted no one at all to go, and asked me, "Aren't you worried that our luck will run out and we will lose one of us? Could you bear losing one of your children to this?"

"My children are on loan to me from God, and he has sent them to this earth for a purpose," I responded. "I believe that each of us should decide what that purpose is, and attempt to fulfill it. If God decides to reclaim what has always been his, then we should accept his judgment and give him back his loan gratefully."

This was another reason we believed our youngest should stay home. We felt he was not old enough to define what his purpose in this life was, and we didn't want to impose our own mission onto him. We wanted him to stay at home and assist his father in keeping track of our whereabouts and be there for his father if action needed to be taken. One of the parents had to play this role, and as a leading member of Sixth of April, I could not sit this one out.

My youngest wasn't happy with the setup, but we were not open to negotiations. When he was done with high school, I told him, he was free to pursue a career fraught with protests and possible arrests, like his mother. I was being facetious, of course. I was hoping that by the time he was done with high school, we would be done with this regime.

PART TWO

EGYPT WILL NEVER
BE THE SAME

A "FRIDAY OF ANGER" REVISITED
(FRIDAY, JANUARY 28, 2011)

9.

(Khaled Bichara, 40, Chief Operating Officer of VimpelCom Ltd.
and Group Executive Chairman of Orascom Telecom Holding)

On the night of January the twenty-seventh, I received my second
phone call from Karim, my brother and the Chief Executive
Officer of LinkdotNet, the largest Internet service provider in
the Middle East and a subsidiary of Orascom Telecom Holding of
which I was the Chief Executive Officer. We had been contacted
again by our government liaison at Amn El-Dawla and we had
some decisions to make.

The first contact by Amn El Dawla was on the twenty-fifth, when
the government ordered us to change the front page story on

Masrawy.com (our Egyptian news web portal that I partially owned through LINKdotNET), an Egyptian ISP and Internet company. The regime was ordering all news outlets to keep articles about the protests off of the front page. On the twenty-fifth, I refused, and we told the liaison that we could not do that as making such a move would destroy our credibility with our readers.

The liaison's reply was simply, "We will shut you down."

"Well, you will have to just go on ahead and do that," was our answer.

But it was obvious that, this time, we had no say. The man's voice was dead serious, Karim explained to me as he relayed the phone call.

He gave the order, "We need you to cut off your company's Internet and mobile telephone services."

It had taken Karim a couple of minutes to digest the request and ask, "When would you like this to take place?" he asked.

"Right now."

And that was that. This is how the regime handled Class-A wireless and data communication providers. This meant that Vodafone, Etisalat, TE Data, Nile Online, and EgyNet had already received the same call or would receive it shortly.

"If you don't follow our orders we will come in and break the equipment, in case you were wondering about the seriousness of my request.", the voice had informed Karim.

If the police break the equipment, the company would incur severe losses and more importantly, would not be able to resume service for its millions of customers for a long time. However, if we followed orders, we would be able to resume services as quickly as possible when we were cleared to do so.

Even if we had arrived at a different conclusion, legally, according to Egyptian law, we really had no other option than to comply with government orders. I do not believe that the Amn El Dawla liaison had any clue of how big of an adversary he created of me, someone he hardly knew, at that moment. I was instantly on the opposing team of whomever this guy claimed to be with.

In fact, so was the majority of the Egyptian population, which was enraged by the government's callous and dangerous move to cut off all of its citizens' rights to use modern communication technology to communicate with their families and loved ones on the Friday of Anger.

By 1:00 a.m., I managed to disconnect our Internet services and by 10:00 a.m. of Friday the twenty-eighth, all phone communications from our end were disabled as well. The regime informed us that government mobile telephone services, as well as some key individuals' phones should be left active. My brother's phone was one of those. The regime decided that he was to remain reachable in case they had further orders.

That was the extent of my professional compliance. On the personal level, my family had spent all of the twenty-seventh since that phone call holding a massive gathering of friends at our house and putting together a plan of how we would participate in the next day's protests.

The mood was almost festive. Our two sons, age nine and fourteen, kept walking in on us and asking all kinds of questions.

"What is a protest, Daddy?" "Are the police the bad guys now?" "Will you be in danger?"

Some questions my wife, Marianne, and I tried to answer and some we just had no time for. None of us had ever done this before. It was eerily strange to be planning to do something "anti-regime" in Egypt, where we had never even attempted to vote in our entire lives.

I was in Italy on a business trip when the twenty-fifth took place, and even before I had known that the government would pull the plug on our communication equipment, I was already sold on participating in whatever the activists planned next. I just didn't know that it would be so obviously dangerous.

I had even contacted my boss, Naguib Sawiris, the executive chairman of the telecommunications companies Wind Telecom and Orascom Telecom Holding, and explained to him that I was planning to participate in the protests. I told him if my participation was in any way an embarrassment to the company or presented a conflict of interest, I was prepared to resign.

"There is no need for that, Khaled," he said. "You just keep yourself safe and do what you feel is necessary."

Marianne had argued with me for hours that she wanted to come as well, but I really thought that, given the expected danger, one of us should be out of harm's way for the children's sake.

We had moved our family to Italy from 2005 to 2009 for a temporary position I held there. Like every young Egyptian family that experiences life abroad, we began to discuss the possibility of pursuing a life outside of Egypt where day-to-day life was seemingly so much easier.

We are Christian Egyptians, and many of our friends believed that it would be an easy transition for us to move out to the West or Europe, and set up a life for ourselves. My father had always taught us growing up that we should never forget where we were from or feel that we were any less Egyptian than anyone else just because we were part of a religious minority. "We will not leave our home because someone believes we are too outnumbered," he'd said. "We will not leave Egypt to those who believe it is better off without us."

Marianne and I had had a definitive discussion on the subject just a few weeks back, after the Alexandria church bombing on New Year's Day. We had been on vacation in Egypt's Red Sea Coast resort El Gouna. The bombing had taken us out of our rest-and-relaxation mode and into the ugly debate of whether or not Egypt was the right place to raise children from a minority faith.

We walked along the beach that night, oblivious to our surroundings, after seeing the heartbreaking images on television, discussing our children's futures. We wondered if it was safe for them. Would they prosper? Would they be welcomed and loved? Should we leave? And if we did, when would we make the move? At that point, we grew wary of where the discussion was taking us and sort of had an epiphany then and there.

"This is a stupid discussion," I declared to Marianne. "If we set a deadline for ourselves now when we are supposed to consider leaving then we will most definitely leave." I held her hand firmly and continued, "But if we decide right here and now that there is no way we would leave, we become committed to staying in our own country and remain first-class citizens of Egypt, as opposed to a 'naturalized' version of whatever it is we would be. This is *our* country and it is our children's as well, and we should never leave."

That night our friends, both Muslim and Christian, who were on vacation with us, gathered in our beach house and mourned the Alexandria bombing with us. They made plans to join us for the church mass on January 6. We would all pray together for the souls of those who lost their lives so senselessly and their parents. We would pray that Egypt perseveres in spite of those who wish to see it divided and conquered.

On the night of January 6, as we loaded our children into the car, our nanny kissed them and said a small prayer for us to return to her safely.

Marianne and I joked while we drove away about how paranoid the nanny was becoming in light of recent events. We were then interrupted by our elder son, who asked, "But Dad, aren't *you* scared after what happened?"

It wasn't his question that shocked us. It was the manner in which he asked it. He was implying that he was afraid and that we should be, too. It hit us then how serious this event was. It had actually affected our sons' feelings of safety and belonging in their own homeland.

It was interesting how, only a few weeks before, Marianne and I had decided that we needed to be more politically active and create an environment in which our children experienced the Egypt we did growing up. The one in which we never felt like we were targeted or were any different from our Muslim friends.

This was definitely our revolution, too. Egypt had so much potential, and we needed to be more involved for it to be realized.

On the night of the twenty-seventh, with all our friends there in a gathering that mimicked the dozens of parties we had held over the years, we planned for something entirely different.

We planned to participate in an event that allowed us to voice an opinion for the first time in our lives.

ᘒ᷉ ᘒ᷉

(Hoda Rashad, 36, Educator/Writer)

The Cairo-Alexandria desert road is a long, dark, and lonely place. It has sections that are well maintained and others that are downright treacherous. I spent the bulk of my stay in Egypt on this road. It is not a road that sees a lot of women driving with two children in the back seat without a man in the car.

To reach the suburb in which we lived in at the time, it was a fifty-eight-kilometer drive that took about forty-five minutes. It took a little less time to drive back from my mother-in-law's house or from my son's school, which is located in the nearby Sixth of October City. At the end of the day, the time spent in the car was not all that bad, considering people in Egypt spend an average of five hours a day in transportation due to traffic congestion.

My father had moved out into the desert a long time ago. "He has culture shock," I remember people saying that about him when we moved back from Boston in the eighties, before I even knew what the term meant. Later, I figured out that it meant, psychologically, he found it difficult to deal with the challenges of a still-developing country.

It meant he would experience anger, frustration, disbelief, and maybe even some shame. He moved back to Egypt after close to eighteen years in the United States. He had made a commitment to retire there, close to his elderly mother and siblings.

He ended up building a house in the middle of nowhere, where it was almost like he wasn't in Egypt at all. He had access to Cairo during the day, but after 5:00 p.m., he went home to his isolated farm in the desert, where none of it could get to him. When I married Basil, an American-Egyptian from the South, and we had to pick a location for our home in Egypt, I thought it would be wise to have the same setup.

Like Dad, once we hit the desert road, despite its bad reputation, we left everything and everyone behind and went back into the world we had created for ourselves.

The desert road was dangerous because travelers abused the speed limit as they sped through in wild disbelief that there was no bumper-to-bumper gridlock on this less-traveled road. There was no threat of theft or crazies on the loose or anything like that, despite the fact that large strips of it were entirely cut off from any services or facilities.

I often reflected upon my day during the long, dark ride back home. It was in this desolate setting that I found myself digesting the decision that Basil and I had reached together about a half hour ago. We had both attended our son's soccer practice, but were now in separate cars because we had arrived at practice separately.

I watched the taillights of the Hyundai he usually borrowed from my father to use for his six-week visits with us in Egypt. It was the farm's extra car, and it was beat up and struggled on the bumpy parts of the road. I often wondered how someone who spent the bulk of his life in the United States—coped with all that was thrown at him here.

That question was particularly fresh in my mind as I mulled over our decision to be a part of what was happening in Egypt through Basil's participation in the next morning's protests. I watched the car and thought of him sitting inside thinking about it, too.

He was thirty-eight years old, out of shape, and a little heavier than he should be. He had broken his ankle a few years ago and it was still giving him trouble. He was as sheltered as the rest of us, and he had not grown up in Egypt nor mastered the Arabic language completely.

Furthermore he had basically been a Californian for the last five, years and you know what they say about California making you too soft…

What would he do in an Egyptian protest?

To add to the complexity of the situation, he had decided that he wanted to hide the decision from his parents until he had left for the protests, when I would then inform them after they could no longer reach him by phone.

This scenario was particularly difficult for me, because it was our weekly routine to visit his parents on Friday morning for brunch. They were American-Egyptians as well, who had retired in Egypt after twenty-five years in the States. They owned a two-story town house in a gated community in Sixth of October City on the outskirts of Cairo.

Basil's plan was for us was to arrive there as a family as usual. He would excuse himself to go upstairs, where he would grab some items that he needed to take with him from there (namely, a copy of his American passport, an old pair of goggle glasses that he used to wear during basketball games, and some old soccer shin guards that he wanted to wear under his clothes on his forearms and legs in preparation for police beatings). I was supposed to help him sneak back out to the car, see him off, and then march straight in and break the news to his mother, father, and brother. (It was kind of ironic, when you thought about it, that he was willing to face the Egyptian police, but not his mother.)

I had argued with him that this was very unfair to me. My son kept looking to us from the soccer field to check if we were watching him, so I kept talking as I smiled and pretended to watch.

"Hoda, listen," Basil said. "If we are really deciding that it is important for us to do this for the country, let's take the necessary steps to make it happen. If my parents find out I am going, they are going to do everything in their power—and I mean *everything* in their power—to stop me, and they will probably succeed. It will be a downright emotional disaster that will end with all parties upset and me not going, lest they have heart attacks right then and there. But if we tell them *after* the fact, there will be no struggle. All that will be left is the initial upset and then they will accept it, and I will already be in the protests. Believe me, I know them better than you do. This is the only way I can do it."

I knew what he meant, and he had a point. But what I would face after he left would be my own Friday of Anger, except without the police. On the road, I called my father from my cell phone.

"Hi, Dad. Is Mom there?" I asked.

"Yes, she is right here. Do you want to talk to her?"

"No I want to talk to you both. Put me on speakerphone."

"Hi, dear," my mom said. "What's going on?"

"Basil is joining the protests tomorrow. He thinks it is really important that we participate and support the people out there. He wanted to take the Hyundai."

There was a short pause. "I understand his decision and, *insha Allah*, he will be fine," Dad replied. "Don't worry about it. And of course he can take the car. Just tell him to park it as far as possible from where all the action is." I could almost hear him smiling as he said this.

This was the beginning of a series of interactions that I had with my father throughout the revolution and beyond that really introduced me to a side of him I had not known. I had watched him mellow out throughout the years, but his cool resolve in situations like these would continuously take me by surprise.

"Sure Dad, I'll have him park it in a safe place. What do you think about him going?"

"It will be fine, Hoda. Don't worry about it," my mom pitched in. "It probably won't be too big of a deal anyway, *insha Allah*, although they will be cutting off cell phone services you know…" her voice trailed off, and I think the ramifications of what I just said had started to sink in a little. No one else from our family that we knew of had decided to go.

"Yeah, Mom, I know…"

"We will pray for him," my dad said, dismissing the drama that appeared to be taking over the phone call. It was obvious he felt there was no place for it. "You do what you see is right, and I think that it is an important cause. Would you like to come and stay with us while he is there?"

"Well, that's the thing, Dad. We'll be spending the night at his parents' house—except they don't know that. In fact, they don't know that Basil is going…" I went on to explain our little plan.

My mother thought it was an awful way to go about it, but I explained that it was out of my hands. I had butterflies in my stomach. *Big* butterflies. The kind that carried your dinner out to meet you. My mother-in-law was a kind but strong-willed and confident woman with very clear guidelines on what was and was not safe in Egypt.

"You'll survive," my dad said, once again in a dismissive tone. "Now focus on your driving and get your family home safely. Call us from your in-laws' house tomorrow."

And that was that. I hung up and I was alone again on the desert road. I thought of what it had been like at work today. The faculty room in Hayah International Academy, where I worked part-time, had come alive. The K-12 school had been pro-change for a very long time, so naturally everyone was celebrating what happened on the 25th of January.

As I walked through the hallways, I noticed something that almost made me cry.

I had set up a civic responsibility website with a group of high school students there that had launched in the beginning of the school year. We held a ceremony for it on the International Day of Peace and had designed T-shirts for that day with an all-encompassing campaign slogan, "Not in My Country."

The slogan reflected the students' commitment to tally up all they deemed unacceptable for their generation and stand against it. The website had struggled to stay afloat as it competed with their study workloads and transportation and funding challenges, and I had lost hope a bit for the campaign.

Today, however, several students had the T-shirt on. They wore it proudly with a sense of ownership and purpose. They had finally connected with the slogan. Even if the website did not take off the way I wanted it to, they had found the part of the message that counted. They were on board with the movement to make their country what they wanted it to be, and the twenty-fifth had given them the inspiration they needed.

I thought about this as I pulled up to my home. I could face the drama tomorrow for this cause not only because I believed in it, but also because it had the ability to inspire our youth in such a manner. I was not a coward. Basil would face the turmoil outside the house and I would face the turmoil inside. We would both get through it, I prayed.

ᏣᎳ ᏣᎳ

On Friday morning, January 28, Basil and I woke up groggy and shaky. Both of us had gotten very little sleep and, to be honest with you, were scared out of our minds. The kids had awakened us at 7:00 a.m., oblivious to the fact that it was the weekend and were running around in their crazy morning routine. They spilled the milk from their cereal and watched *Dora the Explorer* in Arabic on TV. I went through my typical mommy morning in a daze.

Basil had printed out an e-mail from my sister from the night before, before the government had cut off the internet. It was a forwarded message that had circulated wildly ever since news of the Friday of Anger had spread nationwide.

The e-mail read as follows:

Hi All,
 I don't know which of you are planning to go to the demo tomorrow, but here are some tips a friend of mine who protests a lot in France sent so I thought I'd share. We need to be prepared and safe so we can go on! Feel free to pass it on.

Best of luck to everyone
Rou

What to wear:
—Long sleeves and pants, sportswear, non-bright-colored clothes. Hoodies are not advised, as you might be dragged by it. Long hair tied and put under collar. Multiple layers might soften shocks.
—Sport shoes; *no* flip flops or any opened shoes.
—Scarf to cover mouth and nose, and should be wet with vinegar or lemon juice to prevent tear gas inhalation.
—Good tip for the head: Get a small bike/scooter helmet and cover it under a *keffieh* [a scarf] to make it less obvious.
—If you plan to throw back tear gas canisters, gloves are a good idea.

What to bring:
Everyone should have a backpack with:
—Water (1.5 L), snacks, tissues, medicine you might need, *saline solution* (which is excellent for clearing tear gas from the eyes, and super-cheap in any pharmacy).

—Bring money, metro tickets, notebook, pen, but not your entire wallet. Stay light.

—Bandages and disinfectant could come in handy.

—Swimming goggles, even scuba masks, are excellent to protect your eyes from tear gas.

—If you can bring some vinegar or lemon juice in a plastic bottle to rewet your scarf, *yalla* ["come on"].

About IDs: The best thing is to bring a copy of your ID with you and leave another copy with someone staying home.

About phones: Make sure you have credit and a battery, and behave like you're going use it a lot for a long time (i.e., disable Bluetooth, 3G, etc.).

Legal aid numbers: Get the latest legal aid numbers from http://egyprotest-defense.blogspot.com, save them on speed-dial, and write them on your forearm in case you lose your phone.

Find also *someone staying home*, write down his/her number, and have him/her ready to help in case of problems. Have him/her follow Twitter and Facebook to keep you updated.

Behavior:

Well, that is common sense: stay with friends, be ready to run fast but don't overly panic at the first mass movement, help people around in need, try to watch for plainclothes cops.

Setting up a meeting point is tricky as the scene moves fast. Horreya is a good one, though. :-D

Don't throw rocks or anything really solid, as they're going to throw them back. If you run into empty bottles, well, that would be smarter, as they will crash upon arrival.

What to do in case of tear gas:

Put your scarf on your nose and mouth, don't open your mouth, run away from it as fast as you can.

Don't wear lenses; in case you still do, have them removed ASAP.

Spit, cough, rinse with water, don't swallow, keep running; it fades quickly.

Rinse your eyes with saline solution (or water if you don't have saline), but *don't touch them* with your hands, which are covered as well with tear shit.

Then rinse other people's eyes; you'll make new friends!

If you're close to being arrested:

RUN the hell away, try side streets, and keep running! The police want you away from the scene more than they want you actually detained.

If you're arrested:

DO NOT give them your IDs, phones, or anything else unless they demand this of you. Say as little as possible, and if there's an opening, as it often happens in Egypt (personal experience), RUN! Discreetly text your emergency contact as soon as you can and send your names to legal aid, try to call them. Let people know *where* you've been taken. And keep looking for openings.

Accordingly, Basil was preparing the recommended gear and writing a list of what he would need to pick up from his parents' house. As I washed out an old plastic bottle of children's cough medicine to fill it with vinegar for Basil's demo kit, it finally hit me that I was sending the father of my children out to a dangerous, unknown situation that would most likely be violent.

I started to panic but kept it to myself. To stop him from going now was against everything I believed in and everything I had ever told my students throughout the years—and most recently the website kids. I had always taught them that you shouldn't complain if you didn't intend to be part of the solution. I could not stop him from going. In fact, on many levels I could not see a future for myself with him if he didn't want to go. To me, that would have meant he had no investment in Egypt's future at all and no compassion for its people, and I could not live with someone who felt that way.

I took the bottle of vinegar, with the cute, little teddy bear on it, and walked out into the living room to give it to him. He was taking pictures of the children on his phone and his eyes were glistening.

He was scared, too. I had already sensed that because of the number of times he had visited the bathroom in the last hour. I think I felt closer to him at that moment than I had ever been throughout our eleven-year marriage.

I picked up the phone and began to call a friend of mine who, because of his Facebook status, I had known was going to the protests. I told him that my husband didn't know many people in Egypt and he was going alone. I wanted him to meet Basil somewhere and keep him with his group. I needed to know there was someone there who kept track of what happened to him.

My friend Ahmed was helpful and offered to call my husband himself and pitch the whole setup to him. Ten minutes later he did, and I had the partial comfort of knowing that Basil would not be out there alone. Basil would drive out before the prayers and meet Ahmed at the entrance of his apartment building, where a group of about seven men were gathering to go together. This was a first-time experience for all of them.

As we packed the kids into the car, still plagued by that stage-fright-like feeling we were experiencing, my mother-in-law called on my cell phone. Cell phones were still functioning, but were likely to be cut off soon.

"Hi Tante Gigi," I said to her.

"When are you guys coming," she asked cheerfully.

"We are loading the car now," I answered.

"OK, I will start frying the falafels so they are warm and ready when you arrive," she said.

For the first time ever, I believe, neither Basil nor I were excited about her delicious, warm falafel. We could not even think of food. Basil was barely able to get through some cheese and bread for breakfast. I was plagued with feelings of guilt and apprehension at what we were about to put his mother through. The feeling was so overwhelming I could not bear it.

In the car, I said to my five-year-old son, "Ferris, Tatta"—(our word for "Grammy"—"and I may discuss something that may make Tatta a little angry. If that happens and it starts to look like Tatta is too sad, Mommy is going to take you and Layla to my dad's house until Tatta feels better. I don't want you to get worried or anything like that if that happens."

"But I wanted to play with my cousin," he said, slightly disappointed but somehow grasping that what I was saying outranked his desire to have a play-date. I have found that children have the tendency to be oddly intuitive when we least expect it.

"I know sweetie…we can visit him a little later if that happens, OK? It may not happen at all so don't worry. Maybe we will just talk and she won't be upset…" my voice trailed off, as Basil and I made sad eye contact.

As we approached their home, my mother-in-law came out to the front porch.

"Khalas"—"That's it"—"the cell phones aren't working! You were the last phone call I was able to make," she said to me, smiling nervously.

She kissed us both and took Layla out of her car seat. Layla held on to her in a tight hug that was part of their routine together. Tante Gigi was really close to my children. She made a point of taking care of them and being part of their lives as much as possible.

She was their closest adult friend, and the one with whom they would most likely feel most at home if anything should happen to me. It came so naturally to her. She was a mother in every sense of the word, and she was that way to everyone around her. She mothered her two sons, their wives (me included), and her own husband. She ran her house with the efficiency and care of a five-star-hotel manager and everything was always *just right.*

Ferris tagged along at her side and told her something silly about a cartoon he had been watching. I prayed that he wouldn't let our conversation in the car slip out before it was time for it.

After some small talk that I could barely get through, I managed to get away from my brother-in-law and his wife, who were helping my mother-in-law set the table, and join Basil in his room upstairs. He was trying on the shin guards under his clothing. He had his American passport on the bed together with a water bottle that was designed to be carried on one's back. He was attempting to conceal that under his clothes as well. He wanted to make sure that if anyone stopped him on the road, a common occurrence under Egypt's thirty-year-old emergency law, he didn't appear to be on route to the protest.

He handed me the passport and said, "Can you make a copy of this without anyone noticing? That e-mail your sister sent said we shouldn't carry the real thing on us."

There was a scanner/laser printer in my father-in-law's office across the hallway. I hurried to the desk, sat down, and turned on the computer. My brother-in-law was climbing up the stairs. I quickly hid Basil's passport on my lap under the desk.

"Hey, checking e-mail?" he asked with a smile. There was really no need to be flustered, since I regularly did check e-mail on this computer and he was just politely acknowledging that I was there.

I think I managed a nod. I was too tense to reply. The minute he went into his parents' bedroom, I pulled out the passport again, put in on the scanner, and turned it on. It made a noisy sound the way scanners do when they reposition themselves at the beginning of a document.

I was shaking my leg nervously under the desk.

For some reason the scanner/printer icon was not appearing on the computer screen. I checked the cables and realized that it wasn't hooked up. I fished around at the back of the computer and managed to find where the cable was supposed to go in.

I checked the screen again...nothing. I had no time for this. I pulled the passport out of the scanner and ran to Basil in the room.

"I can't photocopy the passport," I whispered desperately.

He ran his fingers back through the short hair on his head and said, "I'll have to take the original."

"You can't take the original..." I said through clenched teeth. "What if something happens to you? I will need it to go to the embassy to prove who you are."

"You have my social security number, you can use that, I guess" he said as he paced the room. We were running out of time. He had to get out while his mother was still cooking. That was his only chance.

"OK," he said. "I will copy the information on it, the passport number, and date it was issued and stuff like that. I'll take my American driver's license as well, although I don't know if that is sufficient proof in such a situation." He took a picture of the passport as well as its internal pages with his cell phone. He was taking the phone with him, anyway, in case the connections were reestablished.

"You know what," he said, suddenly standing still after we had both been pacing the room nervously. "I am ready, and I suppose I'll just go now. Let me use the bathroom one more time."

My heart sank. It was like the climb up on a steep roller coaster. You go up slowly, but once you are at the top you have little time before you are rushing down at breakneck speed with everything around you in a big blur.

We went downstairs together quietly. His mom saw us and smiled at us as, and I believe she said something, but my heart was pounding so loudly in my ears that I didn't catch Basil's answer. The kitchen was right by the front door. We were standing at the kitchen doorway, but the minute she turned back toward the stove, we slipped out.

We both walked very quickly toward the parked Hyundai. There was no time for goodbyes and he was too nervous to even look me in the face. I think we hugged briefly—I can't remember, it was so quick. He promised to find a landline whenever he could and call me when the timing was right.

Before I knew it, he was driving away, and I was alone in the street looking at the taillights of the car and wishing that I could just walk away and not face the mother in that kitchen preparing a meal for a son that had just leaped off of the ledge of everything we held familiar.

What had I done? What had I helped him do? Did I just kill the father of my children? Would I regret this for the rest of my life? At that moment, I did not feel like a patriot at all. I felt like a wild animal with her cubs at her feet, frightened and apprehensive of her surroundings.

I believed 100 percent this was the right thing to do. What would happen if we all held onto our men and kept them among us? I asked myself.

But why, then, did I feel so bad?

∽ ∽

When I finally willed myself to go into my in-laws' house, I was having a severe panic attack. The whole scene I was about to disrupt was breaking my heart. My children were playing with their four-year-old cousin in my in-laws' well-manicured backyard, the food was laid out on the table, my brother-in-law and his wife were talking about the news coverage from Al Jazeera that showed the protests forming on streets across Cairo.

I looked into the kitchen, but Tante Gigi was no longer there. She must have gone upstairs to tell my father-in-law that the food was ready. My brother-in-law's wife saw me in the kitchen, my face ashen, and immediately she knew that something was wrong.

"Are you OK?" she asked, placing a hand on my shoulder.

I was so relieved that she was the first person to whom I would break the news. She was always so warm and welcoming with me. She was the kind of person who made you feel that your opinion was really important. She was an attentive listener and had a permanently warm disposition. I spilled the whole story in seconds. I was in shock, and it came out in this strange, monotone voice that didn't feel like my own.

Her eyes welled up with tears and she grabbed me from the shoulders. "You did the right thing, Hoda. I completely understand. Don't worry. I will be with you when you tell them. I will not leave your side."

I was so grateful to her at that moment. I was not feeling strong at all, regardless of all my convictions and speeches to my students. I was afraid and needed someone to console me, but instead I had to defend my position in an agonizing battle with a mother I had just stabbed in the heart.

"I will go with you and we will tell my husband first," she said as she led me out of the kitchen with her arms around my shoulders.

My brother-in-law looked up at me, away from the television screen he had been watching. "Your brother has gone to join the protests just now," I said in as strong a voice as I could muster. He stood up immediately and was in an obvious panic.

"How…when…when did this happen…can we catch him at the gate?" he asked in a strained tone, referring to the gate of the housing complex we were in.

"I don't think so. He must have passed through it by now." I weakly checked the clock on my cell phone.

"You know there are no cell phone communications today. Were you two aware of that?" Some anger was seeping into his voice.

"Of course we are aware of that. That is one of the reasons we felt everyone should join the protests. The protesters have to protect each other on the ground because they can't call anyone for help."

"Perhaps you should go upstairs and tell your parents," his wife said to him as gingerly as she could. I did not know that she was going to ask that, but once she did, I held onto the suggestion for dear life. It would *really* help me if the initial shock came from someone else.

"I certainly will not," he retorted. "If she wants to kill them she can go upstairs and do that herself."

All of a sudden, in my desperation for him to do it, I addressed him with a seriousness and strength that appeared to catch him off guard.

"I cannot go up there and do it. I am in shock myself, and you have to understand that I am in a lot of pain right now. If you do not go upstairs and tell them now, I will take the children and attempt to drive to my father's house, without a phone, so that I can wait for Basil in a calm environment."

He stared at me for a second, as if to gauge how serious my threat was. I think my eyes said it all. He moved right past me and up the stairs.

The minute he was up there, I slumped down into the couch and put my head in my hands. His wife kept rubbing my back and saying it was going to be all right.

At that moment, my son came in with his cousin and Layla, and I immediately placed my hand on his shoulder and said,

"Remember what we talked about in the car?" He nodded with a sudden mixture of seriousness and excitement on his face. "Well, I am going to have that conversation with Tatta now, so please take your sister and cousin into the garden and don't come back in here."

Layla somehow could tell that there was something wrong with me, and accordingly refused to budge; instead she climbed on top of me and held on tight.

It was not long before Tante Gigi appeared at the top of the staircase with an expression of utter pain on her face. "How could you keep this from me? *How could you?* How could you both do this to me?"

"Tante Gigi," I said quickly but quietly, "he instructed me not to tell you…"

"It doesn't matter what *he* wanted. You had no right to keep this from me. He is my son…he is my son!"

Tante Gigi was in the worst situation a mother could be in. Her child was in danger and she could not reach him. She could not even speak to him. She did not get the chance to discuss it or try to change his mind or to even tell him goodbye. She was stuck in a state of panic and grief, and I was an accomplice to the crime.

The conversation went in a circle, from "What were you thinking?" to explaining all the danger involved to how Basil could have contributed to the country positively in so many other ways, to "How could you keep this from me?" and back to "What were you thinking?" Layla held onto me tightly the whole time. At times, she cried for her grandmother because it was so distressing to see her like this, and at others she buried her face in my chest.

At one point, Tante Gigi said, "I am calling your father and telling him what you did."

To which I replied as quietly as I could, "He already knows."

She just looked at me like I had just insulted her, raised her hands up in the air and dropped them, and walked out of the room.

The scenario repeated itself throughout the day. She would advance on me and then retreat in disbelief at my responses, as if I had just broken the news to her all over again. She gathered all the information from me about who he was with and how many were with him, what he was wearing, and what he was carrying on his person. She grasped at every piece of information that may somehow assure her that he would be OK. Ultimately, nothing could do that for her, so she paced the house like a caged animal, trying to flee the worry and the pain.

At one point, I was so exhausted and Layla was so distressed that I repeated the threat I had told my brother-in-law, "I will have to leave if we can't find a way to discuss this calmly. I am really sorry, but I am heartbroken as well, and I need to find some peace right now." I felt terrible saying it, but I was beginning to fall apart on the inside and couldn't let that extend to the outside for the children's sake.

My father-in-law did not leave his bedroom for a few hours. My brother-in-law had told me that when he heard the news he got back into bed and closed his eyes.

I went upstairs to lay Layla down to sleep in one of the bedrooms. She had fallen asleep in my arms and had escaped the tension for the time being. As I closed the bedroom door behind me and exited into the hallway, my father-in-law was standing at his bedroom's entrance.

"I have a simple question, dear. Why did you really do this? What is the logic behind such irresponsible behavior that is so unlike you and Basil?" His voice was calm and his facial expression was soft.

"Uncle Aly, this is exactly the kind of thing Basil and I *would* do. Haven't you known us at all, all these years? We had an NGO together, and left jobs to work for organizations that looked like they were out to make this a better country. We did what we could and most of our efforts failed or met with resistance. This is the first time we feel we could be part of something that could really make a difference. Nationalism is not a hobby to us; this is who we truly are. We both feel that we have not done enough and that we benefited from living in America for such an extended amount of time that we owe it to Egypt. He really wanted to do this. Please understand. I heard that you had done something similar when you were young, during the English occupation."

"That was entirely different, I was not married and I did not have children."

"I am qualified enough to take care of his children, and he knows that. This is what he wants and what he wants his children to know he did, no matter what the outcome is."

He gave me a calm, serene smile and I couldn't believe I was even getting that. He was eighty-three years old, I am sure he had seen it all...or at least most of it. He patted my shoulder lightly and went back into the room. He never discussed the matter with me again.

By five o'clock, Basil had been gone for over five hours and had not called. Tante Gigi was exhausted and no longer came to talk to me. She watched the television and did not speak to anyone. In fact, from this point onward, the television was never off. It blared bad news continuously.

Local channels were at war with satellite news channels such as Al Jazeera, El Arabiya, CNN, and BBC. The truth had a wardrobe change every time you switched channels, and it was almost comical to watch how differently the events were spun into what was supposed to be factual news.

I never left for my parents' house. It was way too dangerous for me to even consider doing so. As we pieced the news together from the television and from relatives and friends who called in and shared whatever they knew, we quickly came to the realization that all hell had broken loose. Protestors who had called their families reported live fire and dead bodies. They spoke of betrayal on the police's end and of the protesters fighting back.

We were too far out to hear or see any of it, but we had family members who lived downtown, and they were witnessing an all-out war. The NDP building was on fire and so was the local police station nearby. Police appeared to be fleeing.

I finally gathered the strength to get the overnight bag I had hidden in my car and bring it into the house. It showed premeditation on our end, but I was too tired to be ashamed when I brought it in. As I set up Basil's bedroom upstairs to house my children and I for the night, I thought of Basil taking a picture of the kids on his phone. I wondered what he was going through and if he was looking at that picture for comfort.

"He will come home safely, *insha Allah*. He will come home safely, *insha Allah…*" I repeated it over and over until I believed nothing but that.

❧ ❧

(Mohamed Shafei, 39, Co-Founder and Partner
of Deraya Sales Services)

On Friday, I finished my prayers at the mosque near my house and walked out to see the first signs of the protests. A group of young men carrying anti-Mubarak signs were walking the streets of Nasser City. This was such an unlikely sight given that the presidential palace was located nearby. It would be a long walk from here to Tahrir, but they didn't seem to mind.

They chanted *"Inzil Inzil"* ("Come down out of you houses") and *"Eish, horreya we adala igtimaiya"* ("Bread, freedom, and social justice"). Their ranks expanded as they moved on. I took a deep breath and looked around my apartment's building for signs of the danger I had sensed last night. It had been a rough night for me. I was overcome by worry of what would happen to Egypt. I had my fair share of reasons to believe that today had the potential of turning into a bloodbath. There was already no Internet on my computer and BlackBerry, and cell phone services were cut off two hours ago.

I had viewed the protests as a political conflict with the current electoral system that reflected a democratic adjustment that was probably on our horizon anyway, but the move to cut off communication from all Egyptians made it much more than that. It was as if the government just sent the people a written invitation to join the Friday of Anger. If one hundred thousand Egyptians had originally planned to attend this protest, now millions would.

It was a shame because we had a country of which I was very proud. My wife is a dual American-Egyptian citizen, and I have been married to her for over fifteen years, yet we decided to live in Egypt. This is where I belong, and where my extended family lives. I am the only son, with three sisters, and both of my parents are happy and proud Egyptians. I have three children and a wife I love, and this is the life that I want and choose to protect.

It was hard to believe that this was where we were at, just a few weeks into this new year. We had barely recovered from the church-bombing incident, and now we were facing mass demonstrations.

Just a few weeks back, the company I own was launching a new product, an apartment building complex in a decent area with a solid payment plan. Everyone was in deadline mode, and the thirty-plus employees were completely absorbed in the excitement that precedes a new sales launch.

Most of us who had Facebook accounts in the office had received some form of an invitation to the protests taking place on Tuesday, the 25th of January. It was a national holiday, Police Day, but it was already taking a different form. Protests in Tunisia had been the topic throughout the month, and we were all in awe that an Arab nation nearby had managed to uproot its president and his regime.

We had been seeing the images of Tunisian citizens and their children in protests and hearing of the violence and looting for weeks. It all seemed foreign and chaotic to me, and emotionally, I held it at a distance. The relevance escaped me. There was no parallel or sense of connection between that story and the protests being planned for Tuesday the 25th. The last ten years in Egypt had seen some protests. A few thousand here and there, but nothing that took up more than a half hour of dinner conversation.

I was not the kind to get involved in politics. Like every Egyptian, I knew the system was heavily flawed, but logic told me that attempting to push against the large sand dune would inevitably result in me slipping into it and becoming engulfed in it once again. The system was massive and fluid; there was nothing concrete to push against that I felt would result in any true accomplishment.

The words "civic unrest," "revolt," and "popular uprising" were in no way part of my vocabulary as a citizen either. In fact, before this, the most "unrest" I had ever been through had occurred only a few weeks earlier while on a trip to New York City with my wife.

We had left our three children with my in-laws and headed for the Big Apple for a weeklong vacation. Instead, we dealt with a massive snowstorm that closed down subways and stranded people in the streets. I remember the sense of panic I felt when we heard announcements that police would be overwhelmed with rescue efforts and that people should assume that when they call 911, they might not get an immediate response.

Before January the 25th, to me, that was the greatest feeling of danger I had ever experienced. The idea of the absence of governance because of a storm had shattered my sense of security. When we returned to Egypt and the sun was shining, there was no way I could have seen this next storm coming.

By Monday morning the buzz about the invitations to protest that were circulating on Facebook had made their way into our meeting room. Managers started to strongly suggest to me that launching our product on the twenty-fifth could be a bad business move. At a minimum, people would be distracted and the ad campaign would go unnoticed. So reluctantly, we all agreed to push the launch back a couple of weeks.

With what I was seeing as I walked through to my apartment building's entrance on the twenty-eighth, I figured we would need to push it back more than just a few weeks. When I entered the apartment, it seemed as if no one was there. I looked through the rooms for Amina (my wife) and my three children, and quickly found that they were all gathered on the master bedroom's balcony.

Our apartment is on the twelfth floor of what was once dubbed "The Ministers Building," because of the number of retired ministers who lived there. Therefore, we had armed security at the entrance. Most of the old ministers had passed away, but I am sure that their widows and families were as shocked at what we were experiencing this past week as we were.

From our balcony's bird's-eye view, Amina, the kids, and I could see that the group I had seen around the corner by the mosque had now swelled to what appeared to be about five hundred men. Their spirit was positive and the mood was contagious.

I saw nothing of the danger I had felt watching the news when I saw a young man from Arish, a small oceanside city north of Sinai, get shot by Egyptian police for no apparent reason, other than the fact that he was standing in the middle of an empty street.

Maybe the satellite channels were reporting images out of context or wanted to exaggerate the situation to hook viewers. It didn't look that bad from where I stood. Still, in the papers and on local news, if you read between the lines, the government seemed to be warning citizens. It was clear to me that the regime was sending a message that what it had let slide on the twenty-fifth would not fly today.

Today, it was implied that police would strike back from the get-go. But none of that attitude was apparent in our neighborhood so far.

"It doesn't look that bad, Mohamed," Amina said. "What if we were to join the marches around our building?"

The kids excitedly jumped at this suggestion; it was the weekend and it already seemed more exciting than any other weekend plans they had experienced.

The chants had gotten to me. "I'll tell you what," I said. "Let me take the car and drive around and check things out first, and then I'll come back and see if we can maybe join the small protests in our area."

I drove around the five-hundred-man group that we had witnessed from above. Up close, they seemed a little more serious, and they were multiplying by the minute. I noticed that I was the only car on the street. Right in front of me, I could see a massive protest coming my way, and to my right, a bunch of police officers appeared and signaled for me to take a left. I complied, got onto the sidewalk (not an uncommon move in Cairo), parked the car, and got out.

As I moved back into the street on foot, a stone flew by me, and I realized that the second group of protesters were being chased, and in turn, a few of them were throwing stones at the police.

The image of the fellow from Arish being shot was fresh in my mind, as I noted that I was pretty much standing alone at an intersection with one protest to my left and another to my right.

I turned around and quickened my pace in the direction of my parked car. I got in and drove up the street. A policeman heard me approaching and aggressively whipped around and looked straight at me. I made a visible effort to slow my car down and show him that I merely wanted to make a U-turn and had no intention of running him over. He appeared to be as scared as I was.

When I got home, I immediately told Amina and the kids that we probably shouldn't go out of the apartment at all. Amina appeared to have an internal dilemma of whether she and I should help out with the protests or simply watch them from afar. I needed to adjust her thought process to fit what I had just experienced firsthand.

"I believe it will be flat-out violence in the streets, Amina," I told her. "I do not think protesters' demands are clear and I do not think that our police force has a ceiling to their retaliation maneuvers today. I believe it is our responsibility as parents to protect these three children, and that includes not attempting anything that is even vaguely irresponsible."

Around four o'clock, televised reports reflected that my prophecy was being fulfilled. Dozens of deaths were being reported due to clashes with police in Cairo, Alexandria, Portsaid, Suez…the list of cities went on and on. I prayed that the tragedies would not extend to our family, as I listened to Amina consoling her sister, Hoda, on the phone. Her husband, Basil, had gone out to join the protests and they had not heard from him for the past five hours.

My parents had been a little concerned as well. Accordingly, my sisters, who lived near them, had decided earlier in the day to go be with them. It was a tradition to spend Friday as a family in my parents' home, and they felt that today would be a day when that tradition served a higher purpose. Our parents' apartment building was located in the Gameat El Dowal area, right next to the Mostafa Mahmoud Mosque where many of the protests were being initiated. My sisters felt that it was important that they be there for our parents in case the situation escalated.

I felt it was my duty to be at my parents' side as well, especially since I was the only son in the family, despite the fact that my home was completely across town. I do not know if my decision was right or wrong when you consider the children and their safety, but as the hours dragged on I found myself becoming increasingly frustrated with my own marginalized state in the confines of my apartment. On the one hand, I could not see myself as a father dragging my family through the unknown. But on the other hand, I could not see myself as a son staying home and not being with my parents and sisters.

I discussed it with Amina, and we rationalized that most of the protests were probably focused in the Tahrir area right now, so if we headed out before dark and stuck to our route straight through to my parents' home, we should all be OK.

The only caveat was that our route actually took us onto the twenty-kilometer Sixth of October Bridge and Causeway, which crosses the Nile River, continuing through downtown Cairo above Tahrir. We would have to drive toward the Gezira Island to El Mohandiseen, the neighborhood of Gameat El Dowal and Mostafa Mahmoud. In fact, there was no route from Nasser City to my parents' apartment building that didn't pass through, above, or intersect with Tahrir.

Nevertheless, with an air of apprehension and excitement, we all got into the car as a family. The children were in awe of everything that was taking place. My fourteen-year-old daughter and eleven-year-old son, in particular, seemed thrilled that we decided to go out and give them the opportunity to possibly catch a glimpse of what was going on.

Sure enough, when we reached the segment of the Sixth of October Bridge that went above Tahrir, we suddenly found ourselves face to face with a big mob of people running towards the car, obviously panicked and scared. If we were hoping to catch a mere glimpse of the action, this was much more than any of us had imagined.

I instantly regretted taking Amina and the children with me. None of us had ever witnessed anything like this before. The car was suddenly enveloped by a crush of humanity. I had no idea that from this point onward the Egypt I had known all my life would never be the same. It faded away as quickly as my car disappeared into the mob of disheveled and injured Egyptians, who appeared to be fleeing.

The faces we saw go by held expressions of a solemn determination that suggested that their flight was only temporary. This was not a crowd that was going home. This was a crowd that was getting out of the way, but planning to turn around and go straight back in.

We were in the middle of the active protest ranks that were fighting the police as we watched. And there was nothing that distinguished our car from the group that surrounded us. We had just involuntarily joined the protests with three kids in the car, the youngest being four years old.

I inched the car slowly through the crowd and made eye contact with a few of the protesters as I drove. They were mostly males in their twenties and thirties, but you could tell from their attire that they were from different class levels. I wondered if I would see my brother-in-law Basil among them.

We began to enter into an area that was thick with smoke, and I couldn't tell if it was tear gas or something burning. We heard something slam onto the side of the car, and we all jumped a bit in our seats. Apparently, one of the protesters had slammed his hand onto the car, but it seemed he did it to keep himself from falling. Nevertheless I took that as my cue to quickly exit the bridge. Shoubra was the exit on the right.

Shoubra is an impoverished district with a population upward of one million. It had absorbed a lot of migration of farmers from rural areas over the past twenty years, and had very narrow roads with random unlicensed buildings and shantytowns. Truth be told, I wasn't sure I knew how to get to my parents' home through Shoubra, but I had felt that any locale outside of Tahrir would be safer than the bridge.

Once again, I was wrong.

My Jeep Liberty, with my wife and three children inside, had just been placed within an active combat area, and there appeared to be no way back up to the bridge or anywhere else from where we were.

There was no specific road or direction to go. The road we had exited onto held ten times the amount of people we had encountered on the bridge. People ran in all directions with tissue paper, cloth and/or articles of their own clothes draped across their mouths and noses. We quickly discovered why, as our own car began to fill with the stink of tear gas.

My heart beat harder in my chest as my children began to say that they were feeling the effects of the tear gas and the car filled with a chemical stench akin to bug spray. My visibility had also become inhibited by the mass of people and waves of thick smoke.

In the distance, I could see the bridge we had been on. I tried to move alongside it in the general direction of Mohandiseen. I was determined to get my family out of there as quickly as possible. The fact that I could not tell where the tear gas canisters were coming from only added to my panic. I was afraid I would drive straight into the police when there were no other cars in sight. Would they shoot at the car, unaware of its inhabitants?

It began to sink in that Egypt's fight on this Friday of Anger extended far beyond Tahrir and a mere unhappiness with the electoral process. This was a popular uprising, one that should definitely not be attended by women and children.

I made eye contact with an older man on a sidewalk and decided to drive up to him and ask him directions. He was surprisingly calm and friendly. He took a look inside the car and understood the urgency of my request for assistance. He instructed me how to get to the main Shoubra square, dubbed Dawaran Shoubra, which led to all exit roads.

At the square, we drew closer to where the combat was. We could hear the tear gas launching and see the canisters catapult into the air. We witnessed men picking up the blazing-hot tear gas canisters and throwing them back into the air. Some appeared to have big, bloody lacerations on their heads, indicating that the tear gas canisters had hit a few of them.

Once again, we were surrounded by protesters, but these were oddly at ease with the tear gas. They had appeared to be in battle for so long that they had gotten used to it. Here, there were none of the multi-economic and varying class levels we had witnessed on the bridge. These men were seasoned Shoubra men who were not fazed by police batons and tear gas.

One could say that Shoubra inhabitants had seen much worse in their lifetimes of struggle. They lived on streets lined with garbage and inhaled the dense air pollution of downtown Cairo. Their apartment buildings were built mostly with cheap redbrick, and their exteriors were left unfinished. The sewage systems were old and damaged and the streets regurgitated human waste on a regular basis. Running water in many of the homes here was a luxury afforded only by those who could buy a private water pump.

In short, Shoubra inhabitants had little to live for and a whole hell of a lot to die for.

According to the directions the man had given me, I was supposed to head west to get to my destination. Instead, my surroundings kept forcing me north into rural areas adjacent to Shoubra.

The children grew quiet as the immense poverty of these areas shocked them into silence. They had never seen this side of the country before. We were in the middle of winter, yet children stood barefoot in the mud with no pants on. They smiled and waved wildly at my kids in the car as if they had seen celebrities.

My children stared blankly across the unpaved streets with the broken-down homes and drank in this oddly informative experience. They had no idea that they were being introduced to their country on a day that would make it in bold print into the history books of Egypt's unknown future.

Amina and I hardly spoke to each other in the car. Every time I drove up next to someone to ask directions, she would attempt to ask for directions on her side as well, in an attempt to get a consensus on the path out of our massive forced detour. We managed to get directions that led us into Imbaba, which was not in our desired westward direction but was south of where we were, which was better than continuing north, farther and farther away from my parents' home.

Urban Imbaba was slightly better than the rural Imbaba that we had just driven through unknowingly, but it was actually more impoverished, if that is even possible, than Shoubra.

Accordingly, it had almost no cars at all. Hybrid vehicles called "tok toks" ruled the streets. These were akin to rickshaws pulled by motorcycles. They zoomed through the muddy streets, packed to the gills with customers, at breakneck speeds. They had to swerve left and right to avoid potholes, pedestrians, and donkey carts, and they did it with the skill of racecar drivers.

I realized that the only way of getting out of there was to become a customer as well, so I situated my car in a way that it actually forced one of them to slow down. I explained to the driver where I had wanted to go in as rugged a manner as I could. Had I been in the United States, what I was doing would be similar to one stopping in the projects to ask for directions to the mansions at the top of the hill. I couldn't help but feel nervous as he scanned my face, the car, my wife, and the kids.

To my surprise, the man was utterly friendly and eager to help. I paid him to drive ahead of us and get us to the nearest point he possibly could to Mohandiseen.

"Do you know El Kitkat area?" he asked.

"Yes, yes I do. Is that nearby?" I knew El Kitkat because it was the closest underprivileged area to my parents' home, and it was where we used to go to distribute meat and money to the poor during religious feasts and holidays. In fact, I knew a butcher there who knew my family.

The tok tok took me to an area in Kitkat that looked familiar, and I was able to locate the butcher. He welcomed me with a big hug. He was very surprised to see my family and me there at a day like this one.

It was 5:30 p.m. We had been on the road for about ninety minutes on a trip that usually took us only twenty-five minutes. I decided to use the butcher's landline to call my family and inform them of my whereabouts.

About twenty minutes later, I was hugging my sisters in my parents' apartment. They were joking and eating and did not appear to fully grasp the danger that was rampant throughout the country. They had been at the apartment since the early morning and all they had witnessed were sporadic peaceful protests.

As was customary on family day, they attempted to feed me all kinds of food and desserts, but I could not take my eyes off the reports and videos on the Al Arabiya satellite channel. It had just announced that the Egyptian army would be joining in to bring the situation under control and an immediate curfew was taking effect. The regime expected *all* law-abiding citizens to remain in their homes until it was clear that there was no danger.

At that point, I saw a clip I would never forget for as long as I lived. I saw an angry group of four or five protesters who looked just like the young men I had encountered minutes ago jump on an armored police car in a vengeful frenzy, open the upper entrance door, and throw a Molotov cocktail into the car.

We could see the policeman inside burn to death in the car. He flailed about in a panic, batting his arms about before disappearing from the camera's view. I imagined him screaming in pain and dying with his own fear alongside him as the tortuous flames engulfed him.

Did any young Egyptian deserve this? Was that policeman any different from the rest of us? Low-ranking Egyptian police officers were known to be very poor and struggle to give their families a decent life. He was following orders, and refusing to do so would have landed him in jail. It was difficult to pick a side in this sad tale of a tigress eating her own cubs to ensure their safety. My heart was irreparably broken.

૭ઌ ૭ઌ

(Khaled Bichara, 40, Chief Operating Officer of VimpelCom Ltd. and Group Executive Chairman of Orascom Telecom Holding)

We took a taxi to Batal Ahmed Street, where we had set out to meet our friends on the morning of the twenty-eighth. The taxi driver who dropped us off in front of the Ceramica Kleopatra store could tell we weren't there to buy ceramic tiles. In fact, he refused to take money from us and told us to take care of ourselves and to not get our hopes too high.

"It's no use, you know," he said matter-of-factly.

I turned to him with a big smile and said, *"Ya akhy inta nikady!"* ("My brother, you are one hell of a killjoy!") He laughed out loud.

"No, but seriously, it is an honorable thing you kids are doing, and I hope for your sakes you can turn things around for this country," he told us.

It was the appropriate sentiment for the day and at first, during the initial honeymoon period of the Friday of Anger, we thought it would all be smooth sailing. The number of protesters on Batal Ahmed Street gave us a false sense of security. We felt untouchable.

The crowds chanted, *"Ya horreya feenik feenik, Amn El-Dawla beeny we beenik!"* ("Oh freedom, pray where are you, the internal police force has built walls between us") in a voice that reverberated through the streets and up the high-rise buildings into the homes and apartments that lined the streets.

We ran into many friends and acquaintances along the way. We would make brief stops and chitchat and hug and joke. It seemed like a large parade. I must admit that it was rather fun at first. I somewhat regretted not letting Marianne come with me. The spirit was energizing, and you felt that you were part of something bold, brave, and brazen. I had never participated in anything like this in my life. This was how people assembled for rock concerts or carnivals, except this gathering had a magical unifying spirit to it, and I loved it.

As we grew and grew, we headed for El Galaa Bridge, which would take us in the direction of Tahrir Square. There seemed to be a unanimous agreement that if you were part of the protests in Cairo on this day, the destination was Tahrir. Its name bore the symbolism the movement required, and it was the location of the recent miracle of the twenty-fifth, which was still as fresh in our minds as if it happened ten minutes ago.

That was where the dream ended and the nightmare began.

There was no time to adjust between the "This is awesome!" mood to the "Oh my God, we may all die!" mood. The minute we came near the bridge, an endless barrage of tear gas canisters were shot at us. There was so many of us packed together that it was impossible to just turn around and run.

The gas quickly engulfed us, my throat constricted, my eyes burned and filled with tears, and I could not get my bearings to make a decision on what our course of action would be. My face felt like it had been set on fire. People gave me Pepsi to rinse out my eyes, and oddly enough it seemed to work.

I had a tight-knit group of fifteen family members and friends with me. We had sworn to our families that no matter what, we would stick together as a core group amid all that took place around us. We were already breaking apart quicker than we had ever planned—and were frankly too inexperienced to know what to do about it at this point.

I heard an explosion to my right and realized that the police had just shot a tear gas canister into an apartment building, and it had broken through the window and exploded upon contact. Shortly after, the apartment was engulfed in flames. There was a police blockade of cars parked side by side to obstruct the way across the Galaa bridge. I followed the instructions of people around me, some of whom bore activist logos and others that looked inexperienced. It felt odd that here, my CEO status meant nothing. I was not overseeing or managing anything but my own safety. Those around me said that the collective goal was to charge the blockade and break it so we could clear the path to Tahrir.

I broke into a run alongside the crowd of charging men. It felt a bit insane to advance at the police with nothing but scarves across our faces, only to run from them as they came at us with sticks, rubber bullets, and tear gas bombs. But this is what I was here for, and I assumed that someone had thought this through, so I participated. At the age of forty, this was probably the first time I had fully entrusted myself to fellow Egyptians in a life-or-death situation. It felt oddly liberating.

For the record, there is nothing "rubber" about rubber bullets. People around me who had gotten hit by them looked like they had been shot with lead. I have not experienced a "live ammunition" attack, but this is what I had imagined one to be like.

The surrounding scenes sent me into a dazed, adrenaline-filled state of shock. Amazingly though, your psyche and your body adjust immediately, and you find yourself pulling together and trying to succeed and survive all at once.

It was funny how even a businessman like me who really had nothing to do with all this did not decide to just run away and deem the experience too extreme. It seems that the human spirit is stubborn and pride-driven, emboldened by resistance if the cause is sound. Consequently, I continued the fight, though my core unit had shrunk from fifteen to about five.

We maintained a position in the back. Those who were inexperienced like us naturally fell into the "followers" group and did not attempt to join the initiators or leaders. It was not out of cowardice as much as it was out of a general lack of knowledge of how to navigate our way across this situation. I looked at the leaders in utter awe. They were obviously younger than I, mostly of a simpler economic background, and appeared to be less surprised by all that was going on.

At that stage, we were far enough in the back of the pack to realize the humor in the situation. My friends and I looked hilarious. We were wearing swimming goggles that we had with us, which we donned after reading the e-mail of protest-gear recommendations. Our hair and faces were a complete mess. Our clothes were disheveled and a few of us had lost a shoe or torn though their pants, and we were coughing and blowing our noses continuously.

A large cheer made its way through the crowd like a giant domino line falling. The protesters had captured the officer in command of the blockade, and the rest of his team, in a sudden panic, had locked themselves into the armored cars that were the blockade itself.

Protestors immediately enveloped the cars and began to kick and bang on them wildly. The captured officer was being aggressively dragged around to the back of the blockade as protesters surged across the bridge. In the crazed charge, protesters began to smash the blockade cars with the police inside them, but I immediately saw a group of people pull them back and say, "*Silmia, silmia*" ("Peaceful, peaceful!"), and as far as I could see, the group on attack stopped its actions immediately.

The idea of the trapped men in the cars made me uncomfortable despite the intensity of the assault that they had just launched against us. However, I had neither the time nor the authority to do anything about it. I fully understood that the only reason we were able to pass was because this team of men had been detained within their vehicles. In any case, we were so far back in the crowd, as well as in the chain of command, that we were literally part of the herd. We had neither the capability nor the responsibility to approve or disapprove of these actions.

In fact, I found it an impressive show of self-control that the crowds had not already beaten the policemen to death, given the sheer number of bloodied and injured individuals who were a testimony to the police's brutality.

When we arrived at the Qasr El Neel Bridge that stretched across the glorious Nile, we unknowingly became part of the now-infamous video that has since circulated through the Internet millions of times over.

A legendary fight for this final bridge before Tahrir bore the brunt of the battle for the square. Crowds advanced and receded, and the police finally began to use live ammunition. The mood became very serious, and my unit began to gravely contemplate the fates of our children if we chose to continue.

We began to witness dead bodies pulled onto the sidelines.

There was no humor anymore, as we barely even looked at each other. Everyone must have been wondering if this was how and when their lives would finally end. I certainly was. A group of men came through carrying a young protester who was literally drenched in his own blood. His hair and body dripped liquid red onto the pavement as they settled him onto the ground. A massive man who appeared to be his friend screamed and thrashed about wildly when he saw him. So dramatically, in fact, that the four men that had been originally tending to the injured man's wounds were forced to turn their attention toward the friend in an attempt to hold him back from charging in a suicidal manner directly toward the gunfire.

"You killed my friend!" he screamed in the direction of the police as he pulled forward the four men who were trying to hold him back. "You killed my friend!"

At that second, the bloodied young protester on the ground took a deep breath and coughed weakly. The massive man turned around immediately, making the other four fall to the ground. He dropped to his knees and cradled his friend's head in his arms. I felt like sinking into the ground myself. I moved away from them, unwilling to witness the end of the sad scene unfolding.

When Muslim protesters lined up for the asr prayers, we stood by and around them as protection. The police pushed in and began to spray those praying with water cannons. This enraged the crowds, and the prayer was disrupted with a heightened sense of determination. At this point things went from dangerous to far beyond the definition of that word. We were shaken and diffused, and we appeared to have lost our footing on the bridge for the moment.

At this point, my group decided to turn into neighboring Zamalek to catch our breath, regroup, and rethink our strategy. In Zamalek we encountered many of our acquaintances who had elected to participate from the outskirts. I saw some of my female friends, who were wisely keeping a seemingly safe distance. I remember feeling awkward that everyone was so surprised to see me there at the protests.

"I can't believe you, of all people, are here," they kept saying, but they didn't explain what they meant. To what were they alluding? Was it my religion? My economic status? My build? What?

"Of course I am here!" I said. "Why wouldn't I be? I am an Egyptian, like the rest of you."

The atmosphere in Zamalek was loving and comforting. Citizens from the affluent area left the security of their apartments to give incoming protesters water and food. Old women stood in the streets and grabbed and kissed us. Like on the sidelines of a marathon, they cheered us on verbally and mentally. There were people waving at us from the balconies of their homes, and some tourists from hotel balconies as well. Not one person questioned even for a second what we were doing and why. You couldn't help but be proud.

After our Zamalek break, we made one last attempt to reach Tahrir through the Fifteenth of May Bridge. Again, we were given the "full-assault" treatment. Reaching Tahrir began to seem like an overly ambitious dream that we felt was beyond our reach. The bulk of those standing their ground and continuing on were the activists. Their chants escalated to *"Yasqut yasqut Hosni Mubarak"* ("Down, down with Hosni Mubarak!"), and they had endless energy reserves.

We were a little too old and out of shape to keep up. We stopped at a small kiosk on a nearby street and asked to use the phone. The man in the kiosk took one look at our sweaty and dirty faces and clothes and said, "The phone is not working."

"Seriously?" I said with a smile. "Come on man, we just need to tell our families that we are OK."

The man took the phone out from behind the counter reluctantly and handed it to us. There was a small television behind him broadcasting the local news. The television announcer was brazenly stating that the protests were small and under control, and were organized and carried out by a small Quila Mondassa ("Infiltrating Few") thugs and mercenaries that had been entirely contained.

I joked with the kiosk owner. "Do we look like thugs to you? Those who are still out there, believe you me, they are anything but contained."

In the end we made five phone calls. In Egypt you usually pay about one Egyptian pound for each local phone call, but the man refused to take our money. The local man in the local kiosk with no access to satellite channels had seen us up close and realized that there was something askew with the image being presented on local airwaves when compared to what he saw before him. But how many had not seen it for themselves? How many really knew the truth? It was a scary question to contemplate.

It was 5:30 p.m., and we decided to give the bridge a few more attempts. We charged and ran and charged and ran until we found ourselves on the frontline for the first time, with everyone else behind us. There we were, my brother and me and my cousin, with not a drop of activism experience, leading a mob of protesters toward an intact police brigade like the one we had conquered a mere hours ago.

As the tear gas intensified, we saw a passenger bus appear out of nowhere and head toward the blockade. Whoever the bus was carrying, the police appeared to have known in advance that it was coming, because they seemed to be ushering it in. This was our chance to get through with the vehicle.

We were a group of two hundred or more, and we ran as fast as we could after that bus, but it pulled forward and we couldn't catch up with it. The minute it passed through, the police bombarded us with tear gas so heavily that it made you feel like it was impossible to draw in air. I listened to my heart beat inside my head and body, as if it was finishing what it had left.

The whole thing was happening in slow motion. I was running and listening to the horrifying heartbeats, acutely aware that I had not drawn in a breath in what seemed like five or six heartbeats. I fell onto my hands and knees and tried to gasp, but couldn't. I felt a damp cloth suddenly come across my face powerfully and a voice forcefully ordered, "Take a breath! Take a breath!"

I willed my whole body with all the strength I had left, and drew in as hard as I could. I felt the stench of vinegar fill my lungs, but it had oxygen with it and I could feel my body drink it in anxiously. As the relief washed over me, so did a strong nauseous feeling that was almost too much to bear.

The minute I had the strength, I thanked the man who had helped me over and over. I had known that my own vinegar bottle was in my pocket, but when I was struggling for air, I did not have the strength to pull it out, pour it onto something, and try to inhale it. He had just saved my life.

When I looked around me, I realized that the three of us had finally been broken apart as well. I did not know where my brother and cousin were, and our parents had made us swear to stick together no matter what.

I made the decision then and there that if I found them I would leave. The decision was a sound one, in my opinion, because people I met informed me that the television had announced that the army was coming in as well. The regime was imposing a curfew to get things under control, and to me, that signaled that the game was over.

We did the best we could. We came together, we participated, and we got to see Egypt in a way we had never dared to imagine before, and thankfully every member of our group was accounted for and would live to tell the story.

We all left around 6:30 p.m..

None of my group had reached Tahrir.

∽ ∽

(Hoda Rashad, 36, Educator/Writer)

At five o'clock the phone rang and everyone jumped. My father-in-law answered. We all slowly gathered around him, as we could tell from his response that the phone call had something to do with Basil.

It was a few tense minutes before we realized that the man on the other end was the father of Ahmed, my friend who Basil was supposed to be with. Apparently Basil had left our number with him so he could call us if anything went wrong.

Ahmed's father didn't have any bad news. In fact, he didn't have any news at all, and was wondering if we had. He had expected Ahmed to call earlier and when he didn't, he began to worry. My father-in-law calmly explained that we knew nothing, and shared the story of how his son had tricked him and slipped out of the house. I stood by and listened to him describe what happened for a few minutes before he handed me the phone.

"Hello dear," Ahmed's father said to me, his voice kind and apologetic. "I didn't mean to worry you all, I just wanted to know if you and your husband had agreed on a cutoff point when Basil was supposed to come home or at least call to touch base?"

"I am sorry. We didn't, actually," I said in as comforting a tone as I could manage. "I am sure they are fine. They are a big group of people and they promised to stick together for their own safety. If I hear anything at all from Basil, I'll make sure I find out everything about Ahmed as well."

"And I will do the same," he said. "Take care of yourself, dear, and God be with us all."

The phone call did nothing but add to the tension of the situation with my mother-in-law. Since 11:00 a.m., every minute had passed with great agony. I could not think of anything else but the possibility of losing Basil, so I could not even imagine what his mother was feeling.

Every time I heard or saw the children playing, it hurt because they were unaware of how the world as they knew it was dangling by a thread.

My brother-in-law's wife took care of everything—the children, the food, comforting my in laws, everything. I just sat on the couch staring into nothing.

My parents called every hour, and my sister Amina called whenever she could.

The hours seemed to move so slowly.

At 6:30 p.m., Ahmed, with whom Basil was supposed to be, returned home and called us.

"Hoda, I want to tell you something, but I want you to trust me that it will all be OK," he said in as optimistic a tone as he could possibly pull off. "I lost track of Basil in one of the tear gas episodes and was unable to find him again."

"What?" I said, trying not to make my voice sound too alarmed. Everyone came out of the woodwork to listen to the call. "I thought you said you wouldn't leave anyone behind."

"Listen, that proved to be very difficult, and he was very confident and kept stepping out on his own. You would have been very proud of him, actually. No one would have guessed he lived the majority of his life in the United States." He attempted a laugh but it came out completely fake. "Believe me, there doesn't seem to be much danger out there now, and he is probably attempting to get home. The army has imposed a curfew and everyone was leaving when I left."

I didn't get much more out of him. All we knew now was that there was no one we could reach with any more news about Basil at the moment.

I filled in Tante Gigi on all the details. She looked at me very seriously and said, "I want you to listen to me and forget everything you discussed with Basil before. When he calls, *insha Allah*, I want you to tell him to find a place to stay, a hotel or something, and stay there and spend the night. I do not want him to go out into the protests alone or to even try to come all the way back here with all that's going on. You need to help me get him out of danger and into a sane state of mind."

I nodded my head in agreement.

Another agonizing two hours went by. The television was still blaring as I changed the children into pajamas and brushed their teeth. We all got into the queen-size bed, and I held onto both of them as they fell asleep. They'd had a fun day, my son told me as he dozed off. Thankfully, he hadn't asked about his father, so I didn't have to lie. Layla slept peacefully as well. If her father comes home safely, I thought to myself, this day will disappear from her memory. She won't remember her grandmother crying or us squabbling. She won't remember my face or my inability to smile at her cute little routines, which usually never failed to change my mood.

But if, God forbid, he did not return, both children will always trace their sorrows back to this day when their parents decided to risk it all in pursuit of a political possibility. I hoped that I would not experience this scenario. I hoped that we had done the right thing.

My sister had described scenes in the streets that contradicted Ahmed's claims that Basil was safe. I kept Amina's accounts from my mother-in-law. Amina's family, including her three children, was forced to spend their night at Mohamed's parents' home because of the imposed curfew. They had seen the army tanks roll into their residential area close to seven o'clock.

Army tanks, in the street.

This did not resemble the unflappably calm Egypt that we witnessed growing up. It had always felt like it was almost impossible to ruffle Egyptian feathers, or so we had thought. Now we had become so ruffled, the ruffling garnered an army presence.

It was frightening to consider that we were at war with the police; admitting that meant that they were no longer our protectors. There was no one to turn to now that we had named the police the bad guys. I had little knowledge of how or if the army could fill that void, but those around me seemed to trust them blindly.

〜〜 〜〜

(Muslim Brotherhood/ Sixth of April Activist: Mohamed Shawky, 26)

At around six o'clock on the twenty-eighth, I realized that I was a lucky man. I'd had the privilege of witnessing a time akin to when prophets walked among us. I'd seen how determination can literally change what you had thought was possible even when it came to your own physical endurance.

The Sixth of April group in Maadi had just completed a twenty-kilometer walk from Maadi to the entrance of Tahrir. This included women who had never played a sport or participated in a marathon in their entire lives—like my own wife and Tante Shahinaz.

Yes, my wife was with me. For a minute there, about eight kilometers into our March, she requested a break and I thought we would part at that juncture. But she rallied after a short rest and continued in her pledge to herself and me that she would not leave my side.

Many have criticized me for allowing her to come along. But, as many activists would tell you, there was a strange comfort in having your spouse nearby. I planned to have her wait for me in a nearby building or café on the outskirts of the battle—far enough away to be safe, but close enough for me to see her quickly should I get wounded and perhaps want to say my final farewell.

Her motives were entirely different. She believed that her presence kept me from doing anything too crazy, because I had a responsibility to return to see her home safely, and that she was here to protect me. Her rationale warmed my heart, and I prayed that for her and my son's sake, we would both return safely.

After such a walk, you needed a rest. However, when we got close to Tahrir, it was obvious that the battle was already raging. There would be no rest for us, as we appeared to be much-needed backup.

Our group formed a massive front. Our width went from one side of the street to the other, with people packed in between and banners raised above the crowds. Our length went as far as the eye could see.

I talked to those around me and shared my doubts about how much of an asset I would be to the struggle to enter Tahrir, given that I could hardly stand. However, I soon realized that everyone had been traveling on foot for kilometers upon kilometers across unbelievably long distances. By the eshaa prayers, close to eight o'clock, we began to come across participants who had started their trek in Helwan, over forty-five kilometers away.

I'm telling you, it was the time of miracles. People were worn to the bone but possessed energy and seemingly endless amounts of adrenalin that pushed them forward.

I left Mona at a small shop on a side street, as planned. The owner had refused to shut down and offered the protesters free water and snacks. We were told that plainclothes policemen were rampant on these side streets, but it was still a relatively safer place for Mona to be than on the frontlines.

I noticed that the "urban elite," which had been character-istic of the twenty-fifth and that I had seen a lot of during our march from Maadi in the morning, was mostly absent. Had they gone home? And who were these people repeating our Sixth of April chants that had been part of our sing-song routines for years.

I was formally introduced to Egypt's poor and struggling at that very moment. The crowd had not come from a specific area, and many were not even from Cairo. It became apparent that men and women had traveled for hours upon hours in buses, trains, and by foot to be exactly where we were now, and were insisting on entering a square that, at the present moment, offered them nothing but a symbolic victory.

This generation of protesters had shed its *Silmia, silmia* mode to face the police's take-no-prisoners approach of tear gas and live ammunition.

When we had first exited from Maadi, it was obvious from the get-go that the Friday of Anger was not an appropriate day for the *silmia, silmia* routine. Even in the early stages of the march, when people were still joining in, plainclothes men carrying swords and broken bottles attacked us.

They charged at us with weapons drawn. We would scatter and regroup, scatter and regroup, losing some here and some there. But ultimately, our ranks recovered into thicker crowds and eventually chased the armed thugs away. We were like a stubborn two-year-old and Tahrir was the cookie jar. Egypt was throwing the tantrum of the century.

So, tired as I was, I grabbed rocks from the ground alongside the mysterious angels of wrath at the forefront and tried to support their efforts. They were pummeling the police force, which was thickly stacked in front of a tear gas launcher.

Several times, Yehia and I witnessed a live tear gas canister land in front of us, sputtering and spewing its poisonous, flaming fumes. The protesters would grab the canisters and throw them back in the direction of the police. In a moment of enthusiasm, Yehia tried to do the same. As he attempted to grab the canister, it seared his hand and he pulled away and yelped with pain. I tried as well, but barely managed to kick it. At that point it was pounced upon by one of the uber protesters and flung back without even as much as a pause.

Were they on drugs? I thought to myself. They didn't even appear to be slightly in pain.

As nine o'clock drew near, it appeared that the police had decided to wipe out this group that kept tirelessly scattering and regrouping. Instead of shooting the canisters at and in front of us, the officers began to shoot in the back of us as well, so we couldn't even scatter. We were becoming trapped by multiple and surrounding canisters. Our eyes were burning and we couldn't run as much as we had before because of our inability to take deep breaths. Running would suffocate us and limit the oxygen that reached our brains.

The dark made the launched canisters' flights easier to trace, and that was the only advantage we had at this point. Each time the officers launched one, we were able to move away from where it was expected to land. This scuffle was pushing us backward and into the surrounding side streets. I intentionally kept to the side that led back into the street that had the shop where Mona was waiting.

Then, in an oddly terrifying coincidence, I could see that the shop Mona was in was in the direct path of a canister that was about to land. She had been standing in front, watching the fight with a tense expression on her face. The whole scene played out before me as if it was in slow motion.

The canister appeared to be going straight down onto her body. I turned around and broke into a run, forgetting about the consequences of such a move in these stifling fumes. In fewer than four strides, I was on the ground suffocating. Amid my struggle to gasp for air, I looked up through my teary eyes and could see that the spot where she once was now was full of protesters. Some were on the ground and others were gathered around those who fell attempting to revive them.

My view was blocked by a few men who gathered around me and tried to get me to breathe. I was overcome by dizziness and nausea, but kept willing myself to gain any kind of strength so I could go to Mona.

I don't know how long it took me to shake off the effects of the poison, and I don't even remember thanking those who helped me. The minute I had any feet to walk on, I stumbled in the direction of the spot where my wife had stood.

I said a prayer every step of the way. I went from fallen protester to fallen protester trying to find her, but my eyes saw nothing but the injustice, sorrow, and pain of those who had either lost their lives or been seriously injured in the last ten minutes. My heart was heavy with grief. Who were we to demand that we survive this when so many had not? Who was I to hope that my wife, the mother of my child, whom I knowingly brought with me for my own comfort, was still on this earth? I was hoping she was alive, but I fully expected that she be among those martyred tonight.

There was a sudden hustle and bustle in the crowd, as we saw *Quwat El Amn* (the Egyptian security forces) heading our way on foot with sticks and Tasers. We scattered, but I was searching frantically as I fled. I ended up at the entrance of the Faisal Nada Theatre on Kasr el Eini Street. The theater was closed, of course, but the entryway was spacious enough for protesters to gather and take cover.

In the crowded theater entrance, with dozens of people huddled around her attempting to revive her, I saw my wife on the ground. Her body was lifeless and her lips were blue. I ran in, pushed people aside, and gathered her in my arms, all the time screaming, "That is my wife! That is my wife!"

As I lifted her face close to my cheek, I realized she was not breathing. The entryway was full of people and tear gas, and I myself felt woozy and deprived of oxygen. I picked her up with great difficulty and my arms shook beneath her. I moved about with her in my arms, trying to get onto a different street, but I could hear bullets and see police running after protesters and beating them into the ground. I went back toward the theater's entrance. I felt that our only hope was to get into the theater itself. It would have cleaner air.

With Mona still in my arms, I went to one of the doors of the theater and kicked at it. I almost fell forward because, as it turned out, that door had not been locked at all. There simply was a heavy table shoved up against it from the inside. I rushed in, lay Mona down, and attempted to elevate her feet above her head, thinking that if her blood pressure was low, it would help bring needed blood to her brain.

I could hear other protesters rushing in and coughing loudly. The theater's security, two obviously shaken, middle-aged men who had been hiding, came out and started begging protesters not to vandalize the theater.

I heard Yehia's voice say, "Don't worry, we are the *silmia, silmia* crowd, except the government doesn't seem to support that stance at the moment." He then saw me and rushed to my side.

As we both knelt beside her, we found that she was breathing weakly, though she was still unconscious. There was a noticeable difference in the color of her lips and skin since we entered the building.

A few women came into the theater out of nowhere and tended to the wounded. They came to us and washed Mona's face and forehead with Pepsi, which was known to reverse the effects of tear gas, and it appeared to be working.

I was so grateful for her survival at that point that all I wanted to do was pray. Yehia and I headed for the theater bathrooms to perform the prayer ablutions. In Islam, when you prepare for prayer, you wipe water across your face, head, arms, hands, and feet three times before you face God on the prayer mat. Unfortunately, we did not know that adding water to a face that had traces of tear gas on it was highly inadvisable.

As we raised our hands in the very first step of the ritual and wiped the water across our faces, Yehia and I simultaneously felt like we poured boiling oil onto our faces. We screamed and jumped about the bathroom, oblivious to why we were experiencing this pain and how to reverse it. It was almost comical to watch.

Two protesters rushed to our aid with the Pepsi and vinegar bottles and applied some tear-gas-specific first aid. In the end, we overcame our symptoms and managed to perform our prayers, which calmed and recharged me.

By the time I finished praying, Mona was awake and conversing with those around her.

I hugged her, then pulled back and said, "Mona, I have to continue. I would take you home if I could, but unfortunately, there is no safe route out at the moment. So stay here and keep yourself safe. I will come back as often as I can."

In many ways, though, I regretted her presence—for her own safety. Still, the fact that I had to regularly come back to her kept me from getting too deep into danger. So in that sense, she was successfully protecting me, just like she'd planned.

She was my seat belt against the evil that lay ahead. If I threw myself violently against it, her presence held me back, but if we pushed against it gradually we would make it together safely to the other side.

❧   ❧

(Mother/ Sixth of April Activist: Shahinaz Meshaal, 50)

The security forces had been easy to fight to this point. Our Maadi group had branched and regrouped along the way, but it only seemed to make us stronger, like Moses in the Pharaoh's court in his face off against the magicians. For every stick the magicians turned into a snake, Moses (through God's divine power) would throw his stick and it would turn into a multitude of snakes that were bigger and more powerful than anything the village had ever seen. Every time they scattered us, we came back more plentiful, determined, and steadfast than ever.

But now I reached Kasr El Eini Street, with a group so big that I barely knew anyone in it, I realized that we walked into a battle that was claiming lives every minute with such brutality that the ground was streaked with blood. The sky was raining tear gas canisters, and we were immediately slapped with the stifling stench.

I had a woman I didn't know named Marwa at my side. I'd met her along the way, and she had asked, "Are you going to Tahrir?" I told her I was, to which she replied, "Please take me with you, but promise to never let go of my hand. I was supposed to go with a group of my friends, but I lost track of them when the thugs came after us."

She was a petite, veiled woman who couldn't be much older than twenty-one. I took her hand in mine and said, "We have conquered the thugs, and they ran like cowards. I will not leave your hand, my child. As long as I am standing, you will be right here next to me, and our hands will be locked together." Her eyes misted but she said nothing more. I do not have any daughters, and her face tugged at my heart.

I advanced into the blood-soaked streets with Marwa and I still holding hands. I looked at her face and saw shock and horror. I strengthened my grip on her hand and threw my shoulders back in a defiant walk that I hoped would inspire her and summon her courage, which was obviously running in the opposite direction. I thought about Shawky and his wife, as we had lost track of each other a few hours ago. I thought of my two sons, who had been marching toward Tahrir with their friends from the Zamalek area downtown. I wondered if they were already here in the battlefield. I wondered if they were among the dead.

The goal of all the protesters was obvious. They wanted to break through the deadly police barricade and settle into Tahrir Square. When I looked up, I could see that the police had snipers on top of surrounding buildings. They were the main cause for the deaths and maiming wounds I saw all around me. They were aiming for the eyes, the knees, and the heart.

To join the quest to move past the police traps and into the square, all you could do was run around madly, trying to get through the gauntlet of dangers. So I pulled Marwa—and any other young person I could see standing around aimlessly in shock—and ran to the left and right in a zigzag fashion.

If the situation wasn't so dangerous, it might have been funny to watch. I was not in the best of shape, I was an older woman, and I was dressed in a long skirt and veil. But I ran like you wouldn't believe. The younger kids could barely keep up with me.

It was no coincidence that the battle was this fierce on Kasr El Eini Street. It wasn't just that it led to Tahrir Square, but that it had strategic buildings and locations of which the police were trying to maintain control. The infamous street had the Maglis El Shoura ("The Consultative Council") and the Maglis El Shaab ("The People's Assembly"). If you took a right off of it, you reached the Ministry of Interior's main building, and if you took a left you were at the American Embassy. In other words, the Egyptian government had all its eggs on Kasr El Eini Street, and the protesters were just about to walk all over them.

After being there for a few hours, if you were lucky enough to survive that long, you began to notice something. There were intermittent periods in which all fire and tear gas would cease and then resume at full force. This seemed to be coinciding with the ambulances that were coming through and allowed access to the square. We assumed that the ambulances were tending to the injuries from the police's side, though all we were throwing were rocks and the occasional fireball or burning piece of fabric. We hoped that the ambulances were tending to protesters as well.

However, in Egypt, an ambulance only comes when a patient's family commissions it and in most cases pays it full price before it transports the patient. So given the fact that the protesters had no working phones, these ambulances were probably only for the police. But why were officers ceasing their attack for the duration of the ambulance's stay, then resuming after it left?

One of the boys came to me and said, "Tante Shahinaz, the majority of men here are having their doubts about all these ambulances that keep coming in. We'll try to stop the next one. We fear that they are replenishing the police force's supplies of bullets and tear gas."

Shortly after our discussion, another ambulance was making its way through, fully expecting us to let it pass as we had done with all the others. Instead, protesters blocked its path, trying to stop it and check its contents. The ambulance immediately ran off, veering to the right, and almost hitting the protesters as it fled. No more ambulances came back, and as time passed it seemed that the police gunfire seemed to be slowing down.

The protesters made the decision then and there to create a circle around the square. They set up checkpoints that prevented anyone from entering the square without being checked first. This would ensure that only peaceful protesters went through and that any further supplies—food, water, medical supplies, and ammunition—were cut off entirely from the police.

This tactic may very well have won the game for protesters on the twenty-eighth.

I wished that the ambulances were real. I wished that somehow this power that governed us regarded us as its children. I prayed for medical help on the twenty-eighth like a mother by her child's bedside at the hospital. At one point, a white Toyota stormed by us in the direction of the protesters on the other side of the square. I could hear protesters' screams over the bullets and tear gas. My body cringed, and I said a prayer for everyone out there.

We had to win this battle and end the bloodshed we were seeing on the streets of Cairo. Everyone seemed to know this, and we buckled down and worked harder and harder to gain ground. With every charge we made at the barricade, the police officers intensified their efforts, and we were bombarded by live ammunition. The bullets flew by Marwa and me and hit the guy next us in the stomach or the guy in front of us in the face. We would stumble over fallen bodies as we ran. The screams of pain and anguish will stay with us the rest of our lives.

It became so intense, I was fresh out of fear. You know when someone says, "I ran out of tears to cry"? I discovered that it's possible to run out of fear. That must be the case with Palestinian mothers carrying stones with which to assault armed Israeli soldiers to avenge the loss of their child. Your fear grows so large it reaches a critical stage at which it just explodes, turns into shock, and can hurt you no more. If that was happening to all the protesters around me, which I felt was the case, then it was a mere matter of time before this square was ours.

As Marwa and I stopped to catch our breath, a young man a few feet away caught my eye. I could not see his face because he was looking in the opposite direction, but I was almost 100-percent sure that it was my youngest son, the one who was supposed to be home with my husband.

The one we had forbade from participating.

I ran up to him and placed my hand on his shoulder and he turned around.

It *was* him. I grabbed him by both of his shoulders, looked him in the eye, and said, "How did you get out of the house without your father's permission?"

"It wasn't like that, Mom," he said hurriedly, "I was at the Friday prayers and I saw a group of men chanting for us all to join. I couldn't help but follow them."

"Did you call your father? Does he know where you are? Or is he searching for you now?"

"I didn't tell him, Mom, and I never got a chance to call."

The Friday prayers were at noon and it was now past 10:00 p.m. My husband must be absolutely beside himself with worry for all the family members that were at large, I thought. Was he here as well? Did he head out to look for us since our youngest was no longer with him at home?

I didn't have much time to think it through because a tear gas canister was launched and hit the very spot we were standing. It was followed by a barrage of rubber bullets and gunfire. We scattered under the intense assault and though Marwa's hand remained in mine as I had promised, my son and I had oceans of people and bullets between us. As hard as I tried after that, I could not find him.

⚬ ⚬

(Muslim Brotherhood/ Sixth of April Activist: Mohamed Shawky, 26)

At about 10:00 p.m., we witnessed a historical moment. Army tanks were sauntering in and taking flanking positions on both sides of the square. They were not interfering with the fight, and protesters appeared to welcome them, though it was hard to tell in all the chaos.

Almost simultaneously, we also witnessed the Haram (the pyramids area) branch of Sixth of April arriving, together with an endless stream of that area's poor and struggling. The faces of this incoming group's members said it all: the poverty, the mistreatment, and the humiliation of living without a backbone in Egypt. They wore their fatigues on their faces. These were Egypt's most downtrodden coming out of the woodwork with absolutely nothing to lose.

They were already bloodied and bruised. We'd been hearing that the pyramids area had been hit hard and that nightclubs and police stations had been burned down, though it was unclear who did it.

For the past half hour I had been worrying about how long we could withstand the police onslaught. Dead bodies had begun to line the pavement. But things began to turn around as this battered group of men entered the field. At face value, the dead multiplied and quadrupled on our side, as these protesters threw themselves into the battle devoid of any caution. However, upon closer examination, you discovered that they were making unprecedented headway regardless of the sizeable casualties.

Not only were they fearless, but they also exhibited the same strange characteristics that I had witnessed earlier with some of the rougher-looking protesters—namely, a lack of feeling when it came to injury and pain.

Not only did these guys pick up tear gas canisters and throw them successfully back at the police, but they also would take bullets to the arms and legs, literally go to the sidelines, get first-aid treatment, wipe themselves off, and go right back in, Rambo-style.

They wore cutoff T-shirts and heavily worn clothes, but even in the dead of winter, this didn't slow them down. It was a spectacle as exciting as a Hollywood movie. In fact, I saw several individuals filming the scene, including some who appeared to be reporters from other countries. It was hard to tell given how dirty everyone was.

Over the course of two hours, we inched forward with them, creating a sizeable perimeter to the square and claiming it as property of the revolution. This was it. We could finally call it a *revolution.* The thought choked me up even amid the heartache and loss I was witnessing. We were getting our revolution. We were part of it right now.

We started to come across members of the Sixth of April Maadi group from whom we had been separated earlier in the day. They explained to us about the mysterious ambulances and cars that were bringing in ammunition and how they were manning the entrances to the square and finishing off the police's supplies. This invigorated the Haram group, and they became part of the security teams, thus making them impenetrable.

The police's tear gas supply was definitely coming to an end, as the inflow was noticeably slower. Our side also ensured that almost every can that was fired at us was returned back to their area. The police had to have been as suffocated and tired as the rest of us, no matter how prepared they were.

They still appeared to have an arsenal of bullets, but protesters were breaking through here and there and seeking out the gunmen. The more ground we gained, the more the army tanks inched in with us. There was still little dialogue between them and us, and we were still experiencing a high rate of casualties.

At one point when we were being fired upon left and right, I lost Yehia. I couldn't find him anywhere. As I advanced, following the lead of those ahead of me, I asked people about him, but they didn't know anything. Finally, one Sixth of April member told me that he believed Yehia had been shot in the face.

My heart sank.

I ran and the bullets started again. I vowed to try to find him the first chance I got.

It was midnight before I finally had that chance. We had already penetrated through to the midan but were still under fire. I was regularly running from one end of the square to the other trying to find him. At one point, I went to Mona and checked on her, and some of the people around her said that I should start searching the hospitals for Yehia.

The French Kasr El Eini Hospital, named so because the French government had donated the money to build it, was situated in the middle of the battlefield, and most of the wounded were being taken directly there. However, there was another location in the square that was so obviously a miracle in its own right that even a pagan would have been able to make the connection.

At the heart of Tahrir Square was a medium-sized mosque called Masgid El Rahman ("The Mosque of the Merciful"). As the battle intensified, the mosque opened its doors to the fallen and injured protesters. Instead of simply housing and finding water and food for them, the sheikh went into the minaret and, using its microphone, started to call upon protesters and homes in the downtown area, saying that the mosque was in need of doctors and medical supplies to treat the influx of victims.

That was a mere few hours before I walked through its many doors, which were designed to welcome the faithful. When I arrived, although the scene was chaotic, you could already see that there was a system in place. The very first doctors who arrived on the scene must have immediately set it up. They designated one area for people arriving fresh from the battle, another area for those being operated on, a first aid area, and a makeshift morgue.

There was a person at the microphone still repeating the call for doctors and medical supplies. The wounded lined the floors of the ad hoc waiting area in the hope of receiving treatment or relief. Their wounds prevented them from running around and dodging bullets to get to the French Kasr El Eini hospital. This place was their only hope.

I searched the faces of those on the ground to find Yehia. Some were shot in the face with what they call *khartoush*, a bullet that breaks into pellet beads all over the body, so instead of one bullet, these men looked as if they had been spray-painted with a thousand of them. These pellets had lodged themselves in eyes, noses, and ears. When they hit the torso area, they would lodge in the spine or groin or other vital organs. Doctors and volunteer nurses were busy trying to extract life-threatening ones and leaving those that would not kill the patient. Understandably, this was one of the many reasons the painful moaning was creating an almost symphonic humming of agony.

I still could not find Yehia. But I did find Tante Shahinaz, visibly shaken, and examining the faces of the wounded like I had been doing. She had a young woman by her side who I had never seen before. She looked at me with gentle eyes and never let go of Tante Shahinaz's hands.

"What are you doing here, Tante Shahinaz?" I asked. "Seriously, you should have been home by now."

She just patted me on the shoulder gently and said with sorrowful eyes, "I cannot find my youngest son or my two elder boys."

She filled me in on what had happened, and said that she was heading to the French Kasr El Eini Hospital to check there as well.

"You know what my advice is to you, my dear, "I told her gingerly. "The pharmacy inside that hospital has a phone. Call home first and check if they'd headed out without you. You are so tough;

you assume they held out as long as you did. You may be pleasantly surprised to find that they'd called it a night."

I hoped that she would find them, and that she and that poor girl would finally get away from this awful scene. I, for one, needed to get my wife out of there as well. We entered the hospital together but parted ways when she headed for the phone. There was a long line there of people trying to call their relatives and I had to keep looking for Yehia. I said a prayer for her to be with her family soon. That woman was damned tough and determined, and it would be a shame to have grief slow her down.

❦ ❦

(Hoda Rashad, 36, Educator/Writer)

Finally, at eight o'clock, Basil made his first phone call. His voice was oddly detached as his mother and father took turns bombarding him with questions about his whereabouts and safety. He had prayed the Maghrib prayers with an old work colleague he had come across in the protests shortly after he had lost contact with Ahmed. The prayer took place in Zamalek on Twenty-Sixth of July Street, a fifteen-minute walk away from Tahrir Square. He had not successfully broken through to the square yet.

His colleague's name was Ahmed, as well—Ahmed Gomaa. I knew him and his wife from work functions and company dinners. Gomaa had his own group of friends, and Basil had joined them. Basil was calling from one of Gomaa's friends' homes in Zamalek. He couldn't stay on the line because there were several men waiting to call their families. He did say that he noticed that in the last hour or so the majority of protesters available in and around the square appeared to be of a lower economic status.

Most protesters of higher economic levels seemed to have adhered to the imposed curfew and taken the army's move into the protests as a sign to quit, at least for the night.

"Are you quitting for the night, Basil?" I asked as his mother waited on the line for his response.

"I will see what's going on. The people here are considering sleeping in this apartment and not trying to reach our homes," Basil said.

"You stay where you are, Son," my mother-in-law interjected. "There is no need for you to go out there again. Just stay where you are and come home to us first thing in the morning."

"OK, Mom," Basil said.

She hung up. I was still on the line.

"*Are* you quitting for the night Basil?" I asked again.

He took a deep breath. "I am heading out again in ten minutes."

"Are you sure?" I almost whispered. "Haven't we fulfilled our role for the day? Most people we know have gone home or are staying put from this point forward."

I was asking his opinion, as I didn't have one at the moment. Deep down I didn't want to hang up the phone, knowing he was going out there, since that would render the call of no real value. It simply meant we had heard from him, but in reality he could be dead in the next few hours or even the next few minutes.

"What I saw today...what the remaining people are doing and trying to achieve..." his voice trailed off. "At least Gomaa believes so as well, so I am going to head out there again with him."

"What do I tell your mother?"

"You do whatever you feel is better for her," he said. "If you can keep her thinking I am still here, maybe that is easier for her."

"She has caller ID, Basil. She is not an idiot. She is going to try to call you again and make sure you are there." I was a bit angry.

"Then do as you wish. I have to get off the phone."

I could sense that the man who had left this house hours ago was not the same one on the phone. Whatever he had seen had changed him. I made a conscious decision not to lose his trust in me, so he wouldn't start lying to me about what he was going to do. It was imperative that I know where he was heading so I had an idea where he was last, should our contact be severed for the night.

"Can you at least try to call us every few hours?" I said as delicately as I could.

"Yes, I will do my best to keep this system going. I gotta go." He hung up. There was nothing sentimental. No messages for the kids. No "I love you." No "if I don't come back, do this or that..." Nothing. It was out of character and far removed from what I was used to or expected. I put both of my hands on my head and slowly looked up. My mother-in-law was standing in the doorway.

"He's going back in there, isn't he?" she asked forcefully.

I didn't have much time to consider my answer, but in the split second that I did, I decided that the worst thing we could do to was to feed her another lie. She had already lost her faith in us as a couple, at least for the time being.

"Yes, he is."

She threw her hands in the air and said, "I do not understand you. How can you encourage him to continue with this? It is over. He has participated. Why is he insisting on placing himself in danger to finish something he was not a part of to begin with? He doesn't know who the organizers of today's activities are or what their plan is. He is not familiar with their demands or their methods of execution. What is he doing?"

"I did not encourage him," I said gently. "I simply supported his choice to do what he believed in, and apparently this is the right thing to do at the moment. We didn't even get the chance to discuss why. There was a cue for the phone and he seemed to have a lot of people around him."

She was right back where she was when we first informed her that her son had left to join the protests. The pain and the worry circled her like an angry mob. She had nowhere to go in her mind that made her feel better, and she held Basil and I accountable for her torment.

I understood her sentiment completely. I didn't know what to do about it, but I understood it. I don't know what I would do in her shoes.

In my heart and head I prayed for God's guidance and forgiveness for causing so much pain to a parent who had done nothing but love and support her children her whole life. I prayed that we were doing the right thing. The sane thing. The responsible thing.

❧ ❧

(Mother/ Sixth of April Activist:
Shahinaz Meshaal, 50)

As Shawky and I walked toward the hospital, we could see the National Democratic Party's building on fire and hear the people start to chant at and to the army, *"El Geish wel Shaab, eid wahda!"* ("The army and the people are one hand together"). The protesters were wooing the otherwise neutral soldiers into the battle like the promise of a woman: Join us and there will be great things to come.

Shawky went to find Yehia, and I stood in line with the fortunate ones who were calling home to report that they had survived so far. In that line, I came across a Sixth of April Maadi group member in his early twenties, who had a patch over his eye and a cast on his left ankle.

"Tante Shahinaz!" he said like a little boy who had found his mother in the crowd, "I think the army was shooting at us."

"Oh no, my child, they would never do that," I said reassuringly. "There were snipers all over the rooftops. The army is here to protect us. We must hold onto that with all the faith that we have within us. They are our biggest hope now. They can stop the madness, or take all this ugliness to a different level."

I knew in my heart that our army would not be our enemy. The police had no regard for it. The army was neither feared nor paid much attention at all. But its dramatic entrance suggested that it was time to wrap things up.

I eavesdropped inadvertently on the phone calls that took place before mine. Most delivered good news. None were like me, looking to see if I could get good news from home.

When I finally got my turn, the phone receiver was musty and hot. I dialed. It rang twice.

"Hello?" said my husband's anxious voice. I immediately guessed that he was frantic about our son, and my heart sank. All his warnings flashed across my mind, and in a split second I could feel the guilt rising up within me.

Had I led my son by my example straight into his grave?

"It's me," I said weakly. "I am in Kasr El Eini Hospital…"

"Oh my God! Are you hurt? I knew something was wrong when everyone showed up except you!"

Just like that, all my fears were laid to rest.

"The two elder boys returned hours ago, but our little daredevil youngest here just walked in a half hour ago. He is grounded for a whole month…except if Mubarak leaves." He forced a laugh. "Are you OK, Shahinaz? Please be honest with me."

"I am fine," I told him. "I've been looking all over the place for our daredevil since I caught him here and we got separated by the shooting. Tell him he had me frantic." I was too relieved and drained to be angry.

"Please come home Shahinaz," he said desperately, "Please come home to us. I have heard awful things and I need to see you all here together and intact."

When I hung up the phone, I was shaking. This time it was Marwa who was holding me up. "We have to go home my child," I managed to say to her, "But give me a second to rest here first."

I sat on the front steps of the hospital like a heap of rocks. I had walked over thirty kilometers over the course of the day and had been standing for eight hours. I had not eaten at all and had very small amounts of water here and there. I had been exposed to hours and hours of poisonous gases. I was over fifty years old.

I could still hear Masgid El Rahman's makeshift hospital calling for doctors in the distance. I thought of all the men I had seen die today. I thought of them lying there cold in the Mosque or the hospital, their anxious families by the phone waiting for that call that would never come.

A few tears found their way down my face and Marwa, the girl I knew nothing about, put her arms around my shoulders and squeezed a little.

"Let's go home, Auntie," she said tenderly. "I believe we have done all we could tonight."

I handed Marwa over to a trusted member of our movement who was going in the direction where she lived. We hugged and parted and she and I never met again.

I took backstreet after backstreet in the pitch-black night. There was no one around but I was too tired and numb to be scared. I found my way out to a segment of Corniche El Neel, the Nile promenade that leads to Maadi, and walked alongside it until I found a microbus that was willing to stop. It was packed with people who appeared to have been stranded like me amid the chaos taking place downtown.

I was the only women in that cramped space. Everyone kept repeating that it was insane for me to be out at this time of night under these circumstances. When the microbus reached the end of its line, I went back out into the night. I was very close to my home at the entrance of the Maadi area.

A car slowed down alongside me. A man rolled down the window and smiled. I knew him. His face looked very familiar, but I could not remember his name. I believe he was a neighbor who lived a few apartment buildings away from me. We must have passed each other on the street a dozen times.

He offered me a ride and I accepted without much thought. Without him, I had little hope of getting home at all. I had lost all ability to walk and there wasn't a bus, cab, or any other form of transportation in sight.

My husband swung open the apartment door while I was still fumbling with my keys. He had seen me arrive from the balcony. He and the boys had been stationed there since we hung up the phone together. We hugged and cried and told each other about the paradoxical day of victories and violence and marveled at the privilege of being an Egyptian at this time.

Satellite channels were raving about the revolutions in the Arab world, and Egypt's revolution specifically received top billing. We congratulated each other repeatedly, and I kept stealing glances at my sons, who were listening to the worldwide praise and beaming.

These same boys who had wanted to get a visa to whatever country would take them could not be pried away from Tahrir Square with a forklift, let alone be convinced to go anywhere else but here.

I got up immediately with my last vestiges of strength, cleaned myself off, and prayed. I prayed to God to accept my sincere gratitude for saving my family tonight. I thanked him for giving us the honor to be a part of this. I prayed that Shawky, his wife, and as many Egyptians as possible had made it home safely tonight.

But most of all, I prayed for those who were still there: the ones awaiting their burial, the ones who were being treated for injuries, and the brave young men who were spending the night there in the cold to guard the territory that had been won.

Shawky called before I was about to doze off. He and Yehia were ok, though Yehia had been shot and had to remain in the hospital because of bullet fragments still lodged in his nose and sinus area.

I was told that by 3:00 a.m., Tahrir belonged to protesters, and the police were nowhere to be found. I was told that the tanks had formed a perimeter around the one that the protesters had set up to control who came into and left the square. I was told that doctors and nurses didn't get a wink of sleep.

I was told that Egypt was almost ours tonight, and that it was only a matter of time now, and she would be ours forever.

༄ ༄

(Mohamed Shafei, 39, Co-Founder and Partner
of Deraya Sales Services)

At around 6:30 p.m. on the twenty-eighth, my sister had showed up again with her son at my parents' apartment. It had only been twenty minutes since they had left in an attempt to get back to her husband before curfew. She was in a terrible state. She was crying uncontrollably, and we could barely make out what happened.

Her twenty-one-year-old son and eighteen year old daughter, filled us in on their terror-filled ride. They described how there were almost no police in the streets, and when you did catch one, the officer was fleeing. There were car tires set ablaze and the police stations were on fire. All the decent, law-abiding citizens who had a place to stay stayed put, and all the protesters were in Tahrir, so the vast majority of people left on the city's streets were there to take advantage of the situation. Some looked like seasoned thieves, while others simply looked terribly poor and destitute and searching for an opportunity to salvage anything for their families.

Amina and I decided against going home as well, and so we were three families now in one home, as my other sister had managed to get to her husband safely. My parents had not prepared for any of us staying over, so there was a grocery shortage that needed to be resolved. We barely had enough to keep us going through breakfast tomorrow and we had all these kids to feed.

It was ironic because back in my apartment, the fridge and pantries were stocked because I had been worried about the situation escalating after the twenty-fifth and stocked up. I also took five thousand pounds out of the bank just in case. That turned out to be the smartest move I made all week.

The money was on me, but the groceries were out of reach. The only three men in the household now were my elderly father, me, and my twenty-one-year-old-nephew, who was to a great extent very sheltered and had as little experience as any of us of situations with elevated danger levels.

I made a decision to take him with me and try to get groceries before it was too dark.

My sister was right. It was crazy out there. The streets were full of young men who were obviously devoid of a cause. The chaos delighted them. They were keying cars and trashing the street and propagating a sentiment that had little to do with what was going on downtown.

We moved our car to a position where we could see it from a back window in the apartment and where it was not on the main street that seemed to be getting most of the beatings from the street mongrels. All the grocery stores in the vicinity were shut down, and we returned home empty-handed.

"We just have to be creative," I told my mother. "I will go to my apartment in the early morning tomorrow and we can share some of what we've got."

We wanted to watch from the front balcony that overlooked the main street, but we noticed that when the looters saw people witnessing their crimes from above, they would start pelting them with whatever was within reach and threatening to come up and attack them. So we took our seats a couple of steps into the living room where they couldn't see us and turned off the lights throughout the apartment. It was like watching a war movie live from our living room. Gameat El Dowal Street, normally a huge, high-end shopping area and home electronics hub, was being ravaged.

At 8:30 p.m., we witnessed one of the strangest spectacles we had ever seen in Cairo. People appeared to be descending from poorer neighboring areas in droves. They went clamoring onto Gameat El Dowal Street and Shehab Street, which was perpendicular to it (and also known for its variety of stores and boutiques). What they were carrying, though, seemed to come from an office building and not a store: office furniture, chairs, tables, mini-refrigerators, and generally odd items.

I was worried that they were attacking residential apartment buildings and the hotels on our street, so I went downstairs to check with my doorman for updates. He told me that the looters had attacked an entire building owned by NDP leader and locally loathed billionaire businessman Ahmed Ezz. It was alarming, though everyone believed the man entirely deserved it, but not as scary as it could have been had the looters targeted random Egyptian homes with occupants.

At one point, it got to be too much for my parents, and they decided to go to bed and leave us the nightshift.

After an hour or more of the same chaotic and highly sporadic behavior, we began to witness an evolution of the looting. It became a more sophisticated form of burglary. Young men came in organized groups with a predetermined division of labor. They brought motorcycles and tok toks to load merchandise into. They claimed spots and became territorial, and they seemed to be willing to keep going and gathering as much as they possibly could before the authorities tried to stop them.

The interesting thing was that I truly believed that none of this was premeditated. For most, it probably started with the Ahmed Ezz building as a form of revenge, or it was simply Robin Hood behavior. But then they realized how easy it was and how nonexistent the consequences were, and things began to snowball.

You could hear them calling to each other, "Hey check this out...they got the CD store unlocked!" or "There is an eveningwear boutique that is wide open!" It was contagious, and unlikely participants began to stroll into the vulnerable stores in an apparent daze.

The items they carried down the street became stranger and stranger. One man had an entire toilet mounted to his shoulder, while another had a door—an entire door that had been removed from somewhere! I saw a middle-aged man walking around with a naked, female store mannequin under his arm, and others were actually trying on clothes from the boutiques in the street and seeking each other's opinions on the fit and color. A truly bizarre spectacle, indeed.

I don't know which part of it got me to go down there. But I do know that I had a strong feeling that if the law-abiding citizens didn't stop what was happening, looters would start coming into our homes.

I took my nephew Ahmed, who was very excited about the prospect of getting close to the action. We went out into the street in an attempt to gather like-minded individuals to stop the looting.

As soon as we were in the street, Ahmed started giggling nervously, and I began to think that maybe this was too much for him. I also considered the fact that he may be a liability to me and would actually jeopardize my safety. It was too late for second thoughts, though. I couldn't very well get him to go back into my parents' apartment now even if I wanted to.

Up close, the looters seemed much less threatening than they did from the balcony—like a bunch of kids having fun. Beyond all their street talk, they had no true intention of harming any human beings. They were obviously of a poor economic background, and many of them were simply giddy to be so close to all this quality merchandise. It was strange how when watching them, you couldn't help but feel somewhat happy for them in this brief, kid-in-a-candy-store experience, even though what they were doing was so obviously wrong.

On a bench in front of a building, a group of about ten men were gathered around a bounty of about twenty to thirty stolen business suits. They put on the jackets and sauntered around in mock runway fashion to make each other laugh. I heard one of them say to the other, "What do you think? Like I was made for one of these, huh?" The other sheepishly answered back, "Where are you going to wear it, Mister Eveningwear, to your bullshit mechanic sidekick job or to your mother-in-law's luxury castle?"

Banter like that reflected the sad reality that when the dust settled, if it did, none of them would ever get to own such things and even if they did, the items had no function in their world.

That is why it was rather ironic when another young man of a similar background came by on a motorcycle and snatched a bunch of the suits on the bench and took off. The group hurled insults and rocks at him, and he looked back and laughed as he sped away.

On Gameat El Dowal Street, quite close to where my parents' building was, the looters were breaking into the coveted duty-free shop that was so big that its front window wrapped around two large sides of a huge twenty-story apartment and office building. It was unclear why they targeted this particular store, as the Ogeil store, left untouched, equaled if not surpassed it in girth and expensive products and was almost next-door.

The merchandise in the duty-free shop ranged from electronics to pricey foods, and if looters were already looting each other, the lure of what was in there was sure to create a street brawl. It occurred to me that they may even set fire to the building and occupants could be at risk.

Accordingly, that was the first group of people to whom I decided to speak. I rushed to the building and started to engage one of the people instigating the break-in. I utilized all my Procter & Gamble sales training to try to convince this individual to walk away from what he was attempting, as well as maybe convince a bunch of his friends to walk away with him.

"Hey man," I said in a friendly tone. "We don't have to do this. What about the people who run this place and have jobs here, man. This is *har'ram*. We can be better than this."

Some of them ignored me altogether, while others responded dismissively, "Oh, the owners have enough money as it is. What is the harm in just one day of looting. Let them try what we go through. We are hungry, *ya basha* ['sir']," they would say with a chuckle, half-joking and half-admitting that they knew what they were doing was preposterous.

But small groups were listening to me, and I could see an obvious influx of other well-intentioned people who must have thought what I thought when I left the safety of my parents' apartment. Gradually, groups of three here and five there were convincing their friends to just call it quits with what they have and to not cause massive losses just because no one was watching.

Like I had feared, fights started to break out, as men beat each other up over phones and microwave ovens. Citizens had begun to attempt to protect the particularly expensive items by creating human shields, and they were getting beaten as well.

A plainclothes policeman entered the equation. He was obviously not present on behalf of the regime. He was there as a self-appointed representative of the owners who were not there to protect their interests. He was performing his duties as a real police officer, and people were preparing to attack him as he announced his vocation and intentions.

He pulled out his gun, and it was at this particularly dangerous moment that I realized that Ahmed, my nephew, was not by my side.

I moved away from the officer and began looking wildly to my left and right. The officer began shooting into the air, and people started running around, still trying to grab items here and there. Since I was near the store's entrance I was getting pushed around by people trying to hastily exit. I began to see some shots ricocheting, and the situation turned from mildly dangerous to deadly in a few moments.

I tried to force myself further into the store, yelling, "Ahmed! Ahmed!" into the chaos, but to no avail. Looters were emerging from the back of the store carrying full-size refrigerators! Yes, refrigerators. This was the first time in my life I had seen one man carry a fridge on his back and move with it while an accomplice helped by keeping one hand on the fridge and directing the laboring thief with the other.

I fought my way through, but when I reached the back of the store, Ahmed wasn't there. It occurred to me that he might have ran with the first shots, so I headed toward our building and asked the doorman if he had returned. He said he didn't. I could not bring myself to go upstairs to my sister without him, so I hung out in front of the building first, trying to think it through.

I had only been there five minutes when Ahmed showed up, pale and nervous. He *had* run out when he heard the first shots, and had since been on his way home.

We both went upstairs, but neither of us could ever find enough calm to permit sleep, so we kept our vigil from the balcony from midnight until dawn broke.

As the sunlight began to slowly trickle in, I heard the call for the dawn prayer. In Muslim countries, right before daybreak, microphones mounted on mosque minaret's broadcast the voice of the lone *muezzin* [prayer caller] of each mosque. The *muezzin* makes the nightly journey in the dark to his mosque to call into the microphone for people to wake up and pray. I had never appreciated the beauty of this ritual and the miracle of a new day as I did at that moment.

As the prayer caller sung his song to the faithful, looters began heading home with whatever they could carry. The duty-free store was the hardest store hit on the block. At around 3:30 a.m., when the store had been almost completely emptied, it suddenly went up in flames. I wondered where the plainclothes officer was now. He had obviously failed in his mission.

By four o'clock, the army tanks had rolled in. The looters weren't scared at all, much to my surprise. Instead, they acted like this was their revolution, and they immediately jumped on top of the tanks, dancing and singing.

Each tank had about five officers operating and guarding it. In that sense, the army was grossly outnumbered, but it made up for it by being heavily armed. The soldiers diplomatically got the excited youths to step off of their vehicles and keep their distance. They sporadically shot in the direction of the looting, around shops, and into the air. It was obvious they had no orders to fight these people, so their tactics were all precautionary and there were no injuries.

The situation began to get under control and as daylight shined brighter, I felt that now was the time to move my family off this street and back to Nasser City to my apartment, where it was generally safer and the pantry was full.

I woke my father up for the dawn prayers and told him that I wanted to head out as early as possible to ensure the absolutely safest route for our children. My brother-in-law came for his wife and son and helped us pack our cars for the move.

My parents had slept through all of the drama, so they were fighting us all the way, saying that we were panicking unnecessarily. However, when they saw bullet marks in some of the walls and saw two thieves sitting next to a fridge in our own building's entryway, they began to cooperate.

The doorman explained that he had an agreement with the thieves. They would help him guard the building, and he would help them guard the fridge until they found a way to move it. I attempted my last bid of lobbying and approached the two of them.

The first rule of a successful sales pitch is to make sure you are addressing the person in charge. I directed my words to the one who looked me in the eye when he saw me approaching—the other made a point of looking away— and appeared confident about what he was doing.

The second rule: Point out what the person is doing wrong by asking him an open-ended question that makes him reflect on his actions.

"You know it's not right to take something that doesn't belong to you. Do you really want this fridge following you around on judgment day?"

"Come on, man," he said with a grin. "You know that if I don't take it, someone else will."

The third step is to offer a solution that appears to be the better option. "Well then, let us allow that other person to use it as a ticket to hell—and you know what, it doesn't even have to be that way. I can ensure that this fridge will be returned to the store if you decide to do the right thing."

The fourth rule is to offer an incentive: "You know there may be rewards set for those who return merchandise. I can keep you in the loop on that one."

And the fifth rule is to attempt to close on the spot: "So how about you set it up with my doorman here, and I will personally see to it that everything goes along smoothly?"

He paused a few seconds. "Sure, why not? I wasn't making any progress finding a way to transport it anyway."

We shook hands and exchanged numbers, and I left proud and full of hope.

I would later learn that the thieves took the fridge with them shortly afterward.

On our drive back over the bridge, we could see the NDP building burned down and overturned police cars on the Sixth of October Bridge. Cars were burning below us as well. As the children *oohed* and *aahed* about what they were seeing, my father's eyes were full of tears. He and my mother watched from the car windows with a pained expression on their faces. They had often mentioned how their days in this country were so much better than the Egypt we shared now—I believe that what they were seeing was almost too painful to bear. It was still unclear to them who started this revolution and whether it would result in anything positive.

The "Friday of Anger" was definitely the end of all things familiar to Egyptians, but it was also the beginning of the steepest uphill climb the country had been faced with in a long time. I had a strong feeling that we were in for a tough ride, and I hoped that we were headed for the better.

As I looked at my children's faces juxtaposed against that of my parents, I felt my spirits lift a little. The children were inspired by the possibility of a different reality than the one they had experienced so far. For them, this was a new beginning.

∾ ∾

(Hoda Rashad, 36, Educator/Writer)

It was 4:00 a.m. on what now was officially the twenty-ninth, and my last phone call with Basil had been a couple of hours ago. I had moved my children out of the bedroom and onto the hide-a-bed couch in the living room upstairs. I wanted to be in a room that had a television, so my brother-in-law's family and I made the exchange.

The sight of my children so beautifully sound asleep helped me stay calm. The TV had been on all night set to Al Jazeera with the volume low. It hummed away, repeating headlines and taking phone calls from protesters on the ground as well as Egyptians at home. The feed would announce one piece of news and then adjust it according to fresh information, it would tally a death toll and then update it…if you had a loved one who was still out there, it was almost impossible to turn off the television.

I could hear the TV in my in-laws' bedroom as well. They couldn't sleep, either. I closed my eyes for a second and leaned my head back, thinking about our last phone call. Basil had been keeping his promise to call every two hours or so.

Our conversations were short and sad. He was getting an eyeful of some of the craziest scenes he had ever come across.

He described a particular incident in which a group of men threw a wood log from a building-site scaffold onto an incoming armored vehicle to force it to stop. They yanked out the officers in it and confiscated bullets and tear gas supplies meant for the police. He described how protesters took the captured officers and handed them over to the army unharmed. In fact, every time it appeared that a protester might "lose it" because he had just seen his friend murdered or wounded, surrounding protesters would stop him dead in his tracks. Basil found that extremely impressive.

During every phone call, his mother picked up first, then hung up and appeared in my room. Sometimes she tried to convince him with love, and other times she got really angry with him and said she would disown him for life. But she never gave up on trying to get him to come home. It was almost as if she believed that she had the power to *will* him back. And the funny thing was, I believed that this particularly strong woman had the power to do just that. It was oddly comforting.

In his last phone call, she told him that he was killing his father. He had diabetes and she told Basil how his sugar readings were all over the place and it was his fault. She tried to get him to worry about his work and the possibility of airports closing and his meetings in California being placed in jeopardy. She reminded him that if he neglected his business, he would be of no use to his wife and children. She was relentless and I felt that she was starting to get through to him.

But Mubarak's speech had made him angry, and he didn't want to give up the fight. He was insulted that no apologies were made for the loss of life he had witnessed firsthand.

The phone ringing brought me out of my thoughts and back to reality, and I picked up immediately so it wouldn't wake the kids. It was Basil.

"Hello, Hoda," he said. "I just wanted to let you all know that I am in Ahmed Gomaa's house and that I'll be spending the night here."

"You are not going out again?" I asked, perhaps a little too eagerly.

"We'll be going out in the morning, *insha Allah*." He sounded disappointed that I was among those who wanted him to stop.

"Are you OK?" I asked.

"Yes, I'm fine." He paused for a second. "I saw a lot of people die today." He let that statement linger, and I didn't know what to do with it. We had been married for ten years and neither of us had ever had an exchange like this one.

We were not strangers to tragedy. We had faced a lot together. We had gone through years of infertility and the premature birth of twin girls. We had sat by our daughters and witnessed them leave this life one after the other. Their deaths were slow and painful, a direct result of the insensitive and ill-equipped medical system that Mubarak's Egypt had provided us. In fact, the experience of losing our daughters was the final straw that had broken our relationship with the country.

We had set up a small NGO that initiated educational and developmental endeavors, and we felt that we had done so much in Egypt and it had given us so little in return. We had given it our time and our money and had done what we believed was our best and had very little to show for it. We drew the line at losing our own children to Egypt's shortcomings.

Now he had witnessed someone else's children dead on the street by the hands of those who had sworn to protect them. Someone else's child had died a willing adult to change those things Basil and I had hated so much about Egypt. I felt ashamed at the audacity of our sentiment that we had done enough for Egypt. I felt ashamed for every day I cursed it in front of other people, to myself and in my sleep. I did not know Egypt before January 28, 2011. Now I was seeing it differently for the first time.

CNN was hailing Egyptian youth as brave leaders of freedom, and the network's entire broadcast focused solely on this country. I was experiencing a sense of Arab pride that had been absent my whole life.

The channel had presented a translated version of Mubarak's speech, followed by President Obama's reaction, in which he stated that he found the Egyptian president's remarks to have fallen short.

In the past I had felt indebted to Egypt because my parents had told me I should, but, deep down, I had viewed my duality as a nuisance. Now I had nothing but love for this country. I felt the need to reprimand her for not introducing herself to me like this before. Where had these people Basil told me about been hiding? How could there have been activism at this level and Basil and I were not part of it?

"I am glad you are safe, my love," I whispered. "Come home to us tomorrow if you can."

"I do not want to, Hoda. Please understand and support me on this."

His mother appeared at the door and took the phone from me. "Listen Basil, just come home first and let's think this through and then you can go back out there if you choose."

"We will talk in the morning, Mother," he said gently, "I am very tired now, I need to sleep. I will call you, I promise."

She hung up the phone and looked at me kindly. This was her first break from the whole ordeal. "I think we all could use some sleep, don't you?"

I smiled and slid further down into the bed.

She walked out and closed the door behind her.

~ ~

I woke up two hours later. My son was sitting up in bed, looking at me.

"Mom, did Dad come home last night?" he asked in his usual upbeat manner. He was not worried, just getting his facts straight.

"No, honey," I said, half asleep. "He spent the night at a friend's house."

"Is he coming back today?"

Good question. The whole of last night came crashing into my head. I crawled out of bed quietly so as not to awaken my one-year-old daughter, Layla. I opened the door and took a peek out to see if anyone else was stirring.

My brother-in-law and his family were awake and fixing their breakfast in the kitchen. My brother-in-law's wife came over to me and put an arm on my shoulder. "How is Basil?"

I filled her in while my brother-in-law listened intently. "I received a call from a friend in the American Embassy," he said, "An evacuation plan has been set up at the airport for American citizens wishing to exit Egypt. In fact, they are advising all families to do so. If you and Basil are interested, you need to call this number and give them your names and passport numbers and book a spot. But you have to be serious about it. If you book a spot and then you do not show up, you fall to the bottom of the list and have to wait for you turn."

"But we don't have anything there at the moment." I said. "We have no house, our stuff is in storage and Ferris is in the middle of a school year. I am not sure Basil would…" I let my voice trail off as I thought of him.

"Well why don't you call him then," my brother-in-law said, pushing the phone toward me. "The evacuation will probably only go on for two or three days."

"Are you evacuating?" I asked him.

"My case is different, I don't have a job there. My work is here. But I *am* going to present my parents with that option. My father needs medications that would make staying here detrimental to his health if there were shortages."

Layla called out to me from upstairs, interrupting our conversation. But as I changed Layla and made breakfast for the kids, all I could think about was whether Basil should quit the protests now and come home or continue the fight for the country. Was he taking chances with his work that we couldn't afford? Should it matter, considering that Egypt was in crisis?

But I couldn't help but think, what would happen to my job and my father's job and my brother-in-law's job and my father-in-law's job? The only person in this group whose source of income came from outside of Egypt was Basil. Was it wise to let his work go on hold as well, when it could carry the rest of us through if things got really bad?

I couldn't make heads or tails of it no matter how hard I tried. In a revolution, these are the arguments that present themselves. It is not all about who throws himself at the guns first. It is also about those who survive the fight and have to deal with the aftermath. If I learned anything from the thought process I went through, it was to eliminate judging others from my skill set.

Then it occurred to me to consult with two individuals with whom I worked when I was doing the civic engagement project with my high school students. These two particular people's opinions had guided me through a lot of work-related issues the past few months, and I'd learned a lot from our interactions together.

They were also vehemently nationalistic and worked tirelessly in every venue they has access to that was of benefit to Egypt.

Hatem Azzam was a successful entrepreneur who funded some of my website's activities and also did some life-coaching. Wael El Zoghby was the executive director of a prominent NGO called *Baladnaa* ("My Country"). I knew that both of them had been attending protests since the twenty-fifth and strongly advocated the participation of all Egyptians across the board, regardless of their activism experience or the nature of their careers.

First I called Hatem on his home phone, and his wife told me that he was still in Tahrir. I then called Wael, who had been in Tahrir all of the previous night but returned to his family at dawn. Wael's accounts of what he had witnessed were yet another reminder of how dangerous it was to participate, but he still emphasized that he believed that it was everyone's duty to be there.

No matter how "nationalistic" you were, it was not an easy decision to take part in something as life-threatening as these protests, let alone something that may cost you your children's father and livelihood.

When Hatem called back, I was in tears because of what Wael had shared with me and I went on and on about my family's dilemma. I didn't realize that my problems were very much secondary to the tragedies from which he had just walked away, and for a moment I sensed that he lost his patience with my breakdown. "I *cannot* tell you that it is OK to leave the country, Hoda, if that is what you are expecting me to say."

There was an uncomfortable silence, and I think he felt bad about being terse. "Listen," he said gently, "There are people in the square now who cannot go back to their homes. If they do they will get arrested. If the numbers in the square drop, then they will be arrested as well. The only thing holding the police back is the sheer number of people out there. If everyone wants their son, their husband, their daughter, or their father to come back for their own personal reasons, we will lose this fight, plain and simple."

"I know you are right. I am just really worried…" I trailed off into some more tears.

"OK, look, regardless of all the issues now…" he said, and he really seemed to be trying hard to remove himself from his own emotions and judgments and assume the role of a life-coach, "if I was to be totally objective about the situation, and consider only what is within your control, I would ask you what your plans were before all of this happened."

"Basil had an important business meeting on February third and he had booked tickets for the second. There is no Internet and he has lost the capability of working remotely. I am scared they are going to close the airports and then everything will stop for his work and we will run out of cash."

I could hear him take a deep breath. "Well, then maybe he can go and you can find a way to participate on his behalf," Hatem said. "No one expects him to quit his job in the States if that is where he works. There are two of you—maybe he can go catch his meeting and come back. But this is everyone's cause and everyone is losing money and much more in this fight. We must keep Egypt above all else."

I was at my weakest point when I hung up. Wael's stories and Hatem's views had me feeling confused and small, and reduced me to a helpless mother clutching her children at home, and that image did not sit well with my own ego.

My mother-in-law had awakened, and she was waiting for me to get off the phone so she could discuss Basil. I kept the phone to my ear for a few minutes after Hatem hung up, just to give myself a minute to think.

It didn't help much. I had reached no magical solution with which to present her. We analyzed the situation to death, and I was getting weaker every time. She turned on the TV and showed me the reports. Local channels were calling it mayhem.

We didn't know it at the time, but later it became apparent that there was a plan in place to create mass fear among Egyptians. This plan was to show Egyptians that if Mubarak left, there would be utter chaos and everyone would lose. It was a simple choice: stability or freedom. The regime wanted us to trust that now that the government had heard our voices, changes were on the way and we should fall back and wait for them to take effect. But it was hard to shake away the equally plausible scenario that now that they had heard our voices, they would hunt us down and kill us.

Television shows featured individuals calling in live on air, hysterical, reporting break-ins, kidnappings and rapes. The media made Egyptians feel that every family needed every male member to come home and protect his loved ones.

My lack of sleep coupled with the trauma of the last twenty-four hours chipped away at my resolve. I was ready to fold. Like a suspect in the interrogation room, I was ready to give up the goods. When my mother-in-law finally handed me the phone, I told Basil that he absolutely had to return home.

I cited his father's health, his work, our safety, and my relationship with his family. I pulled all the stops. I finally managed to convince him that he should come home and discuss things with his family and then go back if he so chose.

He was angry, but he finally gave in.

His brother was going into the city to get some clothes and supplies from his apartment so they could continue to stay in his parents' house. Families across Egypt were following similar plans, consolidating their members in one home so they could all protect each other. He would pick up Basil from Ahmed Gomaa's house on his way back.

Basil had left my father's car at a gas station, and had stopped a lone cab on the desert road to drive him to the agreed-upon meeting point on Friday morning. Since then, he had traveled on foot all over Egypt for the first time in his life. Now his brother was coming in to collect him. He felt like a teenager being brought back from a night of partying.

Basil was offended and angry, but he would be home in a matter of hours.

There was no relief for me. I felt like a deserter in the most important war Egypt had. I sat down on the couch, numb and separated from my beliefs and convictions, which I'd thought I had known so well. I was at a loss.

I began to dread facing Basil. As I looked at myself in the bathroom mirror, I started to apply makeup to my ashen face. I stopped midway and looked deeply at my reflection. I hated who I was. I made no sense at all.

When Basil came home, he looked none of us in the eye. He almost brushed passed me entirely. He hardly spoke to the kids, and stared at the television for hours.

He had graphic pictures on his phone and he smelled of something almost medicinal. His attitude lasted for about six hours, until the panic that the media created started to hit our area. The news channels began to mention thugs targeting the affluent suburbs surrounding ours with trucks and machine guns. The neighbors came back with a flier from the homeowners' association calling for a meeting. The men of the family went to an area inside the housing complex, where home owners gathered, pooled their weaponry, and created a system of shifts to guard the area and assist the four armed guards at the complex's main gate.

Basil began to feel that he played a role in keeping us safe, which appeased him somewhat. He still experienced some conflicting emotions when his friend Gomaa called and said he was heading out to join the protests again, leaving his elderly father, his own wife and newborn child behind. Basil told him he would have to skip tonight until the threat in our area cleared.

I was running out of diapers and starting to ration the remaining amounts. All stores were still closed and we were running out of fresh supplies. My in-laws had stocked up on canned goods regularly, even when they lived in the States. They were the kind of couple most likely to be prepared for a nuclear apocalypse. Consequently we had access to their emergency food reserves.

We ate so much canned corn and kidney beans during the first ten days of the revolution that I wouldn't mind if I never saw them again. There were no functioning gas stations, so many establishments wouldn't deliver and we were unwilling to drive around to shop for luxury items. Our plan was to use one of the three families' five cars at a time.

My parents called frequently, as did my sister. She told me how her husband, was joining their building's neighborhood watch as well. Her ten-year-old son was joining him, armed with his baseball bat that he had bought during a visit to us in America. My nephew reportedly said that this was the most exciting time of his life.

That night Basil's brother returned from his security shift frazzled, informing us that the guard at the gate was warning all homeowners that armed thugs with guns were expected to attack our complex in about thirty minutes. They were looting a complex nearby.

We decided on loading everyone into the main bedroom and stacking it with food, water, diapers, and all the knives and broomsticks we could put together. I called my parents and sister to tell them what was about to happen. There was really nothing they could say. I was close to tears, mainly worrying about what the children were about to experience, but I was prepared to fight whoever it was who I was faced with to protect them.

After thirty minutes had passed, we heard sporadic gunfire and a general commotion from the housing complex's streets. Thankfully, the children were oblivious. It was close to their bedtime, and there was a television in the in-laws' master bedroom. As far as they were concerned, this was the most fun campout ever, complete with snacks and drinks previously not allowed in this particular room.

After about an hour of intense fear, the gunfire ceased all together. Basil went out to find out what had happened. We were informed that none of the expected looters had shown up. The gunfire we'd heard came from our own guards at the gate shooting in the air when they spotted vehicles approaching. But no one actually saw the thugs. We had just experienced what it was like to buy into the government's psychological warfare.

When the kids had fallen asleep, all three families discussed the America option. We were all dual nationals and needed to weigh what we would do next. The only person with a business engagement in California was Basil. So every discussion ended with someone telling him, "But no matter what Basil, you should catch the evacuation flight, lest your pre-revolution booking be canceled." And that was always followed by whether or not he should take the kids and me.

We were still on the fence decision-wise, but we did have to face the fact that I had actually neglected to take my own and my children's passports in our overnight bag so we needed to go home to get them in addition to some other items that we would be needing for travelling

Our house was about forty minutes away, and would use half a tank of gas round trip. Furthermore, it wasn't wise to travel such a distance on the desert road alone, so we would have to take two cars, hence using the equivalent of a full tank of gas. After intense deliberations, we unanimously decided that it was worth the gas to get some of our belongings.

We'd heard so many stories about the thugs on the road. They reportedly preyed on owners of villas on the isolated desert roads who were making trips to bring their valuables into the city. So my father, the only family member on either side to have a licensed gun, decided to meet us at my house and oversee the packing process.

We decided that I would drive the second vehicle because I had a current Egyptian driver's license. My in-laws' driver had already informed us that there were army check points on the road and that anyone who did not have a license would be temporarily detained.

I drove past the complex's gates and onto the road and immediately was struck by the abundance of tanks. When we approached the first major square, we were stopped immediately, and you couldn't help but be a little nervous. A soldier with a gun slung across his chest checked my driver's license and ID, the trunk of the car, gave the vehicle a quick inspection, and let us through.

It was an insanely surreal experience for me. Basil seemed entirely immune to it, perhaps because of his time in Tahrir. He began to argue with me that he wanted to drive on the isolated segments of the road, but I thought that stopping to switch would be even more dangerous. As we squabbled, the U-turn we needed to get into the highway approached. We were distracted from our debate by a big group of men that we noticed were camped at the turn.

"You gotta speed through it! Do not slow down! Do not slow down!" Basil exclaimed. I approached the turn without slowing down, which made a few of the men jump back, alarmed. I made the turn in a screeching, wide angle, and as I did, I could see the men's faces; they looked tired and haggard. Their expressions turned to surprise, which no doubt came with the realization that a woman was driving. I think I caught them laughing to each other for a split second. We must have looked like a bunch of scared kittens in a sedan.

When I processed the whole thing, I realized that they did not look like thugs; they just looked stranded. I was embarrassed, but rationalized that we were better off safe than sorry, I thought to myself. Basil insisted that we stop after that and switch, so we did. I ran around the car to the passenger seat, but he motioned to me to get in the back.

"Could you stay out of view as much as possible?" he asked.

"What do you mean?" I asked.

"Just lie down if you can," he said. "I am sorry but I heard all these stories of kidnapping women on TV last night..."his voice trailed off. "It's just safer, I guess."

So I did and I felt scared just by admitting that we needed to do that. I felt ridiculous and weak, too. I was so used to the Egypt that I knew, which was almost too safe of a country to be true. In that sense, I had always looked forward to bringing the children here to visit and not having to worry about them being kidnapped or molested or whatever other danger American television warned us about every day.

From here on out, it seemed we wouldn't be letting our guard down in either country. The world was generally just an unsafe place.

My parents were waiting at the house. My dad stood next to his Mercedes with his gun in his holster. It would have been a funny sight, except everyone was too serious to think of it that way.

There were a lot of emotions struggling to come to the surface, and my family wasn't used to open displays of emotion. Everyone was tight-lipped as we entered the house. It was exactly the way we left it Friday morning, with the typical weekend messiness that is usually characteristic of a house with young children.

The toys were lying about where they had last been held and played with, and the children's pajamas were still on their beds. We had drawn the curtains before we left, so I went over to the living room curtains and pulled them back. The sun lit the house in a bright-yellow hue and the green of the backyard looked moist from the sprinklers. It felt almost cruel to be considering ransacking this home to grab whatever we could and bolt.

We were faced with one of those scenarios that are often posed as a fun hypothetical to consider at dinner parties: "If you had one bag to pack and you had to leave suddenly what would you take?" I think I actually had that as an essay question in an exam I took as a child. I remember writing things like "my camera, my favorite toy, a picture of my family…"

It was nearly the same thought process. I did take the camera and a number of warm outfits for the kids. I didn't have much time to make a selection, so it was basically whatever was clean and in front of me.

We emptied our safe of jewelry and cash and switched off the gas and electric appliances. Later, we would have to figure out how to properly close down the house and get the rest of our things. It was too much to consider now. I chatted away to my parents as I packed in a feeble attempt to lighten the mood.

I wouldn't let the silence get a chance even when I went into another room. I yelled across the house whatever silly statement I could think of. But when I came back into the living room, both of my parents had tears in their eyes.

There was no way around it after that. There was no stopping the grieving of two parents/grandparents who were about to be separated from their loved ones. It began to occur to me then that this was not the way I wanted to leave Egypt. If I had to leave, it would be in a well-planned manner that gave everyone the time to process and adjust to it.

My father, a dual national as well, could not leave for America at the moment nor visit me for more than two weeks at a time. He owned his own portfolio management firm and stock brokerage company in Cairo. He had about forty employees and their livelihood to consider. He had an elderly mother and all his siblings to think of; they in Egypt as well.

My sister had a similar setup, with her husband owning a company and being the only son to elderly parents. So it seemed that, at least on my side of the family, if I were to leave Egypt, I would leave with just my nuclear unit. The choice of America versus Egypt always held my family on one side of the globe and the United States on the other. We would not even share the same time zone.

There were no tearful goodbyes when we reentered our cars. My father stated that gas problem or not, if Basil and I decided to fly to the United States in the next couple of days, he and my mom would come see us and the kids before we left.

Basil insisted on driving until the checkpoints to avoid situations like the one we faced on the way over. But one checkpoint appeared out of nowhere and when we stopped to make the switch., an army officer came over to our car.

"Step out of the car," he told my husband, with a snide smile on his face. His demeanor was cynically friendly and I was immediately uncomfortable.

"Is there a problem?" I asked the officer nervously.

"Don't worry," he said. "I'll bring him back."

I saw my in-laws' driver park and walk over to where the officer was standing with Basil with his arm patronizingly around Basil's shoulder. The driver and Basil appeared to be engaging in some nervous banter, and I sat there in the car not knowing what to think or do, and having no access to a phone since cell phone services were still cut off.

After a tense few minutes, Basil and the driver headed back toward the car. Basil seemed uncomfortable and a bit embarrassed.

"What was he saying to you?" I asked.

"Nothing, just trying to scare me. He's on some sort of power trip, I guess. He said he just wanted to verify that I wasn't a threat because he caught us trying to trick them. It's not important. Just drive."

I knew that it was not exactly his comfort zone to speak in Arabic with other Egyptian men in stressful situations. I wondered what he had been like in the middle of the protests with all the chanting and communication in Arabic.

I felt bad for him. This whole experience continually forced him to be a few steps away from where he wanted to be. He wanted to be everything he could for our family. He also wanted to be part of the men of this country who told the regime to go. We had him here packing bags and searching for groceries and ultimately leaving to provide us with money.

After a full night of debates and some shouting and tears, Basil agreed to catch the evacuation flight out of Egypt and not wait until February 2, when he was originally supposed to travel. We also agreed that the children and I would not go with him.

The evacuation process was reported to take as long as twenty-four hours in the airport. Furthermore, when you finally got on a flight to what was called a "safe haven," the nearest safe country, you had to find your own way back to America. We felt it would have been too much for the children, and we believed that it was too big a decision to make so soon. Every scare we'd had so far had been a rumor or an exaggeration fed to us mainly by the media.

So I decided I would stay with his family because it was near Ferris's school and should it reopen, it would be safer to drive him there from my in-laws' home. They also were surrounded by pharmacies and grocery stores that we could access easily when they reopened. My brother-in-law's family was staying as well, and though it was cramped, it also meant that the kids had their cousin to play with as we endured this indefinite house arrest.

As Basil packed his bags, I stopped him and hugged him. We had not talked in depth about what he had experienced, and he was in no mood to do so. The group that he had been with on the Friday of Anger had already continued on without him on the twenty-ninth and thirtieth of January. He bore the guilt and worry for them quietly, as was his nature, but it rendered him alone and beyond our reach.

When it was finally time for him to go, he held onto the children for a minute. Ferris appeared confused. "I thought we were going with Daddy this time?" he asked.

"No, sweetie," I said as I knelt down in front of him. "But he is only going for a short trip this time."

"Then why are our bags packed, too?" he asked.

"Because we are staying here with Grandma and Grandpa until the schools open again."

"Cool!" he said, and ran off. We all smiled for a second before we were reminded that we did not have the luxury of being so easily distracted from our situation. Basil's mother cried when she hugged him, but I held onto my feelings for later that night. I was determined to channel the emotions positively. It was bad enough that he had to leave the protests for our personal engagements. I didn't want to be even more selfish by being too preoccupied with his departure to find something that I could do in his stead.

The minute his car was out of sight, I went back inside and called Wael El Zoghby. His NGO was holding emergency meetings to see how the developmental efforts and projects we had all been working on before, could shift gears and serve this sudden surge of patriotism that was becoming evident across Egypt.

It didn't matter which kind of Egyptian you spoke to. Whether they were for or against the regime leaving right away, they all had taken sudden interest in being part of the solution. That was an energy that was precious and needed to be harvested and positively directed. No one knew this better than Egypt's budding civic society, which had seen an increase of activity in the last ten years or so with the advent of the Internet and international political awareness.

"I want to be part of whatever you can think of that would be of help, *Ostaz* ["Mister"] Wael (in Egypt "Mr." is added to one's first name)," I told him emphatically.

My relationship with Ostaz Wael was a strange one. We had met in the website-launching ceremony we held for the students at school in September. The event was designed to be a networking opportunity for the students to meet with leading NGOs in Cairo.

Ostaz Wael was the executive director of *Baladnaa*, which focused on leadership training initiatives for all ages and backgrounds. Its mission was to train a multitude of leaders in various fields to help the country move forward as a strong and inspired unit. It selected members of society who were already accomplished in their fields and were capable of bringing about true change within their realms.

To enroll these volunteers and convince them to attend a six-week intensive training in development and civic engagement, it would take an inspiring and talented salesman. That pretty much described Ostaz Wael.

He was skilled in becoming a close acquaintance very quickly. There was no such thing as a superficial conversation with him. He went down deep into your psyche with ease to harness what motivated you to do more for the country, which seemed to be his constant ulterior motive. He could figure out within the course of one conversation what your strengths and weaknesses were and how they could be of benefit to your community. That was his gift.

The reason I addressed him as *Ostaz* instead of just "Wael" was because of a subtle Middle Eastern decorum that I had picked up on in Egypt after a few awkward situations. If you were a woman with a male friend in Middle Eastern society and this person was not the husband of a friend, a childhood friend, or a friend of the family, and especially if he was an acquaintance from work, it was considered more appropriate to keep up certain formalities to maintain "propriety."

At times the title was difficult to inject into dialogue when it came to Wael specifically because he was so laid back and personable. But both of us stuck to it and took comfort in the pre-set boundaries.

"Tell me what *you* think you could do," he responded. "We are all focusing now on rallying people up for a million -man march tomorrow, since it is a Tuesday. You know activists have been calling for Fridays and Tuesdays to be mass days of protests. I have even seen quite a few celebrities and religious leaders call for this on television."

"Well, I can't leave the house because I have the children to care for and they need me. Still, I can't believe that I am of no use when all this is going on. There must be a way to add the voices of the people at home like me to those in the streets." And then I had an idea.

"Ostaz Wael, I just thought of this, but it might be worth a try. What if those at home hung signs on the exteriors of their houses and apartment buildings that said "*Irhal*" ["Leave"]. *Irhal* signs are already all over Tahrir, but what if *every* home in Cairo and all the other governorates had that as well. It would be as if we gave the concrete buildings a voice. It would be something that could be captured and broadcast on news channels worldwide, and it would send a powerful message that would be hard to erase."

"You know, that might be worth trying," he said genuinely "It will be a challenge to campaign for it without the Internet or text messaging, but if you want to start by calling people you know on landlines, I can dig around and see if I can get it on television. Go for it. I think the idea has potential."

I was very excited, as I was absolutely convinced that this would be a historical image to create. It would show the world that *every-one* wanted the president out, even if we couldn't go into the streets and shout it at the top of our lungs.

I grabbed my cell phone, as it had all of my contacts, and sat next to a phone in the house and I started calling people in alphabetical order. Some I had not spoken to in years, and they had not even known I was in Egypt. My mother-in-law was getting a little frustrated because I had stopped watching the kids and was seemingly occupied with something work-related at a time when Basil was still stranded at the airport. I didn't have time to explain.

I didn't get that far into my list before I realized that the plan was not exactly working. For the first time it hit me that Egyptians truly were not of a consensus when it came to Mubarak leaving. Many of them were vocally afraid of the change and felt things were getting out of hand.

Some found it terrifying that there was no police presence and stores were closed. I could see their point as I had gotten diapers with me from my house, but those would be finished in about a day and a half. It was daunting that we had no access to the basics or even essentials like medicine and it was the thirty-first of January, three full days after the Friday of Anger. Tourists and foreigners were evacuating at such a speed that the tourism industry was losing millions of pounds by the day. Many believed that the protests and any foreseeable accomplishments they may attain were not worth it.

I refused to give up for another eight hours. I stopped for breaks to tend to the kids, change diapers, and get into pajamas. Basil kept calling and updating us about his wait for a seat on the plane, and I kept cold-calling my friends and acquaintances, trying to convince them to have their homes protest on their behalf.

Somewhere close to midnight, it started to dawn on me that this idea may never take off. I called Ostaz Wael, and his wife told me he was at the protests. She sounded weary, like maybe she had hoped that my phone call was from her husband.

I hung up, defeated, once again feeling like there was little I could do but take care of the kids while the men and stronger women got to change the country.

The kids were unruly when I attempted to put them to sleep. They were obviously frazzled from spending another day cooped up in the house.

At one point my brother-in-law's wife and I had attempted to take them on a short walk within the complex. Ferris had run up ahead of us and was about to turn into a blind corner where cars, not expecting him, could possibly hit him. I screamed, "Stop!" to catch his attention, and to our surprise a bunch of people from the surrounding houses came running out.

An angry father, with two young kids trailing behind him looking desperate for any kind of excitement, said to me, "Why are you screaming? You scared us!"

"My son ran into the street..." I began to explain but the man forcefully interrupted me.

"You really should *not* have children walking about in the street in these circumstances." His voice was polite but curt, and barely covering his aggressive body language.

Our kids started crying, so we gave up the walk and went back into the house, where the Al Jazeera channel was blaring. I managed to get permission to interrupt the news and put on *Bee Movie* for the kids to watch before bedtime. At one point in the movie, the bees actually came together to protest against the exploitation of bees for their honey. Later, as I tried to get the kids to settle down onto the hide-a-bed, Ferris kept jumping up and down and saying, "Free the bees! Free the bees! Look, Mama, I am doing what Dad was doing!"

I smiled at him, and was suddenly very proud that he had made the connection and that our little boy here, just five years old, now held within his frame of references that it was possible to protest against what is unjust and actually bring about change.

OK, so I wouldn't wake up to an Egypt that had all its buildings uniformly calling for the president to leave his position, I thought to myself. But I would wake up to an Egypt that had gone through a full perceptual shift. No matter what happened next, our children had just witnessed something that would enable them to have ambitions far beyond what their grandparents had ever thought possible.

THE MILLION MAN MARCH
(TUESDAY, FEBRUARY 1, 2011)

10.

(Mohamed Diab, 33, Screenwriter and Film Director)

The local media lies, and it should go down with the regime. That is what I'd learned since January 29. It is such an integral part of what keeps us shackled. The regime has held Egypt back for thirty years by controlling the airwaves and with them, people's vision and imagination.

Now the media was attempting to warp the realities of our battle. It had shifted gears and adapted to the situation by adopting the stance that it was supporting what happened on the 25th of January but that protests had spun widely off course since. The "purity" of the "original" revolution and revolutionaries had been hijacked by a fictitious enemy that was out to get us all, or so we were told.

Sometimes the media claimed that America had trained Egyptian youth to destroy their own country; other times Israel was the villain. When newscasters got really creative, it was Israeli plots carried out by Americans.

For a while they claimed it was the Taliban, which had ties to the Muslim Brotherhood—that story killed several birds with one stone, and had the potential to distance the people from the Brotherhood, divide citizens among each other, and label the Brotherhood as an enemy that lurked among the Egyptian people.

The way they threw around these rumors with no facts to back them made it so bizarre that even the pro-regime people half-expected them to claim it was aliens or our friendly neighborhood Spiderman at fault.

It didn't matter what BBC, CNN, El Arabiya, and Al Jazeera were showing, because local media was claiming that these networks were all in on it, too. According to our pathetic local channels, the whole world was ganging up to tear down Egypt by infiltrating the protests. Egyptian youth, who initially had "valid democratic demands," as the president so eloquently put it, were being tricked into tearing down our nation because of its strategic significance. The cowards sung the president's tune like a pied piper across the airwaves.

It was no surprise that international journalists and the offices of Al Jazeera and Al Arabiya were sporadically attacked by mysterious individuals who were most likely plainclothes policemen.

I thought of this as Moez and I walked through the beautiful, chanting crowds on Tuesday, February 1.

Whoever called this a million-man march did it a grave injustice.

There were at least eight million of us in a multitude of Egypt's squares, and this time we obviously had the support of the older generation. This was not just the youth and it was not just individuals. Actors and actresses, union leaders, prominent businessmen, physicians…it was a massive turnout of well-known and successful leaders in Egyptian society, together with a huge number of Egyptians from Cairo and beyond.

We were packed so snugly together that you could barely lift your arms above your head. It was odd how the weather was perfect and you didn't feel claustrophobic or stifled. Any other time of year, this revolution would have failed.

The insane number of protesters, which would have been fatal had it been any hotter, were our impenetrable barrier, and the police were nowhere in sight. Camera crews were everywhere, and I could see reporters taking pictures and filming the spectacle from the balconies of buildings overlooking the square.

People stopped Moez and I frequently. Several men told Moez that his TV appearance the previous night was the reason they came. He appealed to the youth by insisting on a true democracy. And on a parallel level, his ideology appealed to older generations because he was not viewing the regime as represented by Mubarak personally but by an entire corrupt system much bigger than Mubarak himself. Accordingly, his abstinence from disrespecting the elderly leader spoke to many "old-school" Egyptians.

This mentality represented a sizable segment of the population, as we spoke to quite a few protesters who expressed to us that they were turned off by personal attacks on Mubarak. It was hard to explain to the outside world, but in Arab culture, it was considered of low character to trash a leader, especially in his old age. It was definitely not looked favorably upon by many religious speakers.

The idea of vilifying a man as opposed to his actions was believed to be a product of the ego. A man of faith would focus on the actions that harmed society, try the person for his crimes, and then act accordingly.

Despite the fact that I was not a representative of any particular religious stance, as a public figure I wanted to portray this image as well. I wanted the revolution to be represented by determined but level-headed youth. This was not a witch-hunt; this was a political movement. I wanted the president to resign because his reign represented an affront to democracy, and the courts should resolve any other issues I had with him.

My mission was clear. I longed to be the clear surface that reflected the beauty of the revolution's intentions to Egypt and the world and prevented its waters from being sullied by untruths. I had my own camera and was filming for my video blog. I wanted to document this for the history books, and I wanted to have proof that, at least for today, there were no foreign agents or hidden agendas, just an honest drive to move beyond what we had been. One of my videos went viral with over 120,000 hits in just one day, and was picked up by Al-Arabiya news channel and aired constantly. For days after it aired, many people approached me and told me that my video was the reason they decided to participate.

There was a distinct difference at this point between the protesters in the million-man march and the Tahrir inhabitants who had been, for the most part, living in Tahrir since the twenty-eighth. You could tell who the protesters on strike were by how tired they appeared and the condition of their clothes.

As the two groups mingled and exchanged ideas during the march, you could witness the budding theme circulating. Protestors were becoming convinced that all marches should turn into a unified strike in which people stayed in Tahrir until their demands were met.

The march was like a brush fire in that sense. The unprecedented situation was a fertile field for passionate ideas, and no one was exactly sure where they were coming from. Was someone from the preexisting movements making these suggestions? Were we being influenced by what we had seen or heard about in Europe or the West? Or could it possibly be that the almighty had a plan for Egypt and the ideas were whispered to us by God's angels?

If you were in Tahrir this day and you could see what millions of us were seeing, that last possibility would not have seemed farfetched.

By the end of this experience, Moez and I were fired up to continue our media efforts. It was true that millions who marched had witnessed it firsthand, but Egypt has a population of over eighty million breathing minds, many of whom were still weighing this situation at home, absorbing and analyzing every new facet of it.

I would spend a lot of my time at home calling into local television shows and voicing my opinions to make it difficult for them to paint a picture that served the regime's interests above all else.

Because of the various comments we received about Moez's appearance the night before, we decided to go salvage a copy of it from the Mehwar channel to ensure we had a copy for documentation purposes.

We both agreed to briefly visit our families and then meet up at the station.

∽ ∽

(Moez Masoud, 32, Religious Scholar and
Television Program Host)

As I waited for the Mehwar channel to give me the copy of Monday's episode, a producer came out and asked if they could interview me about the protests today. I declined, stating that today was not over yet and I would rather wait twenty-four hours before giving any commentary because the true impact was still unclear.

A few minutes after I said that, the station staff began buzzing with the news that the president was going to give another speech in response to today's turnout. Diab and I feared that if we attempted to head home, we would get caught up in traffic and miss it in the process, so we asked if we could stay and view it at the station.

We waited for the speech with the anticipation of two students awaiting their grades for an exam they felt they'd aced. Tunisian president Zein El Abideen's speech, in which he explained to his people that he had heard them loud and clear and begged them for the time to prove he had learned his lesson, was fresh in our memories and offered a glimpse of what was possible for those who persevered.

As President Mubarak appeared on screen, the entire station grew deathly quiet. No one moved a muscle, but I could almost feel the emotional fluctuations of everyone around me in this station and throughout our beloved, conflicted country.

Many analysts saw the speech as a tactical maneuver that was artfully delivered by a man and his team who knew Egypt well. Others perceived the president to be honestly expressing what he personally believed to be the truth about the situation Egypt was in. This is why, to many, the speech came across as genuine and thus utterly confusing.

He went on to mention the vandalism and looting that the country was experiencing and stated that he wanted to put an end to it for the safety of Egypt. He cited that we were at a difficult crossroads and it was up to us to choose between order or complete chaos, and that both the population and its leaders were in need of deep wisdom to be able to make it safely to the shore.

Then the speech took and unexpected emotional turn as he stated on air for the first time, that even before these painful times, he had no intention of running for another term in the presidency of Egypt. He followed this statement by listing all the battles that he fought for Egypt, all the tough times he withstood with this complex country and the very nature and fiber of his character that he hoped the Egyptian people knew well by now.

He stated that for the remainder of his time in office, he would focus on a peaceful transition to the democratic state that the youth had called for, recognizing that the voice of the people clearly stated that it was time for change.

As he reminded Egypt of his patriarchal role and the history he shared with them, he stated that he would die on the Egyptian soil that he loved and had pledged his loyalty to for the thirty years of presidency and nearly sixty years of public service.

For many, he hit a strong emotional nerve. However, a number of people noticed what Diab and I had throughout the speech. He had not mentioned the martyrs and their families. He had not mentioned trials to investigate their deaths. He had not apologized for anything.

You could almost hear the country split down the middle into pro-revolutionaries and Mubarak sympathizers.

Popular talk show hosts made teary appearances labeling the president's speech as "historic" and a "victory" to the revolution, implying that protesters had attained their goals and should consequently pull back.

To make things worse, a third group appeared to supplement the divide, the faction of people who were fed up with the "disruption" that the revolution presented to their daily lives. After all, businesses, banks, schools, and hospitals were shut down. There was a curfew and shortages in gas and groceries. There was no predictable end in sight and the stamina of millions used to maintaining the status quo started to crumble, exposing a decaying, weak core.

As mysteriously as the Internet had been cut off, it would now slowly sputter back to life.

The Internet that had mobilized the Egyptian people before bore signs of the ongoing divide on its walls, and became a battlefield for those with opposing views. In no time Diab's Facebook page was full of insults and accusations. Messages accused Diab of being an agent of the United States and of being responsible for the country's apparent destruction. On my own page, countless questions were pouring in, asking whether it was right or wrong to continue protesting.

The very next day Diab had already fired back with an article about what we had witnessed in the president's speech. He explained how the changes that were made were easily reversible and that we should all remember that Mubarak was not a "parent" to our people nor did he have the authority to *shame* us into inaction.

I finished reading the article and had to step back to reflect. I thought hard about what my role should be. It was a grave responsibility I bore, because people looked upon my opinion as representative of what the religious interpretation of events could be. I had to analyze every move and statement I made to ensure that it did not contradict any facet of Islam's spirit or teachings. I told my wife that I truly believed that Mubarak's regime was over, but we were yet to see exactly how it will choose to disengage.

Little did I know that the events that were about to unfold only a few hours later would ultimately leave Mubarak with no choice but to step down.

THE "BATTLE OF THE CAMEL" (WEDNESDAY, FEBRUARY 2, 2011)

11.

(Hoda Rashad, 36, Educator/Writer)

As I watched the endless sea of people on the television screen that Tuesday, I thought of how Basil would have loved to be among them. He was on his third plane right now from Frankfurt, Germany, to San Francisco. It had taken him close to three full days to reach the Holiday Inn in Fremont, California.

The whole experience had been bizarre and uncomfortable from the get-go. The Egyptian airport was full of Egyptian-Americans leaving the country. Women in burqas stood in line with their blue American passports in hand. He wondered if they had ever lived in America or even understood fully what it meant to be an American. Would they even like it?

Americans sat together and the dual nationals were grouped in another area, and he guessed that that was pretty much how it would be for them when they reached the States, as well. American soldiers, in charge of the evacuation logistics at the airport, gave him a contract to sign stating that he owed the American government all the expenses it would cost to get him to the nearest safe haven. This route would cost him much more than his original booking on February 2. He wondered if we had all panicked him into this expensive alternative.

At one point, he thought he'd caught a lucky break. An American soldier came up to him and asked him, since he was travelling alone, if he would like to go to Washington, DC, since his passport stated he was born there. Basil said he wouldn't mind any route at the moment.

The soldier explained to him that there was a U.S. private airplane that had brought former CIA Director of Plans Frank Wisner over to discuss the situation with President Mubarak. He said if Basil had no problem waiting a few hours, they could fit him in on that plane and he wouldn't have to pay anything. He decided that that would be a huge relief. But as the hours rolled on, apparently Wisner decided that there was much more to be done in Egypt and the soldiers received word that he would be spending the night in Cairo.

So you see, there were much more than just phone calls going back and forth between Mubarak and President Obama. We all knew that this was too grave a situation for America to be simply sitting back and watching it unfold. There was no mention of Wisner being in Egypt on any of the local or international channels, so it probably was not the kind of information that the two countries wanted publicized.

Evacuees did not even know which country they were going to until they were seated on the plane and buckling up. On Basil's plane, they announced on the intercom that they would be going to Larnaca, the third-largest city on the southeastern coast of Cyprus.

248

On the plane, he was seated next to a pale, thin American with light-brown hair, and he ended up sharing a hotel room with this same individual. He was jittery and eccentric. His eyes had the tendency to jerk to the right and left as if he constantly expected someone to sucker punch him at any second. Interaction with him just added to the discomfort of the whole ordeal.

You always wonder what brings these characters to the Middle East. Had they failed to make something of themselves in the United States? Or did they truly want to understand and be part of the effort to further a country in this area of the world? This guy certainly seemed like he needed a few bolts tightened, so it was more likely that he fell into the former category than the latter.

Basil would continue his journey from Larnaca to Athens, and then go on to Frankfurt, where he caught his San Francisco-bound plane. When he finally reached his room at the Holiday Inn he was drained physically and emotionally.

As he entered the fresh-smelling, neatly set-up room, he was officially *not* at home and it hit him how far he was now from where he so wanted to be. The sun was shining outside and the California weather was a perfect seventy degrees. He walked over to the large window in the room, drew the curtains shut, and went to the bed. He grabbed the remote, turned the television to CNN, and spent the next two hours sobbing into his hands.

To make things worse, when he called me Wednesday morning, I told him that the Internet had returned, meaning that he could have accomplished most of his work from Cairo had he known how soon the government would bring things back online.

"You made the best decisions you could based on the information we had, Basil. Please don't be upset," I said. "Finish some stuff and come back in a couple of weeks. *Insha Allah,* you won't miss anything. You participated in the most important protest, dear. Try to find comfort in that, please."

But he would miss a whole lot in those two weeks, and that was just an unfortunate reality. Maybe I was meant to experience this part of my life as an Egyptian without him. Maybe as a woman and as a mother, God had decided that I had better learn to depend on myself. As a woman of Middle Eastern descent, I had moved from my father's house to my husband's house. It is true that I had experienced life without Basil a lot this past school year, but I'd had the full support of both families with their drivers and house-keepers as I did it. Maybe God had felt that since I had that many perks when I was without Basil, I needed to learn a lesson or two.

Well I didn't mind that at all, I thought to myself. I can do this...

But my phone call with Basil had brought back some of the feelings of uselessness that had engulfed me after *"Irhal"* campaign had so miserably failed.

At that point, however, Ostaz Wael came up with a plan that would keep me sane for the next few weeks. He'd been going to protests daily and had spent Tuesday night in Tahrir. He'd been informed that the general goal circulating through Tahrir was that people should stay put in the square and shift this movement from a protest to a mass strike. He asked me if I would be interested in writing a daily diary of what took place in the square and posting it to a blog online? Protestors that he trusted would be given my number and they could phone in the information hence ensuring its accuracy. There was so much to report that he believed was of value and contradicted the image that the media was painting.

Ostaz Wael said the square was now an experience like none other. There were stages and mini-platforms set up in corners of the square that offered the protesters political poetry, songs, and inspirational speeches. Well-thought-out signs and large banners decorated the horizon. There were a lot of women in the crowds and some children, too. It was hard to believe that in the Mostafa Mahmoud area, in reaction to the president's speech, there were a few hundred Egyptians with pro-Mubarak signs protesting against the revolution.

The vendors selling flags were profiting but the ones selling pictures of Mubarak were making a killing on both ends of the spectrum. Pro-Mubarak protesters were buying them to honor him and anti-Mubarak protesters were buying them to deface, display, and/or destroy them. They sold for fifty pounds a picture, regardless of its intended use.

I was excited about the blog and all the details worth documenting and hurriedly sat down at my computer the minute we hung up.

I told my brother-in-law's wife of my plans, and she was very supportive. She offered to care for Layla to get her out of my hair a bit. Ferris and his cousin were busy playing in the backyard, so it gave me a good half hour to focus before we had to prepare food for the children. I took my laptop and tried to summarize what I knew so far.

It was probably about a half-hour later when television channels started to announce conflict in the square. Local channels were reporting clashes between pro- and anti-Mubarak protesters and satellite channels were reporting mysterious attacks by men on horses and camels who appeared to be hired thugs.

As we remained glued to the TV set, the children were shushed and shooed out of the way.

My phone rang within minutes, and it was Ostaz Wael. "You want to write something about what is going on? Grab a pen and take down what is happening now."

I took the phone into the kitchen, grabbed Tante Gigi's notepad that she used to write grocery lists and began to jot down what he was saying. He was talking so fast it was almost impossible to write, so I stopped and tried to focus on what he was describing so I wouldn't forget. I would take notes after I hung up, I thought to myself.

There was a lot of noise around him, mostly screaming and what sounded like gunfire. It was often hard to make out exactly what he said, but I was not about to ask him to repeat anything. In fact, I was concerned that it was not safe for him to be on the phone at all.

I then realized that he must have felt this was important or he wouldn't be taking the risk. This wasn't just about making me feel like I was doing something—I *was* actually doing something. I sat up straight, closed my eyes, and focused every fiber of my being on visualizing what he was describing and remembering every detail of it.

He told a tale of thugs coming in on horse and camelback with clubs and swords. They were killing people on the spot. Stones were being hurled at the protesters from all angles. As protesters attempted to fight back, there was a dangerous crossfire of sharp stones being flung about. He talked about what they were feeling and how they were in danger and how the world needed to know. He instructed me to stop watching television, as I would get the facts of the blog crossed with what was being reported by entities that could be bending the truth to serve their own interests. Without much warning, he abruptly hung up.

I thought about what he had said about the truth being filtered through those who delivered it. Was I the same? Could I keep myself neutral and report only what he said to me word for word? Yes, I could, and indeed I would. I made a serious commitment to try to not even overhear what my in-laws were discussing about what they saw on television. In a sense, I made the decision to sequester myself so I could deliver unbiased information.

My eyes were still closed as I sat in the kitchen reviewing everything Ostaz Wael had just shared with me. I could feel myself with him in the square, and I could picture the men on camel and horseback attacking. One of the kids was giggling, and it brought me out of the square and into my desperate housewife's reality.

I opened my eyes and there I was in the kitchen, where he had left me. The fridge was humming and there was a hot cup of tea on the counter that someone had left to cool. A mere forty-five minutes away in Tahrir, in broad daylight, Egyptians were being killed and my friends were among them.

I was at a loss. I did not even know what to feel. I peeked out into the living room and the scene was as I left it. The adults were glued to the TV and the kids were running wild. It was really the worst timing in the world for me to slink away from the children, given that it was obvious they would be in trouble soon, but I just had to get upstairs where the DSL Internet line was. That was the only connection in the house.

I went online to blogspot.com and began to create an account. I hesitated when I had to write in all my information, and decided to post under a fake name.

It was official.

I was the most cowardly activist in all of Egypt tonight.

With every phone call from the field, I became more and more oblivious to what time it was, whether or not my children had eaten, and whether I was being rude or not by not picking up after them. February 2 in Tahrir was just a day full of horrors, pain, and disappointments, so the calls just kept rolling in.

By 7:30 p.m. I believe everyone had had enough of me and my erratic behavior. I wanted to get the kids ready for bed quickly and take them in before I got any comments or yet another phone call. I walked over to Layla, picked her up, and was greeted by a warm hug, as if she was saying, "Oh there you are, we missed you!"— and the stench of a diaper that probably should have been changed a while ago hit me like a ton of bricks.

I held her tight and apologized into her ear, making her giggle. I laid out the changing mat on the bed and set her down on her back and began unfastening the dirty diaper when my cell phone rang. There was nothing I could do, really, but answer. If I missed a call and there was a lot of action going on, they couldn't hear their phones ringing over the gunfire and commotion when I called back.

It was Ostaz Wael calling from the hospital. He was accompanied by an injured protester who was in immense pain. We hadn't spoken for the last hour, as his phone battery had been low, and other protesters had been filling me in from their phones. His voice was sad and beat-up, but he wanted to talk. It seemed important to him to relay a specific message to the blog.

He wanted to say that he had kissed his wife and three children before he left for the protests today with the full intent of dying for this cause. It became apparent to him that the willingness to perish for Egypt may just be what needed to be done to complete this revolution, and he feared that tonight may be his last.

With all the loss he had seen today, he could not think of any justifiable self-preservation ideology that would stop the revolutionaries short of the complete dismantling of this horrid and evil regime. He wanted his family to know why he was giving up his life with them.

His voice had broken several times, and it was obvious that he was crying.

I could not interrupt him and ask someone to help me with Layla, and I could not tell him, in the state he was in, that I was changing a diaper. So as he described how he felt and what he had seen, Layla reached down and grabbed the brown mess from the diaper into her hands.

With the phone in my right hand held up against my ear, I grabbed her right hand with my left and stopped it from spreading the gunk around. Unfortunately, with her other hand free, she managed to reach down and get some more pooh and put it into her hair.

As Ostaz Wael cried into the phone from the hospital near Tahrir and said what he thought may be his last words, Layla put her dirty fingers onto my face and hair. I closed my eyes and focused on his voice and, despite the smell and sullying that was taking place, was able to disconnect from Layla until he hung up. When I opened my eyes there was poop everywhere. There was nothing I could do but remove the bed sheet entirely and take it with me into the bathroom. Layla and I stepped into the shower fully clothed and tried to wash away the mess.

❦ ❦

(Wael El Zoghby, 40, Executive Director of "Baladnaa" an NGO)

I hung up the phone with Hoda and struggled to compose myself. I imagined my words online in English and imagined them being the last things my children read about me. They would reference them online for the rest of their lives—hopefully in an Egypt that was free of tyranny.

Or maybe it was possible to get though this and live to see the results of this bloody battle. Oddly enough, the brief respite to communicate on the phone somehow recharged me emotionally. Every time I phoned her to report for the blog, I felt that it was not just us dying here in the square with no one knowing any better. Our words were our virtual "dog tags" in this urban battle field.

The image of her I had in my head was of the first time I saw her on stage, proudly presenting her high school students and their civic engagement website. She wore a white outfit with flowing pants and a banded-color Indian-style top with bright blue beads tangling down to her waist. Her energy was contagious, and the other NGO directors were sold on helping her make these children, who were standing behind her in their "Not in My Country" campaign T-shirts, into little developmental leaders.

I had only met her once after that, and so that image of her on stage was the one I that appeared in my mind. In Egypt, because of the severe traffic delays, you could have a fully functional business relationship via phone and e-mail and never need to strive for a face-to-face meeting that could take both parties all day to get to.

We knew little about each other's personal lives, but we had established a comfortable work routine built upon a mutual respect, and we began to regularly depend on each other for help in several educational/developmental endeavors.

She did not know I was a member of the Muslim Brotherhood. It probably would have scared her away. But then again, there was a lot she did not know about me.

I believe that she assumed that I was a man who had lived his whole life in Egypt, as she constantly appeared shy about her ties to the United States. The truth was that before these protests, I had organized a gathering that brought together an entirely different body of ten thousand people in peaceful assembly. Together we stood against another senseless act of cruelty.

In 2001 I spearheaded the University of Maryland's mourning vigil for the victims of 9/11. I had been in Washington, DC when the Twin Towers were hit, and I was among the first to donate my blood. It had shaken the Muslim community to the core and rendered me unable to shake the shame. I knew that it was an important time to send a message of love on behalf of our dear Prophet and hope that our complete rejection of the incident showed how whoever had done this was not— and would never be considered—one of *us*.

I had been in the States for close to two years when the Twin Towers were struck and I had already been exposed to America in a way that cemented a love and loyalty to that country that I had thought would be hard to break. I had initially come to the States on a student visa, but shortly after I had begun taking my courses I discovered that I had a debilitating tumor growing on my spine.

Tests and surgeries were set up back to back and before I knew it, the well thought out plan to come to America, study business, and make something of myself was reduced to a six-month sentence in bed. To make things worse, I did not have access to the amounts of money necessary to cover the expenses required to save my life. When government medical aid covered it completely and gave me the best care I had ever been exposed to, it finally hit me what the role of government was vis-à-vis those who were legally under its care.

I had always known that the Egyptian government was an abusive parent to its children, but it never hurt the way it did when a foreign country gave me more care because I happened to be within its borders when I became sick. This is what I had sought as a child, as a teenager, and as a college student in Cairo, when I had joined student unions and civic engagement initiatives in an effort to find a sense of community responsibility. I was met with corruption and interrogations, and a society that appeared widely disinterested in helping itself.

My first slap on the face—actually my first kick, punch, and slap in the face—came when I was in high school and the people's assembly elections were taking place in Mansoura. I had climbed a tree and seen with my own eyes officials filling in electoral ballots themselves and using citizen ID numbers to make the fake signatures official.

I jumped in through the window and grabbed a bunch of the ballots and threw them out the window into the crowds outside. The move would render their process tainted and ruined whatever chances they had of making this election site lean in the direction of whichever candidate had paid them.

A group of at least six men beat me for close to an hour and threw me out into the streets.

At every juncture of my life after that, though I studied to be a veterinarian, I tried to give a sizeable portion of my time and life to volunteer initiatives geared to fighting corruption and raising awareness. America seemed like the perfect place to get some business background and study nonprofit organizations on the side. I began to see a life for myself among the Arab-Americans there, and constantly thought of ways I could have the best of both worlds.

During my visits to Egypt I had met and fallen in love with a woman to whom I eventually proposed. She held an American passport and had no problem living in America as well. I was working on setting up a life for both of us in the United States, at least preliminarily.

It was all seemingly coming together.

Unfortunately, there was a glitch in the dream and my past interests would come back to take my plans down. I soon realized that governments were often connected with and affected by each other's policies. Like an STD, it was difficult to determine who got who sick first, so I will never know which country was initially responsible for the interruption of my plans.

Shortly after 9/11, I traveled to Cairo to fulfill the religious ceremony of the marriage and complete the legal paperwork that preceded a wedding in Egypt. When I attempted to return to America, my visa was revoked in the airport before I could leave Egyptian soil. The government cited security issues and my ties to the Muslim Brotherhood.

I was never allowed back into the United States, not even to close up my apartment and bring back my belongings. It was like the minute I left the American government slammed the door and threw away the key. I had never even driven through a red light in either country, yet I was considered dangerous because I was part of an opposition group in Egypt.

Where is the freedom in that?

Just like that, I was jobless and shunned from the country I had thought accepted me as one of its melting-pot members. There was no benefit of its doubt. My actions and track record there meant nothing. My donated blood was probably in an American's veins, but I would never be allowed to walk alongside him.

I couldn't help feel that this must have been a collaboration between the oppressive forces of Egyptian government and the supporting forces of the American government.

I had been characterized by President Mubarak as a dangerous man because I believed, along with the millions of Egyptians who considered themselves a part of the Brotherhood family, that a president should not rule a country illegitimately for thirty years.

The Muslim Brotherhood was a sheep in wolf's clothing for the benefit of Mubarak's presidency. We were the boogeyman he waved in the face of the West, and by doing so he killed three birds with one stone. He killed moderate Islam by forcing us underground so that extreme Islam could keep Egypt as polarized and divided as only religion can. He kept a group that had the power to win a democratic election down by giving its members an automatic criminal record, and he "proved" to America that he was controlling the "dangerous" Muslims of the land. We were really only a danger to him.

Our teachings were never a danger to anyone, as we were never crusaders for the Muslim faith. If you were with us you were with us, if you were not it was not a problem—and that is a simple fact.

Another simple fact was that, today, the Brotherhood's presence helped the revolution, as it was useful to have someone who was used to leading crowds and unifying individuals under a common strategy. I could tell by just listening which young men and women were from the Brotherhood and which ones were regular Egyptians with no background or experience with dealing with the regime.

When protesters initially ran, after the camels and the horses charged at them, I could hear Brotherhood youth bringing everyone forward again and pointing out the obvious. They explained to all those around them that no matter what these "thugs" were armed with, they were still outnumbered by protestors despite the fact that protestor turnout was coincidentally at a low after the president's speech.

"Irgaa odam irgaa odam" ("Go back to the frontlines, go back to the frontlines"), they would say. And the people would respond.

This was a perceptual war and the perception that the government could block the will of so many had just been completely shattered. The Brotherhood had preached this theory for years. How can you fight a group that doesn't mind dying to get you? The answer is simple. You can't.

Protestors began to advance against the horses and camels instead of running from them, and though they lost some lives in the process, they pulled their assailants down from the animals and rendered them helpless. Some of the attackers were beaten as the adrenalin and anger from the crowds were difficult to stifle. Others were saved by other protesters yelling, *"Silmia, khalas khalas,"* (We are peaceful, enough beating").

We went through their wallets and found mysterious amounts of cash, indicating that they had been paid. Hired thugs would have demanded full payment before they participated and it wasn't as if they had the time to go to the bank to deposit it or home to hide it.

Many of them even had IDs that showed that they were employees of the NDP. The horses and camels themselves were those used to entertain tourists in the pyramids area. The story they told was that these they were people who profited from the tourism industry, and they were here to exact revenge on protesters who had killed their golden goose, so to speak.

The story didn't hold water, though, because of the way they handled their weapons and were backed by snipers in buildings and alleyways. Protestors tied the animals they seized to the railings and gates around Tahrir, and handed over the captured horsemen and camelmen to the army.

Throughout the camel and horseback assault, the hail of stones never stopped, so for the first time the protesters began to damage public property in the sense that they began breaking apart pieces of the sidewalk to create their own sharp stones to fling at the police.

There was an obvious division of labor in the square. On the frontlines people fought back against the thugs and plainclothes policemen so they could maintain their hold on the heart of the square. Those in the middle chipped away at the sidewalks and gathered stones that had been thrown by the thugs and collected them into piles. Designated protesters were stone busboys, bringing the rocks up to the frontlines, to those who were actively engaged in the battle. I would alternate my position in the ranks, according to how my body was reacting. After all, I was forty and I did not have the stamina of the twenty-year-old fighters. Sadly, because this age group's members were the spunkiest, they were also the most likely to be dead and placed on the sidewalks and sides of the square. Their bloodied bodies were carried to the Masgid El Rahman Mosque that had been turned into a field hospital. The scene of them being carried away steeled the protesters' spines.

The army refused to interfere, explaining that there were no clear sides that showed who was friend and who was foe. In the eyes of the soldiers, these were all Egyptians, and they wouldn't know who to fight and who to save. However, they did allow people who were obviously anti-Mubarak protesters to stand on the tanks and fling rocks at the other side.

I had been calling Hoda regularly, and so did two other people that I knew of. A lot of the calls were cries for help, and I wondered how she was handling it, as I believed she was a fairly sheltered individual. But I saw women among us here in the middle of it all, so everyone had to toughen up to do what was necessary. It was not as if I—or any of those around me, for that matter—had ever seen anything like this before.

By the time I had finished my last phone call to Hoda at seven thirty, it was completely dark and exhaustion began taking people down faster than the bullets and the rocks could. I had an ominous feeling that the worst was yet to come.

This feeling materialized on the rooftops of several buildings when whoever it was that was attacking us began launching Molotov cocktails into our midst. Some men were actually set ablaze and were immediately surrounded by other protesters who batted out the flames and rushed their burned and deformed bodies to the ill-equipped mosque hospital.

Someone had begun to yell that the thugs were hitting the museum. A large portion of us began fighting to get to it as the path went straight through areas of heavy Molotov bombing and sniper shooting. Protestors did their best to protect the museum, as it was a symbol of the riches that were being pillaged by the regime. They would not allow these lowly creatures to deface the history of the Egyptians, as they had done to its present.

We were slowly succeeding in keeping the thugs out of our territory and had been receiving an inflow of fresh protesters joining the battle after hearing about it on TV and reading about it online. Accordingly, the thugs began to create a ring around us that limited those trying to come in. So, we were two strong, consecutive rings, one created by the regime to halt the flow of protesters into the square, followed by protester-enforced ring that kept any dubious participants from entering the heart of the square and the hospital specifically.

As part of our strategy, we would intensify our onslaught of on-foot attacks and rock-slinging and expand our ring a little bigger every time. By increasing our perimeter, we forced the enemy to do the same, making it impossible for them to block every entrance to our area.

We began to feel like we were gaining ground, and the beautiful spirit in the square began to rise up like a phoenix and engulf us. At about nine o'clock, someone began the beautiful practice of banging on metal lamp posts and rails. The practice caught on and a vast number of protesters participated in the drumming, which created a rhythmic beat akin perhaps to those the Vikings would belt out to invigorate the warriors. The sound rocked the whole square and no doubt sent a message to the enemy that we were holding out and we were still strong.

It was like we were a workout class and someone had decided to turn on some music. Everyone began fighting harder and jumping higher. I pulled out my phone and called Hoda. "Can you hear this, Ostaza Hoda?" I said to her, my voice engorged with emotions.

"Yes I can…what is that?" she asked.

"That, my friend, is the amazing Egyptian spirit singing the song of battle. There is nothing more glorious than being present here tonight.

She was quiet for a moment and said, "Indeed there isn't." I could tell that I had made her cry.

∿ ∿

(Hoda Rashad, 36, Educator/Writer)

It was ten o'clock and the whole house was asleep—and thank heavens for that. My father-in-law's office area on the second floor overlooked the hallway that housed the two upstairs bedrooms and the living room that I slept in with my children on the hide-a-bed.

Mine was the only room with the door open because I wanted to hear the kids if they called for me. I had left TV on mute so I could see the kids from my spot at the desk. Protestors were still calling in, and I had vowed to stay up all night if they chose to keep sharing their experiences with me. If they were getting no rest, then neither would I. The least I could do was lose some sleep.

I checked the stats on the blog, and approximately five hundred people had read it so far. Not bad at all, I thought to myself, considering that the blog had only been up for a few hours.

The phone rang and one of Ostaz Wael's friends was on the line. He had phoned his family and they had informed him that reports on local channels said that the police had the square under control and were breaking up the protests. This angered him. He wanted to make sure that I wrote that the protesters were gaining ground all the way into Abd El Moneim Riyad square and had successfully captured most of the men launching Molotov cocktails into the crowd. The police currently had only one post, with about six to eight officers, left on one building, and the protesters were working on getting that group, too.

I promised him I got it all and would post it ASAP. He thanked me and hung up.

At 11:00 p.m. another protestor called and said that the army had helped them and assisted in capturing two thug-driven vehicles carrying ammunition and supplies. Protestors used the ammunition and the vehicles themselves to push out the boundaries of the pro-government ring as far as they could.

A mere twenty minutes later calls came in informing me that protesters were now in control of about 90 percent of the entire Tahrir area. I continued to receive positive news until midnight, when they reported that the army was trying to convince protesters to call it a night and disperse. To announce this and get protesters' attention, they fired sporadically into the air and shifted the positions of the tanks that had been parked in the same manner for hours.

As we passed midnight and rolled into February 3, the night dragged on and the familiar voices that had been calling me started to say that their cell phone batteries were running out. I began receiving calls from voices I didn't know. That scared me, since my number had been given to many people and if we lost this battle and the regime decided to pull phone records, fake name or not, many trails would lead to me. To say the government frowned deeply upon Internet blogs, especially those targeting an international audience, would be putting it mildly.

I fell asleep at my desk and the phone woke me up at 2:00 a.m. A man was calling to say that the fighting was now at a minimum and though a bird's-eye view of the square may make it appear that it is empty, there are still around fifty thousand protesters scattered throughout the area. They were standing guard at the entrances to the square and hiding on side streets and trying to find bedding for those who were planning to spend the night.

I did not know the man, but I asked him how he was feeling. The question caught him off guard.

"I …I think something is wrong with my eyes," he said with some hesitation, "It's probably from the tear gas, but it is not a big deal. So many have died today, so many…" his voice trailed off.

"What would you say the death toll is so far?" I asked.

"Uh…it was pretty, um…I am guessing around six hundred people died since I joined the protests three days ago," he said, his voice breaking a little. "At one point tonight it had gotten so bad that an army officer stood on top of his vehicle, I even have the license plate number here: thirteen-twenty-six. It was parked at the beginning of Tallat Harb Street. He put his gun in his mouth as tears were streaming down his face and started threatening his commanding officer to allow him to help the protesters or he would take his own life. It wasn't long after that the army started to help us disperse the thugs."

He told me how many protesters were seen hugging this army officer gratefully as they passed by him. The thugs were still charging and retreating at varying intervals and there were reports of drive-by shootings. Protestors were exhausted and scared.

Others called in and said that it was rumored that the Muslim Brotherhood and Dr. Mohammed El Beltagy and others were sending in ten thousand back-up protesters to support those on the ground.

One caller was a doctor and said that he had just been with a protester who had brought in his fifty-year-old father, thinking that he had shrapnel wounds and needed some emergency care. The caller said he had to explain to this young protester, who appeared to be in his early twenties, that his father was indeed already dead. The young man was in shock, and insisted that his father just needed treatment. It took quite a few people and a good twenty minutes to finally get through to him.

The sad stories were endless, and the fight was milder but continuing, as it was reported that thugs appeared to be hiding behind the Sixth of October Bridge. I got up and walked around in the dark in an attempt to calm myself. I approached my room where my children's faces could be seen sleeping by the dim lighting of the small TV set.

I knelt over my daughter and breathed in her smell for a moment. She was snoring lightly and had her little leg draped over a pillow I had placed between her and her brother. How many children slept like her tonight while their fathers lay dead in Tahrir Square? How would over six hundred wives, mothers, fathers, and brothers grieve tomorrow while the president remained in his seat?

How many dead Egyptians would it take to change a dead regime?

∾ ∾

(Khaled Bichara, 40, Chief Operating Officer of VimpelCom Ltd. and Group Executive Chairman of Orascom Telecom Holding)

From the Friday of Anger until the million-man march, I was in Tahrir every day. I did not go to work. There was little to do there anyway, with no Internet and sketchy cell phone services.

My routine was to spend the daytime at Tahrir—with some minor discomfort at the hands of the army going through my belonging at the entrance, and then a repeat of this procedure from the Tahrir residents themselves doing an ID check and a pat down—followed by night shifts guarding our own building's entrance for the *Legan El Sahaabiya* ("neighborhood watch").

During my night shift, I often came across a neighbor or two who believed the whole scene in Tahrir was a big disgrace. This category of people, especially those among the older generation, feared that the movement was run by inexperienced children who wouldn't know what to do with the country if it were handed to them on a platter. We all had a fear of the unknown in that sense, but I couldn't see myself leaning toward the status quo as opposed to this once-in-a-lifetime chance to completely turn things around.

Some people even shared with me their belief that people went to Tahrir for a daily wage of fifty pounds that they were allegedly receiving from foreign governments or the Muslim Brotherhood. I would answer them by saying, "But I am there every day and so are my friends. Would you believe that we would go for fifty pounds a day?"

One man laughed at this statement and said, "I don't know man. Why do you go?"

"I go because I would really like it to be different for my children. I would like the chance to be ruled by a government who really had the people's interests at heart or at the very least was held accountable."

I had experienced firsthand what greed could do, and almost lost my career because of it.

In 2004, at the age of thirty-three, I stood trial in the United States for giving a false statement to a U.S. official in a situation in which I never had any contact with the official in question. I was charged with fraudulent statements regarding the use of USAID funds.

Our company had made a deal with the Egyptian Ministry of Foreign Affairs to utilize USAID funds for infrastructural development of telecommunication equipment in Egypt. A stipulation was that we had to buy all needed equipment from an American company based on U.S. soil.

As far as I knew, we had done that. But it turned out that the company we purchased the equipment from had no real presence inside the United States. In fact, all it had was a U.S. address. The Egyptian government had selected the U.S. company from which we were to purchase the equipment.

We would later find out that this U.S. company was owned by an influential Saudi businessman who later became the Minister of Foreign Ventures in Saudi Arabia. If there were any infractions in the set-up of *that* U.S. company, he was never tried for it.

I had never personally been briefed on the details of the agreement between the United States and the Egyptian government, and all bids and agreements were completed on Egyptian soil with the Egyptian government without ever setting foot in America or dealing with a single American. We were merely the company that had made a bid and was selected to be the executers of the project on Egyptian soil.

Yet, on an unrelated business trip to America, as CEO of the company, I was arrested and charged and held in America for nine months. I never personally profited a penny from the transaction at all; in fact the funds ultimately landed in the Saudi company (claiming to be an American company), and as far as I knew they stayed there. I settled out of court and my company paid a fine, but the experience separated me from my family and raised eyebrows back home. I became gun-shy of government deals and transactions for life.

Along the same lines I should have never trusted in the President's words on Tuesday. I had bought into the speech after the million-man march because I believed there was no way he would stand there and lie to us after I saw influential celebrities, politicians, physicians, and businessmen participating in Tahrir who vowed to hold him to his word. These people had a lot to lose by the revolution continuing, so the fact that they joined put lot of very public pressure on the president.

On Wednesday morning, the government had asked us to resume Internet and full cell phone services for our customers. This information, in addition to the promises that the president had given about the guaranteed safety of protesters, along with his insistence that he would not run for another term, made me go back to work Wednesday thinking that we had accomplished what we had set out to achieve. We had a deal.

Furthermore, I had never felt that protestors had the power to topple the regime completely, so my participation was motivated by the need to ensure that the president would never run again and that he would not impose his son on us if he stepped down.

We had thought we had that settled. It was while we were at work celebrating how far we thought we'd come that the Battle of the Camel took place.

As I sat at my computer and watched the outrageous video footage uploaded onto the Internet as the day progressed, I knew that I had counted my eggs long before they hatched.

I felt betrayed, and I felt like I had let those in Tahrir down. I was at a loss at what to do, so I called a friend of mine who I had met during the protests. Mahmoud Salem, a well-known blogger who posted under the pseudonym "Sandmonkey," had been in close contact with protesters in Tahrir throughout, and I felt that he would have good ideas on how I could pitch in.

He told me that one of the biggest challenges the protesters were facing now was the fact that the army was executing government orders to not allow food, drink, or medical equipment into the square. The policy was that if people needed medical help or food and water, they should exit the square. Many refused to do that out of fear of arrest. Consequently, the mosque hospital was encountering numerous shortages of medical supplies in general, and surgical string in particular.

You couldn't readily find surgical string in pharmacies so I had to make some calls to see if I could get it straight from a hospital. Eventually my boss, Naguib Sawiris, helped me by pulling some strings and managed to get the material to a hospital to provide me with about ten boxes of it.

On Thursday morning, we bought boxes of bottled water and juice and a variety of packaged snacks to distribute in the square, along with the contraband surgical string. We stood out in the street and began to pack everything together so we could carry it on foot into the midan.

We were careful with the surgical string because we knew how difficult it was to obtain and how expensive it was. We removed the individually wrapped packages from the small boxes and stuffed our pockets with them. We were a group of five men—two friends of mine, my brother, my cousin, and me. As we walked toward our car in the Gameat El Dowal area we witnessed some sporadic pro-Mubarak protesters, and it struck me how strange and rehearsed they all looked.

First of all, all their signs were all almost identical, which indicated that they had been manufactured in the same place. This was very different than the mostly homemade signs of Tahrir that varied in size, shape, and content. Secondly, they appeared to be there on punched-in time, their passion borrowed, their mannerisms superimposed onto their bodies. These were clearly men hired to serve a specific function, which was serving the regime's image and interests.

On our taxi ride over to the square, the tone with which we were being addressed had clearly changed. The taxi driver openly criticized us for supporting the revolution. He accused us of taking away people's livelihoods and leading the country into the dark.

There was an uncomfortable silence in the cab and it became apparent that the driver didn't even want to take us close to our destination. He began to drive conspicuously slow, and then in front of the Dokki police station he told us to get out and said that this was as close to Tahrir Square as he would go.

The minute we got out of the car, two officers approached us and asked to see our IDs. We had not done anything wrong other than the fact that we were a group of young men near Tahrir carrying supplies. The officer looked at our IDs and looked at us. Our jobs were listed in front of him as CEO and board members of powerful companies in Egypt, but we were dressed in jeans and sweats and the most rugged clothes in our wardrobes.

Now that he knew who we were, he could not claim that we were being paid fifty pounds a day to wreak havoc on the country. He would have no case at all. Still he kept the five of us detained in a corner next to him for about twenty minutes.

I approached the officer and said, "You know, if you are not going to charge us with anything, you should let us go. If you feel you have something against us, you should begin the formal process of interrogating us because we have places to be and people are expecting us."

He looked me in the eyes and said in a threatening tone, "I advise you not to go to *those* places, nor meet with *those* people. If I were you, I would go home."

I stared at him. "We will not be going home, but thank you very much for your advice."

He motioned with his hand to imply that we were free to go. So we walked away from him in the direction of Tahrir. As we approached El Galaa Bridge, there was a thin line of police set up and then within a few feet an army blockade that forced protesters to stop so they could look through your belongings for contraband. As we passed the police, I could almost swear I saw one of them smile at us, as if he knew what was about to happen.

Before we even reached the army checkpoint a group of plain-clothes men armed with sticks and belts descended on us and began to attack us.

In Hollywood movies, when someone gets a beating from a group of individuals, they slow the shots down to show you how each one of the "bad" guys takes a swing at the lone hero. In reality, a group beating is akin to a human avalanche of blows from all directions. If you tried to place it in a movie in the most realistic sense, it would just make for bad cinematography.

There is nothing grand or heroic about a sound beating. You go from dignified human being to an abused animal in a few seconds, and it shakes the very core of your psyche and self-image.

In seconds, in plain view of the police, the army, and everyone else on the street, they pulled us apart as a group and took each of us to separate areas, beat the crap out of us, and confiscated almost everything we had with us. I was slapped, kicked, and punched with such speed and frequency that it was impossible to even see where and in which direction I was being dragged.

Bruised and bloodied and feeling humiliated and defeated, I felt them kick me onto the ground and walk away. They had not found the surgical string because it was tucked away into various pockets in my clothing. I finally had a second to look around and realized that I was probably just a few feet from where I had been with my group but they were nowhere in sight. I limped across the street to a police officer and said in as dignified a voice as I could muster, "Is this something you consider right or approve of? Is this a normal way to treat a fellow citizen and human being?"

My goal was to shame him into a dialogue, but when I heard my own voice it came out as childlike and broken, and all it achieved was embarrassing me further. They had taken the water and snacks from me like candy from a child in broad daylight, and despite my position in society and my career achievements I had no rights as a man in my own country. No dignity. No freedom. I was as shackled as the poorest of the poor at this moment, and it helped me see that no matter how successful you were, it was nothing without freedom.

The officer looked at me with disgust and said, "If you didn't like how you were treated, you are welcome in my police station to file a report."

I looked toward the police station and realized that if I entered that station I may never come out. So I gathered what remained of my dignity and walked away. My group and I finally reunited as each emerged after being assaulted in some corner. We were actually quite fortunate that all of us were accounted for.

To be honest, the whole interaction was my first brush with Egyptian authorities and, as a forty-year-old man, it left me feeling exposed and vulnerable. I called my wife and told her what had happened. I told her it was important that she summarized the event and shared it on Facebook so there was a chronology of what happened to us, and to inform our friends and family that we were insisting on moving forward into Tahrir so they knew where we were last.

I then called my boss, because he had the clout to bail me out if things got very ugly. I told him that we were attempting to pass by near the same police check point that had stood by as we got beaten up and get to an underground metro subway station. This way, I reasoned, if we disappeared he would know which police station we were most probably at.

We took the train to the Opera House station adjacent to the Kasr El Nil Bridge that leads to Tahrir. There we were able to get through to the protester checkpoint, where we were supposed to meet with Sandmonkey to deliver the string. We asked around about him, but he had never showed up, even though the protesters had expected him much earlier.

I found a person I trusted and we gave him all the string we had on us. He took it to the hospital. We began to become increasingly concerned that Sandmonkey had been arrested or harmed. We called his cell phone but he didn't answer, which was out of character for him, especially since we were supposed to meet.

When it was dark and we were heading home, I tried his cell phone one last time; this time, someone answered.

"May I speak to Mahmoud?" I asked.

"We got Mahmoud here, you son of bitch," the voice on the other end said. "And by the way, he is going to tell us who you are, too."

"I am calling you from my cell phone, you already have my contacts, so do whatever you want. You don't scare me," I said, and hung up.

The truth is, it was scary to get a threat from the police, so I decided to respond to calls I had been getting from the media requesting interviews. In the beginning I had stayed out of the spotlight so as not to draw attention to the company over my personal decisions and actions. But in light of Mahmoud's arrest, I felt that I had to take some measures to keep myself safe. So I called the BBC's Cairo office and told them that I was willing to talk about our participation in the protests. We were told to head directly to the station's main office.

On air, I talked about everything, our participation in the protests, the beating we received, Sandmonkey's arrest, everything.

The regime had pushed us completely to the opposing side. We had been moving toward the middle after Mubarak's speech on Tuesday, but these men that ruled the streets instead of protecting them had made enemies of the people. Shame on the president that he did not realize that and put an end to it.

With an "elected" president, the fear of alienating the electoral body pushes him to be a good "manager" of the men who work for him. This president had lost that fear over the course of thirty years of an undemocratic, illegitimate rule on a throne that was drilled deep into Egyptian soil.

This was our chance to infuse this position with a sense of accountability. We would have a regime that was held accountable to its people or we would reject its rule with all its governing bodies, and may God protect Egypt through this process that will undoubtedly be horrific for all.

PART THREE

RISING FROM TAHRIR

CHAPTER TWELVE

A PRESIDENT STEPS DOWN

12.

(Hoda Rashad, 36, Educator/Writer)

From February 3 onward, after the Battle of the Camel broke a vast number of Egyptian hearts, those who believed in the revolution questioned the methods no more. There had to be a "sit in" until the president left his seat.

Tahrir turned into a little revolution city with its own culture and neighborhoods. The banners, hung huge, high, and proud, were artistically situated throughout the square's borders as if an interior designer had selected their locations. Pictures of the martyrs, some postmortem and some when they were alive and happy, were blown up into big posters and hung in the center of the square. They were dubbed "The Fallen Flowers of the 25th of

January's Revolution," and stared down at the square, reminding protesters why the fight could not be abandoned.

There were regular shows and speeches on the stages, and eventually food, water, and medicine found their way into the square. News of arrests, despite the largely absent police presence, were still reported with relative consistency.

However, no matter how positive or negative the situation was reported to be at any given time of the day, the square was never devoid of music in the background. When recorded songs were not being played over the speaker systems, protesters broke into song. Their music was simple and positive, with poignant lyrics that invigorated the crowds.

People who had handheld signs circulated on foot with daily messages that were updated regularly. In a spirit that was uniquely characteristic of the Egyptian revolution alone, one that later earned it its name "The Laughing Revolution," the signs bore statements that were mostly comical in nature.

A protester would be walking around with a blond wig, holding a sign that read "Foreign Agent" to poke fun at local television's claims that the protesters had foreign agendas and were being funded from overseas. Another would have a statement that rhymed in Arabic: *"Ana hafdal fe el midan hata low tala' Suzan,"* which roughly translated means, "I will stay in the square even if he [the president] divorces Suzanne [the first lady]," alluding to the fact that no measures would substitute for the absolute abdication of the president.

Then there were the *Irhal* ("Leave") jokes that varied in content but were consistent in the message. The signs would say, "Leave! My wife misses me"

Or "Leave! I desperately need a shave and a haircut" Or simply, *"Irhal ya tinih"* ("Leave, you dense bastard").

The *Irhal* signs sought to reinforce the sentiment that the protesters could not go before Mubarak did. More serious signs would state that the martyrs' blood would stain our souls until we fulfilled what they had left their homes and families to achieve.

It was *this* crowd that Moez had addressed on February 5th, as he attempted to spread his religious stance of moving forward without making it personal. He wanted us all to focus on keeping our minds and hearts on the bigger political picture for Egypt so we could prosper collectively.

You can see why some could not digest his message. The human losses had to be dealt with first for people to see it.

It was around the time that he gave this speech that I came to know his wife, Marwa. I had met her during a play-date that a mutual friend had set up for us cooped-up moms and children. It took place in a heavily guarded private club near my mother-in-law's house. By then, everyone had started to cautiously venture out of the house on short outings, and I was very grateful to have any place to go that actually offered a fun time for the children.

Women from our neighborhood had been taking children out in cars with personal drivers, as most were still uncomfortable driving alone. I did the same, though I was not accustomed to having someone drive me around.

It was such a relief when I finally got there and unloaded my excited kids from the car. We all took respite in the club's beautiful greenery and colorful playground, which offered the children a healthy break from the news and tension of the house.

I found myself gravitating toward Marwa on every play-date. She had a similar background to mine, as she had lived a portion of her life abroad and experienced life in England with Moez as a young mother. She was educated, confident, funny, and welcoming, and I really began to enjoy our little breaks together. She wore a veil that covered her hair and put her conservatively selected outfits together with a fashion sense that rendered her nothing less than beautiful.

The group also organized food drives in which we would gather in someone's home and have the children help us bag nutrition essentials packages for distribution in areas that were hit the hardest by the aftermath of the revolution. It was during these times that I shared with Marwa that I was writing a blog for protesters. When I spoke to her of how challenging it was to juggle the blog and the children, she made a suggestion that echoed one that my father had been offering regularly.

She suggested that I write about the experience and told me that a lot of women would find my stories interesting. She then did two things that would prove to be integral to this book. She offered to take me to Tahrir Square and she gave me her husband's e-mail address to contact him for an interview.

I couldn't sleep that night at all. I could not believe that I would actually get the chance to visit Tahrir and maybe even meet some of the people I had spoken to over the phone. It was all too exciting.

Equally exciting was the opportunity to connect to a high-profile person like her husband and discuss the possibility of writing a book. It was all too bizarre for me. I had followed Moez on television and knew how popular he was among Egyptian youth. It would be a great opportunity to start the project with someone like him.

I had been a teacher and an educational consultant for over ten years, but writing a book had always been a lifelong dream. I had published some education-related articles in magazines, but had never found the right subject matter about which I felt passionate enough to write a book.

In my head, I started to absorb everything around me, reflect on it, and think about how you would go about presenting such a complex situation in writing as well as in a language other than Arabic. One of the things I knew instinctively from the very beginning was that this book could not have a lead character because the revolution itself did not have one. The movement was a collective voice and the book had to be a collection of experiences.

I was still heavily involved in writing the blog, and maintained my stance of keeping away from the TV and its reports. I even took great care to never spend more than two hours outside of my mother-in-law's house to ensure that the blog was updated regularly.

After the massive turnout of protesters on February 4, the first Friday after the Battle of the Camel, we were seeing a big drop in attacks against protesters in the square. Apart from isolated arrests here and there, revolutionaries were feeling a lot more confident in their numbers.

Most of my entries focused on explaining the protesters' strategies to those at home, since the country still held a considerable population of Egyptians who felt the revolution had gone too far, too fast, and that it was tearing down the country. This school of thought was often referred to as the "Party of the Couch," because they made up their minds in their living rooms without venturing into the field.

Though there was no entity or individual leading the people in the square, there was a consensus on seven demands that I posted to the blog and the protesters posted on a large banner hung in the middle of the square.

The demands, which I found logical and reasonable, were as follows:

1. President Mubarak must abdicate his presidency immediately.
2. The two illegitimate houses of Parliament must be dismantled.
3. The State of Emergency Law must be lifted completely.
4. A caretaker national unity government must be formed.
5. An elected parliament, independent from the National Democratic Party, must amend the Constitution to allow for a fair presidential election.
6. There must be trials for those responsible for the deaths of protesters since the 25th of January.
7. There must be trials for the crony capitalists and corrupt officials who profited illegally from any and all corrupt systems in place.

However, protesters were criticized for having raised the ceiling of their demands to a level that resonated as highly unreasonable, given the suggested timeframe and the nature of what was being requested. It made me feel that one of the most limiting characteristics of the Egyptian people as a whole was that they consistently set the bar way too low.

There was a short, modern folktale that had been circulating on Facebook that illustrated this point. In it, an American asked an Egyptian, "What are your dreams?" The Egyptian replied, "To

be free, live a good life with access to good education and medical care, and preserve my dignity." To which the American said,
"Those are your rights. What are your dreams?"

The story drove the point home that we had been in captivity
so long that we failed to notice that the cage door had been left
ajar ever so slightly. We needed to get up and walk out, confident
that breaking out is the right thing to do.

It was an exhausting debate that was ongoing in most Egyptian
houses. Family members squabbled with each other passionately,
and married couples found that they were often divided both in
their beliefs and the manner in which they wanted to participate
in the alleviation of the current situation. The odd thing was that
the protesters themselves were largely protected from this debate.
They were secluded in the square with like-minded individuals in
a heavenly environment in which all they got was encouragement.
Most of them had told me over the phone that despite all the pain
and the hardship they had seen throughout their ordeal, their
time in Tahrir had been the most beautiful and spiritual time of
their lives. They had never felt more at home or more Egyptian
than they did in Liberation Square.

However, when they visited their families to take quick showers
or grab a change of clothes, they were often shocked by the divisive attitudes in the streets and within their own homes and among
loved ones.

One thing was blatantly obvious to me. I had never seen
Egyptians so "sold" on caring about the country, what happened to
it, and what needed to be done. All of a sudden, Egypt's problems
were everyone's business, and not just economic or political news
that we watched at dinner time and forgot as soon as we looked
away. Human beings are egocentric people; things have to happen
to them firsthand for them to care about it at all.

Egypt was on everyone's priority list because now *all* our livelihoods, security, quality of life, the value of our homes and so on
were at stake for everyone. Finally, we were *all* listening.

I stared at the computer screen at my blog's last entry's title. It
read, "Be Patient Egypt," and was my feeble attempt to get those
who read the blog, now more than eight hundred people, to

reflect on the emotions they were experiencing and put them in the proper context.

It was close to midnight, of February the seventh, and I was tired and worried.

The most dangerous battles are those that are fought in our own heads. There is nothing more difficult to change than a mind.

It's hard to say what came over me at that specific second, but someone seemed to whisper in my ear that I should get up and look at the television set that was on but muted in the room where my kids and I slept.

I noticed that a popular late-night program was on, and I was quite sure that it would be discussing the protests, which I was not supposed to be exposed to. However, I couldn't help but raise the volume when I saw a young man who looked inherently broken down and sad sitting in front of Mona El Shazli, the host.

It was something about his face and the way he sat hunched over and haggard that drew me in. As I listened to El Shazli, I learned that the young man was Google executive Wael Ghonim, who had been missing since January 28. His disappearance had made headlines because of his position with Google and his family's pleas to the media for help.

The police would not confirm nor deny having him in custody.

I sat down at the edge of the hide-a-bed and strained to listen to the interview. I looked at my in-laws' bedroom door. There was no light coming from beneath the door. I could not believe that after their diligent, almost obsessive vigil, watching every bit of news put on air across all channels all day, that they were missing such an intriguing live broadcast. I sat there alone and went through the awe of the whole experience with no one to share it with me.

The host congratulated Wael for his safe release and informed the viewers that it had been confirmed that he had been in Amn El-Dawla's custody as suspected. The very first words to come out of Wael's mouth after this introduction were his condolences to the families of the Egyptians that had died since the 25th of January.

Perhaps the president should have taken notes on how Wael had placed expressing his deepest sorrows for *all* fallen Egyptians and their families, whether they were protesters or police, above all other issues.

He continued: "I will not apologize for what happened or take responsibility for it, because I know that when we organized these protests and set a date for them, we had never in our wildest dreams imagined that we would allow a single thing in beloved Egypt to be broken, let alone allow lives to be lost."

I sat dumbstruck in front of the TV. I realized I was looking at the administrator of the "We Are All Khaled Saeed" page that had set up the very first event page for the Police Day protest on the twenty-fifth. He was not a lifelong activist with a history in political involvement. He was not a struggling Egyptian of humble economic background or a member of a Muslim group. He looked like a little kid who was sincere, innocent, and exhibiting signs of posttraumatic stress. His genuine emotion came across so clearly on the screen that it kept me stuck to my seat.

Behind the cameras where Wael could see them, Mohamed Diab, Amr Salama and Mostafa El Naggar were there for him as he had requested. They were still in shock at what he had revealed to them (all but Mostafa El Naggar who already knew), about his role in the protests. Wael had explained everything to them in the car on the way over to the interview. Moez and Diab had both received phone calls from their friend Amr Salama saying that Wael was released and wanted to meet as soon as possible. He was frazzled and sleep deprived and tried to fill them in as quickly as he could before the El Shazli interview.

News crews had been camping out at his apartment where his family was waiting for him when he was released, but he had kept his statements to the press short. He strongly believed that the situation merited a lengthier and deeper explanation than what he could give them right there.

"Everyone who had ever worked on the protest gathering with me was in agreement that we were asking for what was rightfully ours and that no one can attempt to claim a right by doing something wrong, such as damaging public or private property," he said. "Our highest hope was for all Egyptians to go out into the streets and demand that their rights be acknowledged and pledge to take those rights back with their own voices."

This was the first time I had seen someone on Egyptian television openly admit to these feelings and word them in the way Wael did. Perhaps when an American or European reads these statements or even views the interview itself, he/she may not be able to appreciate the groundbreaking nature of what Wael spelled out so candidly. However, the interview, by Egyptian standards, considering the sparse liberties that we had been afforded, was historical and paradigm shifting.

Viewers were inspired by his courage and shamed by how his simple dream was not something they had all collectively strived for a long time ago. He insisted that people like him, who were what he called "keyboard activists," should never be made into heroes, and that that was one of the main reasons he kept his identity a secret. He had never wanted to be considered anything greater than what he was, someone who shared and published the knowledge he came across onto the Internet and made suggestions of ways to combat issues that were plaguing Egyptian society.

He used his friend and well-known activist Mustafa El Naggar, a lead campaigner for Dr. Mohamed El Baradei and an activist before and after the opposition leader ever materialized on Egypt's political stage, as a living example of true heroes. He mentioned how people like Mustafa had constantly risked their lives and endured horrific torture, not for foreign agendas or funding, but out of love for Egypt and a passion for it to be what it once was.

The interview was a game changer, and I couldn't move from my seat until it ended. I listened to how he had been blindfolded and interrogated in solitary confinement for close to twelve days. He explained to us how even the officers who interrogated him in Amn El-Dawla apparently believed that they loved Egypt and were doing what was right for the country as well.

Accordingly, he urged viewers to consider how to unify our efforts at the moment and settle our scores with police authorities later, so as not to lose sight of our true goals. In fact, to me that was the most profound part of his message. He pleaded that now that the ball was rolling in the right direction, we should put aside our differences, interests, and ideologies and utilize our newfound voice and strength.

He explained that he had sat with the Minister of Interior Affairs immediately upon his release, and was shocked at how this official, who in the past would not have even accepted a phone call from the likes of Wael, had treated him with respect and acknowledgment as his equal. It was the Egyptian presence in the street that gave Wael clout. It was protesters' refusal to leave the square that gave him a negotiating position. It was our love for each other and the country that would see us through.

Wael's appearance unified the youth and reframed what was taking place in Tahrir. The government had heard the youth's voices because they took to the streets, but Egyptians listened to the story because it had come to them in their own living rooms and was personified in the image of Wael, who was unassuming in size but enormous in passion.

It would prove to be another sleepless night for me as I knew that in the morning, Marwa was taking me to the square to add my voice to those that Wael had said helped Egypt stand upright, and take her first few steps toward freedom.

∾ ∾

I pulled my hair back in a pony tail and put on baggy jeans and a loose, long-sleeved shirt. It was a little nippy so I grabbed my jacket as well. I checked myself out in the mirror. Did I look like a protester? What is the dress code for Liberation Square? I hoped I had gotten it right. I felt ridiculous enough as it is, joining in so late in the game.

I was in disbelief that my mother-in-law was letting me go without any arguments at all. My son was out in the yard and she walked me to the door with Layla in her arms. "Are you sure about going with no men accompanying you?" Tante Gigi said.

"Marwa's husband said it was safe for women now, and he has been in the square on a daily basis. Look Tante Gigi," I said, as Marwa's car pulled up to the front of the house, "she even has her eight-year-old son with her." But even I was surprised at her bold move.

"Don't let Ferris see us, "I told Tante Gigi as I motioned to her to walk out with me out front. I didn't want him to see Marwa's son and want to come. I still thought it was an uncertain situation into which to bring him. It was also a lot of walking and I couldn't very well bring a stroller to a protest—or could I?

My mother-in-law placed her hand on my shoulder and said, "Wait…I want to participate, too." She looked toward the garage and said, "Let me send the driver to the supermarket down the street to get you some supplies to take with you to the protesters. There is also a shop by the mall where we can buy a few blankets as well."

Marwa was glad to wait until the supplies arrived, and we took as much as we could. I had told Wael El Zoghby that I was coming and he had promised to have some protesters meet us in the Zamalek area where we were intending to park and help us carry the items in.

As we drove to the square, Marwa proudly explained to her son that we were going to the place where his father had been spending all his time these past few weeks. The boy listened intently and peppered her with questions as street vendors carrying Egyptian flags—a product unlikely to be sold in Egyptian streets in the past—tried to sell us some merchandise. Marwa stopped for one of them and bought us two big flags and a head band with the flag's colors on it for her son to wear.

Approaching the square, we witnessed groups of youth actively sweeping and removing garbage and debris off of the streets. I had grown up thoroughly disgusted at the Egyptian threshold of tolerance for waste on our streets and the areas surrounding our homes in the city. It was deeply moving to see people jump in under these circumstances and begin correcting what had long been deemed sadly acceptable.

Marwa parked the car about fifteen minutes away from the square, and we both unloaded the contents of her trunk onto the sidewalk in preparation for Wael El Zoghby's friends to come help us bring it in.

All around us a continuous stream of people headed to the square in droves.

Men, women, and children, entire families in fact, were all going draped in flags and brandishing broad, proud smiles. Some had the flag painted onto their faces and others held freshly written signs stating their everlasting loyalty to the revolution.

For some reason, Ostaz Wael was not answering his phone, so we stood by our car waiting for him to call back. We had only been there a few minutes when the crowds on their way to Tahrir started approaching us and offering to help. A family of five—a man, his wife, and three children in their teens—told us that they would love to assist us in moving the items, and each carried a portion of the supplies and headed out with us.

No one attempted to stop us or take away what we were bringing in. The days that Khaled Bichara had witnessed directly after the Battle of the Camel appeared to be behind us now. The massive sit-in in Tahrir was serving its purpose, thus granting the revolutionaries, and us regular folk along with them, more strength.

The army motioned us in. As we came closer, the crowds became thicker and appeared to be diverging down the middle into a line for women and a line for men. Due to the sheer number of people, the lines were more like a thick cord of women to one side and men to the other. I could see what appeared to be a checkpoint in the distance, but to get to it the path was intentionally made narrower so when you reached the checkpoint, only one person could get in at a time.

There must have already been at least thirty thousand in the square even though it was still before noon, yet no one lost their patience or appeared angry at the sudden human crunch we were in. Though a lot of the incomers were carrying relatively heavy supplies and miscellaneous items, everyone treated one another with respect and gratitude.

When we finally reached the checkpoint there were volunteers operating on behalf of the protesters. A young woman wearing a badge with her name and the Egyptian flag on it went through my purse and inspected our group and what we were carrying, and no one questioned her authority though we had no proof of who she was or what she represented. She was a fellow citizen and we gave her as much respect as she was so graciously giving us. In fewer than ten minutes we were walking into Tahrir Square.

There was no way to shake the sense of awe of being there for the first time. This was the Land of Oz, and its inhabitants were magically connected, nationalistic, and full of enthusiasm. This was Egypt's Woodstock without the drugs. People were high on freedom.

I felt like I knew every corner of the square from the descriptions I had heard over the phone. I knew where the martyrs' enlarged images were hung, where the tent cities were nestled, and where the stages had been set up. I had never set foot in this noble place that protesters now called home, but I knew the floor plan well.

There were circles of people gathered together chanting and singing, and there were others writing poetry on large banners and setting them up side by side. I could see the entrance to the street that led to the American University's campus where I earned both my bachelor's and master's degrees. It looked oddly out of place. I myself felt oddly out of place, like someone would call me out at any minute and ask me why I hadn't been here when the battles were raging.

Like a wedding crasher, I kept expecting the bride and groom at any minute to realize that I did not belong to either families and kick me out. However, this was Marwa's first time as well, and she appeared entirely at home with where she was and what her role had been. She helped her son step up onto a small perch at the entrance of a building so he could see above the masses of taller people that surrounded him.

She took great care in explaining to him what the banners said and who the people in the photos were. He wondered why there were so many pictures of people who were "asleep," and Marwa candidly explained that those were people who had passed away during the struggle and were now safely and soundly with God.

I tried to get myself onto higher ground, as well, to get a better view, and it was then when I heard someone say, "Ostaza Hoda!"

I saw Ostaz Wael approaching us and he was, to put it very mildly, shockingly disheveled.

In fact, had it not been for his voice, which had become so familiar to me, I would not have recognized him at all. I believe Marwa was taken aback a bit when I introduced them. He looked more like a homeless man who had been on the streets for years than the man I had seen once or twice before in work-related meetings, who was normally well dressed and very presentable.

"Who's this little one?" he said as he approached Marwa's little boy. The little boy was afraid of him, so I tried to chit-chat my way around the awkwardness of the situation.

"Do you know the religious scholar Moez Masoud?" I asked him.

"Of course I do," he said.

"Well, this is his son."

"I can see the resemblance," Ostaz Wael said, looking to the young boy with a smile. He lingered there a little longer than needed and seemed to space out a little.

"Uh...we tried to reach you but you weren't answering your cell phone," I interjected into the uncomfortable pause.

"Oh, I am sorry, I didn't hear my phone. I was in that *maseera* ["march"] over there, and the chanting and singing were pretty loud." He suddenly looked around him nervously like he was being watched and said, "I need to talk to you about something if you have the time."

I looked at Marwa and she gave me an uneasy smile and said, "You know we should leave before it gets too crowded for him," and she patted her son's head

"I understand," I said. "This will only take a minute." I motioned to Ostaz Wael to step to the side a bit, which was hard to do given that we had very little room to move without losing Marwa to the crowds.

"Are you traveling soon?" he asked.

"I am not sure, but I probably won't be going anywhere until the end of the school year," I replied.

"Well, I have some important documents that I want to get out of the country. Documents that expose a lot of corrupt officials.

We want to get them to Wikileaks or something like it." His eyes were still darting around nervously, and all of a sudden I felt really bad for him. He had a tremendous amount of stress built up and no matter how hard he tried, it was affecting his overall mannerisms. This was not the calm and collected Ostaz Wael. But then again, how could he be?

What happens to the human mind when you take it so far from what its comfort level once was?

This man was not a "combat" man, and his health wasn't that great to begin with. I could only imagine what was going on inside him after sleeping on the pavement and being separated from his home and family. How was he processing all the death he had seen, and how would he put it in context for the rest of his life?

This is what people at home failed to understand, especially about the resident protesters who had been through it all. There was no objectivity or time to sit back and reflect upon the situation. There were no economic considerations or long-term strategies that would make sense to them. Tahrir residents were at war while those at home were witnessing the war. There was a distinct difference in mindset and overall outlook.

"I will try to find someone who is leaving the country soon for you," I promised.

"You take care of yourself and try to get some rest. People have been bringing in supplies all day. Go find something to eat and get a glass of warm tea. A group of volunteers showed us where to deliver what we had brought with us in that area over there. I am going to have to leave with my friend here. Please call me if you need anything else. My father and sister will be coming in later in the day."

As Marwa and I inched our way out through the crowds, with me in the front, she in the back and her son sandwiched in between us, I looked back at Ostaz Wael disappearing into the crowds again. He looked so tired and yet, for the moment, he considered himself home.

I began to think about his bravery and my own home abandoned in the desert and I made a decision. I wanted to take my children back to their house.

I was not afraid anymore.

I believed that Ostaz Wael and everyone else in the square were slowly but surely winning the battle and providing the country with better possibilities.

If I was choosing to stay in Egypt for the time being, then I owed it to my children and myself to lead as "normal" a life as possible.

෨   ෨

The tenth of February was my first day back home. The kids rushed excitedly into their rooms and sat on the floor, eagerly emptying out their toy boxes. The house looked and felt beautiful. I felt like an adult again as I set my suitcase down in my own bedroom. I had called on an old housekeeper who used to work for us and offered her a live-in position until we could figure out what we were doing. She welcomed the job offer.

She helped me unload the car as the neighbors came by to welcome us home. A lot of people had chosen to stay and protect their homes in the desert, and they said that they would do the same for my family, as they knew my husband wasn't with me. They filled me in on how the guards at the gate had recently employed armed, desert Bedouins to help protect the compound. The restaurants and hotel areas within our compound reportedly got trashed by their own employees rebelling against the owner.

He was considered by many to be a wealthy, tyrannical manager, and a lot of workers probably considered him a part of the regime that needed to be cleansed. He owned a large house that was just down the street from mine and usually had a fleet of cars protecting it. You could always see bodyguards with walkie-talkies and numerous nannies caring for his grandchildren. None of his posse was there at the moment. He had probably moved into one of the many high-rises he owned in the city.

A large number of these dubiously wealthy businessmen were being targeted. A few were arrested in a public effort by the regime to prove that it was acceding to the revolution's demands. You feared that this corruption-cleansing crusade could very well turn into a witch-hunt in a country that held a lot of pent-up antagonism between the rich and poor. However, so far, the targeted individuals were among those that had a track record of outrageous business behavior.

My mother was coming over to spend the first night with us as my father was driving to Alexandria for one night on business. I prepared for her to be in the master bedroom and I planned to share the bunk beds with my kids.

I had dinner prepared for her, complete with desert, as a mini-celebration of me coming home, but she wasn't interested in it at all. She had heard that the president would be giving his third televised speech in response to the unprecedented numbers camping out indefinitely in Tahrir Square, and she was convinced he would step down tonight. She raced through dinner and went straight to my bedroom, where she could watch in bed.

She watched and waited while I helped the housekeeper clean up after dinner, watched and waited while I played with the kids, and watched and waited while I finally put the kids in bed.

It was eight thirty when I finally entered the bedroom to join her, and she looked all waited out. She had muted the television, put meditation music on her iPod, and had some incense burning. Her eyes were closed but she was not sleeping and she had a little frown on her face. She was sixty-six years old, had arthritis and the cold was bothering her. But I could tell that she was more disappointed than she was uncomfortable. She had been avidly watching through the past seventeen days of the revolution and wanted to see the finale.

She had seen all the footage of the grieving families of the revolution's martyrs and how they died. She watched my father, cofounder of a portfolio management company that was taking a beating because the stock market had shut down, struggle in the ensuing mess. And close to half of her life had been spent watching Mubarak's regime take us down. I knew she believed that we all deserved a happy ending, and she was hoping that she could experience that with me tonight.

I crawled in next to her in the bed and she smiled at me. "I think these sheets are musty," she said, like a typical mother.

"OK, Mama, I'll change them." I made a move to get out of bed but she held onto my arm.

"Stay," she insisted. "I believe the old geezer will be on any minute and I want us to see it together."

"Any minute" turned into a few hours and my mother kept falling in and out of sleep. I spent the time flipping through the channels, until finally, at 10:45 p.m., regular broadcasting was interrupted and all channels, local and satellite, cut to Mubarak.

The channels claimed that the speech was being broadcast live from the presidential palace, though a lot of Egyptians believed that he was already in the beach city of Sharm El Sheikh, heavily guarded and far away from the protests in the capital. We could never tell because all speeches were given with him standing at the same old podium with the same blue background and the same flag. However, his demeanor was entirely different than his previous two speeches. He no longer had the menacing frown that had been affixed to his face in the past two speeches.

In fact, he had a kind look that caught Mom and I off guard. He started by specifying that he was addressing this speech to the promising youth of Egypt in Tahrir Square and beyond. Mom grabbed her cell phone and pointed it toward the TV and started videotaping the broadcast.

He said that he saw the future through these youths' eyes and it looked bright and full of potential. His next statement felt like an advisor had strongly urged him to begin his speech with it: "I would like to state before anything else," Mubarak said, and then paused a few seconds for effect, "that the blood of your martyrs and wounded, as well as our martyrs and wounded, will not have been in vain. And I assure you that I will take no mercy or spare any expense to punish those responsible for it all."

I rolled my eyes. "Put the phone down, Mama, he just said he would oversee the punishment process. He is not stepping down. You'll just hurt your hands," I said as I tried to get the phone out of her hand. She pulled away from me stubbornly and kept it pointed at the television.

Mubarak went on and on about how he would honor all the requests he had heard in the square and how it was his promise to the people. He said it wounded his heart to see our pain and he would seek vengeance on those whose actions caused all of this.

It was interesting how he had isolated himself from everything. The civilian martyrs and wounded were "your martyred and wounded" and the bad guys were also individuals other than him who were classified as "those responsible for it all."

Mubarak's speech made him out to be exactly what he was—a separate, indestructible island out of reach of the Egyptian people. The deaths were ours to bear and the fault was someone else's and he was the only untouched, innocent bystander. The scary thing about it all is that when you looked into his eyes it was apparent he believed what he was saying.

I was crushed. I felt that there would be no way that this human being would ever come to reflect upon his life and realize that he did Egypt wrong. Now it made sense to me. This is why we remained "third world" for all these years. We had been ruled by eyes that could not see, a heart that did not empathize, and a mind that was incapable of thinking beyond the enclosed boundaries of his own ego.

We were doomed.

But Mom held her phone and her hopes up until the very end of the speech. She listened as he argued that all political systems make mistakes and that he would correct them. She listened while he warned us of the youths' message containing directives from abroad and that he would see that we would not be controlled by foreign agendas. He guaranteed us that he was a man of his word and that he had heard the message of Egypt's upcoming generations loud and clear.

He spoke and spoke but the words amounted to nothing, and nothing was what we got that night.

The El Arabiya channel had broadcast the speech with a split screen, with the president on one side and a bird's-eye view of the square on the other. As the president spoke on a large screen that was set up in the square, protesters called out in anguish as they realized that their dream was not coming true. Men held their shoes up in the air, wishing they could throw them at the screen, and women cried hysterically. The television began to report that protesters were already gathering and heading for the presidential palace.

I took Mom's phone from her hand, kissed her on the head, and told her to get some sleep. I turned off the television, which was now airing the newly appointed Vice President Omar Suleiman's speech calling on "mature" Egyptians to heed to the president's "advice." It was not worth listening to.

I went out into the dark house and got my laptop and my phone so I could get an accurate account of what was going on from the protesters themselves.

I called Osataz Wael and his voice was serious but not despairing. He managed to steady me emotionally. Once again, he had the advantage of being surrounded by people who were as brave and determined as he was. He said that the people around him had vowed to not surrender to hopelessness, and we at home should do the same.

At midnight, I wrote the following onto my blog:

Entry 38:
10 February 2011, 2:00 am

This is a summary of what is happening on the ground now. Mubarak announced that he will not be stepping down but will be giving responsibility to his VP. Crowds were disappointed in this speech (please try to view it online), but did not appear violent as was reported on CNN International.

Crowds that were seen leaving were not necessarily going to the TV broadcast building to storm it, or heading to the presidential palace, as was reported by some channels.

From more than three different sources on the ground, I was told that people are disappointed but not violent. There are those who say they will still spend the night in the square. The general direction is to stay in the square, pray the Friday prayers there tomorrow, and then move the protests to the presidential palace after prayers. "–*Bokra el asr hanrooh el asr*—"*Which* means: "–Tomorrow afternoon––to the palace–."

The protestors are PEACEFUL; this is the most important message to relay tonight. They are not intending any violence. They are resuming their chanting, and are clearly disappointed, but that is the extent of their reaction.

It is my personal opinion as well, that they have a lot of thinking to do through the night, like normal people, which makes their decisions about tomorrow unconfirmed.

I repeat: They are not leaving the square –"en-masse-"in a flurry to do any kind of reactionary demonstrations anywhere. If some people are, they do not represent the majority of the organized entities that have been inhabiting the square for the past seventeen days.

God Bless.

Note: These reports are given by phone live, from Tahrir square, by the protestors themselves.

I spoke to a disappointed Basil via Skype and tried to make him feel better, and then fell asleep on the couch next to my computer. I was exhausted but not defeated. I was home and I was hopeful that this house, God willing, would see us accomplish something and I would get to celebrate within its walls.

෴ ෴

On the morning of the eleventh, Mohammed Diab and Moez Masoud were in crisis mode. They were extremely concerned about the protesters' decision to head to the presidential palace. The past week had been devoid of violence and they had not had the chance to take solace in that entirely. They both headed to separate TV channels and tried to make as many call-ins and appearances as possible to deter people from congregating at the president's home.

They both felt that the epicenter of the protests should remain Tahrir Square, with all it stood for. If it moved to the palace, then it became about Mubarak and targeting him. It was important to them to remind people that at this point, bloodshed was not necessary and they shouldn't do anything that gave the regime an excuse to reap more young lives. The protesters had come so far with the aim of correcting a political path, they should not make it seem like they were out to assassinate a current head of state, illegitimate as he may be.

But at Shahinaz Meshaal's home, the picture was entirely different. Her phone had not stopped ringing since the early morning as Sixth of April members hashed out all the possibilities and where and what they could do that day. She had gotten very little sleep. The past week she had been on pain medication to fight the signals her body was sending her that she was pushing it too far. Her daily routine had been to wake up at dawn every day, cook for her family and place the food in the fridge, do laundry, clean the house, and then head out to the square where she would stay until midnight.

Her mother would cry and beg her to have mercy on her own health. Shahinaz's eyes were constantly swollen and her face was pale and sickly. She had been eating poorly and her joints were acting up. But there was no way she was backing off now.

She had visited almost all the hospitals in Cairo in an effort to help Sixth of April gather records to tally the names and numbers of those killed and wounded since the protests started. She had experienced firsthand security forces trying to kick her out of hospitals and distorting the information being released. The process had convinced her that the serpent was still very much alive and in hiding. It slept and ate among us, and she believed the only hope was to cut off its head so its slithering body could squeeze us no more.

Shahinaz considered the eight hundred of Egypt's children that had fallen so far, inaccurate as that number probably was, all her children. She had adopted each and every one of them and grieved for them every minute of the day. As a mother she couldn't let go—and as a mother she wouldn't.

The mothers of the fallen had paid for a new Egypt in advance, and she had appointed herself, and everyone her voice could influence, as the bill collector. Indeed, she would go to the presidential palace today, which was the only thing that made sense to her and her entire group. In Tahrir the night before, after the president's speech, she had witnessed grown men cry and the women turn their faces to the sky and pray for God to intervene on their behalf. She felt her own prayers leap out of her chest, bypassing both her mind and tongue and rise into the sky with all the rest. It was time to leave the place where the children had died and head to where the enemy slept. She prayed the Friday prayers in Tahrir at noon and then took the underground Metro to the closest stop to the presidential palace. She had two young men from her Sixth of April group with her and together, they took a cab.

The driver looked at them and asked, "Do you want to go to the protests at the palace?"

She looked him fearlessly in the face and said, "Yes, we do." It was two o'clock and things were about to get crowded where they were headed.

The cabbie gave them a big smile and took them as far as the car would go. He was as fed up as the majority of Egyptians, and he would spend the entire day bringing in as much people as he could to support the initiative. It would prove to be good for business, too, as thousands upon thousands continued to join.

They were packed in tight with the palace a mere few feet away. The army tanks stood between the people and the armed palace guards at the entrance. The soldiers had grim expressions on their faces and the tanks' cannons were pointed at the protesters.

As the hours rolled in and the crowds grew thicker and longer, their anger began to rise above the surface and the chants adopted the rhythmic beat of persistent drums. *"El Shaab yoreed isqat el raees"* ("The people demand that the president falls") replaced the Tunisian chant *"El Shaab yoreed isqat el nizam"* ("The people demand the fall of the regime").

As the *maghrib* sunset prayer drew near, the crowds began to form lines in preparation for prayer. Almost magically, it appeared that the almighty was intervening and as the prayers were taking place, the army tanks started to slowly move their cannons in the direction of the palace guards and the palace itself. As Shahinaz and the entire group touched their foreheads to the ground, army tanks stood guarding them from the palace and its men. Soon after, soldiers began to distribute biscuits and water to the protesters, and you could see several protesters embracing the soldiers.

The crowd's anger appeared to dissolve with the water and biscuits as they savored the act of alliance they had just experienced. Only minutes later, cell phones all around Shahinaz began to ring as if in complete unison. It was almost scary to see so many people receive phone calls at the same time.

Her own phone began to vibrate in her pocket, and as she lifted it to her ear, her son was screaming, "He stepped down! He stepped down!"

The scene unfolded around her as if in slow motion. She could hear the ululations that are a cultural reaction to all good news, especially weddings and births. She could see men and women jumping up and down and embracing each other. The crowd was going wild.

The palace guards stared on in disbelief as the army soldiers celebrated with the crowds.

Protestors were quickly packing up and heading to beloved Tahrir for celebration. They all walked, skipped, and danced to the nearest underground Metro station and started boarding the trains in groups of hundreds.

When Shahinaz finally got on a train, everyone else was singing and chanting, but she felt a large lump rise in her throat. Without warning, she broke into heavy sobbing, catching the attention of those around her. The young men from the movement immediately surrounded her, filled with concern. These did not seem to be happy tears, and they wanted to know what was wrong.

"Eight hundred lives!" she exclaimed between sobs. "Eight hundred lives for him to stay in power for a little more than two weeks? What did he gain by robbing us of our children? If he was going to leave anyway, couldn't he have left without them? How many weeks are left in his entire life anyway?" The flood of tears was loud and endless, and the whole car fell silent.

The young men and women kept patting her shoulders and kissing her hands and saying, "We will not forget about them or leave what is rightfully theirs. We will avenge them, Auntie, we promise. They did not die in vain."

In Wael Ghonim's apartment, Mohamed Diab and Amr Salama had been with Wael and a few of his close friends and family members. The news caught them off guard as well.

They hugged Wael and each other as Diab started filming the historical moment with his cell phone. Wael Ghonim fell to his knees in front of his laptop, bowed his head, and fought back tears. Everyone kept yelling *"Tahya Masr! Tahya Masr"* ("Long live Egypt! Long live Egypt!"), and as if on cue they all broke into the national anthem. Several of them began laughably filming each other with their cell phones, as they all knew that this was a moment for the history books and documentary films.

Back in my house, I had just placed Layla in the tub and was standing at the bathroom's entrance when it happened. My mom had just left and the television in my room was still on. I could hear bits and pieces of a program she had been watching. Suddenly, the program was interrupted by the announcement that the vice president would be making an emergency announcement.

For some reason, in my heart I knew this was it.

Vice President Omar Suleiman stood with a bodyguard behind him, looking distressed and somber. The statement was short and simple:

"My fellow Egyptian citizens, in these trying times that the our country is going through, President Mohamed Hosni Mubarak has decided to abandon his post as president of the Arab Republic of Egypt, and has instructed the Supreme Council of the Armed Forces to take over the entirety of the country's affairs, and may God be the facilitator and the source of our guidance."

And just like that, thirty seconds ended thirty years of oppression.

I believe I must have jumped up about ten feet into the air and kept saying, "Oh my God, he left! He left!" Layla got scared and began to cry in the tub, and I tried to comfort her but could barely contain my own emotions.

The housekeeper came running down the steps and asked me what had happened. She was illiterate, as most women in her field in Egypt are, and she had a very limited grasp of politics.

"The president resigned," I told her with great enthusiasm.

To which she replied simply, "Really? Then who is going to run the country tomorrow?"

Turns out, that would be the question of the decade.

WE ARE ALL KHALED SAEED

13.

The weeks that followed the abdication were a euphoric blur. I had spent the night of the abdication calling every soul I knew inside and outside of Tahrir and yelling the same things into the phone over and over while my children tried to get a word in with me. Basil's happiness was reserved because he was kind of miffed that he wasn't there. His friends in the States promised him an "Egyptian Revolution" party so he could experience some form of jubilation.

Wael El Zoghby cried shamelessly into the phone from Tahrir as people went crazy around him. I wanted to head out there too, but my father convinced me to wait until morning and we would go together as a family.

This time I did take my children with me in their massive double-stroller. It was Tahrir Square California-style, with the kids in a stroller and the water bottles in tow. The stroller proved to be a bit of a nuisance, as the poorly paved roads made it difficult to push. My poor dad, who was too deep into his sixties to handle such chivalry, insisted that the stroller was his job and labored with it for the whole day.

I took the "Not in My Country!" T-shirts from the high school website campaign and told my students to meet me there, and we planned to give out the T-shirts to people for free. We packed cleaning equipment, brooms, shovels, garbage bags, and plastic gloves, and set out to fix up Tahrir like you would a young bride on her wedding night. Everyone had the same spirit, and by the time we got there, there was almost nothing left to clean.

I hugged my students every chance I got that day, because I was so impressed by how engaged and how hard they were working. I personally wasn't very effective in the cleaning process since Layla kept insisting on "helping" and had my broom most of the time. Photographers kept stopping and taking pictures of her. Apparently many found the image of a one-and-a-half-year-old with a miniature "Not in My Country!" T-shirt on holding onto a broom in Tahrir Square quite symbolic.

We had about sixty T-shirts, and the minute we brought them out into the open they were snatched out of our hands in a little less than ten minutes. My students would take pictures of Tahrir protesters wearing the campaign slogan we created together and post it to their Facebook pages. It was all quite dreamlike.

We had our "wedding" party, and the honeymoon was almost over.

The euphoria and unified spirit of that day and the few weeks after it were very short-lived. In fact, by the time Basil returned to Egypt in the first few days of March, he barely caught the tail end of it.

He and I did have the pleasure of seeing a young boy, not more than ten years old, standing in the middle of the street waving an Egyptian flag for no reason at all. He had the biggest, proudest smile on his face, and we honked the horn for him in encouragement. He waved at us and made a peace sign, and we felt warm and fuzzy all over. These are the moments I miss the most.

The streets were still clean, but they would later fall into almost the same filthy state they were in before. The segment of society accustomed to disposing of their waste in the streets had not been rehabilitated, and the youth couldn't clean the streets *all* the time.

We also saw a lot of young individuals painting sidewalks and old rundown walls in an effort to renovate them. However, there was little coordination between the various group efforts, so they became patchy and inconsistent.

Some streets were freshly painted with opposing colors that didn't match or look very good. In many ways, these efforts pretty much summarized the current Egyptian situation. The spirit was there, but we lacked the coordination and communication to utilize it properly.

Wael El Zoghby's NGO *Baladnaa*, along with several other leading NGOs, scrambled to address the crises of the families of martyrs who had been primary breadwinners, along with the rampant resulting poverty of the sudden and mounting job losses.

To make matters worse, police forces never returned to their posts full-force and crime was rising. Egypt's crime level remained remarkably less than that of heavily populated U.S. cities such as New York or Los Angles, but nevertheless it was a quite a bit greater than anything the country had experienced in recent history.

Oddly enough, many politicians from the old regime remained in power, and appeared to be openly sabotaging the recovery process. Many questioned if the headless serpent still had its grip on the country.

As Egypt spiraled down economically, it began to crush those in its path and with the economic slump, I could feel the spirit of unanimity being squeezed out of the Egyptians.

At my computer at home, I tried to figure out a plan for the book. How could I accurately summarize the recent past to illuminate the near present and the future? I first started with the idea of one hundred stories from the revolution, and I began to group protesters into ten categories with ten individuals in each.

The concept was to represent religions, economic statuses, levels of involvement, whether the protester had survived or died in battle, and so on. As I did the math on the interviews and how long it would take to tape them, let alone write them out, I began to see that plan A would not work. I did not have enough time to even complete taping before I was set to go back to California in the summer.

Plan B was to narrow it down to twenty-five stories in honor of the 25th of January. But even that plan quickly changed as Moez Masoud began to help me set up interviews with his close contacts, and the first few proved to be lengthy and full of information that needed to be shared.

My very first interview was with Mohammed Diab, and it lasted close to six hours. We did it all over the phone and took breaks to eat and go to the bathroom. It was exhausting, but it was so exciting and presented so much information that Plan B too began to seem unfeasible.

In the end I took Mohamed Diab's story, which was such a beautiful overview of the whole situation, and began to map out what the broad lines that defined this one-of-a-kind revolution were.

When I spoke to my sister's husband, he offered such an interesting perspective on how events affected regular people that I was compelled to tape his account as well. From this exercise of comparing Mohamed Diab and Mohamed Shafie, I began to feel that I should cover activists as well as regular civilians who fought their battles within their own lives by trying to survive the aftermath.

I saw the importance of representing key influential figures and entities such as Dr. El Baradei, the Muslim Brotherhood, Sixth of April, the "Kolona Khaled Saeed" page, and the media in how events unfolded, and attempted to select appropriate people to represent each category.

Moez's role was integral to the process as he followed up with me regularly and eventually got me in contact with two characters that added a third dimension to my understanding of the revolution. I had thought I had watched so closely and understood so fully, yet I discovered that I was missing some essential elements.

Moez got me an interview with martyr Khaled Saeed's mother in addition to Dr. Baradei's campaign manager, an activist and a rarely mentioned cofounder of the "Kolona Khaled Saeed" page, Dr. Mustafa El Naggar.

The interviews were set to take place months apart, and in the meantime the fluid situation in Egypt took us all for a ride.

March 19 was the date of the newly proposed constitutional referendum that asked citizens to choose between keeping the current Constitution while making some adjustments or throwing out the Constitution altogether and writing a new one. This would be the first truly democratic experience for Egyptian citizens in thirty years.

In the past, less than 10 percent of the Egyptian population participated in any kind of electoral process that the government organized. This time, almost every able-bodied Egyptian, and even those who could barely move, vowed to make their voice heard. But as Egyptians began to speak, it became apparent that we were not all singing the same tune. In fact, some found each other's voices downright offensive.

Political campaigning was unchartered territory and the mechanics of democracy were unknown. We could not even handle having opposing opinions on anything, let alone handle the electoral process.

I saw Moez and Diab appear in online videos supporting a "no" vote to a Constitution with adjustments. They argued, along with other celebrities, that we should all start from scratch on a new rulebook for our beloved country. On the other hand, the majority of the Muslim Brotherhood favored the amended Constitution and had their own fliers and videos.

Shahinaz Meshaal returned to her grassroots campaigning on the streets of Cairo's impoverished areas. Her efforts focused on awareness and on explaining the difference between the two decisions. In her heart, she feared the Brotherhood and other Islamic groups coming into politics, and she personally opposed the amended constitution. However, she thought that the priority was to have an informed population who had the knowledge to make the decision that they were comfortable with and believed in.

It was a mess when you looked at it in terms of how it divided us, but it was a sight to behold when I held my mother's hand and waited in line to vote in Egypt for the very first time for both of us. Forty-one percent of forty-five million eligible voters turned out to vote, and that was proof of how the revolution had indeed brought about change in people's sense of citizenship.

As I discussed how beautiful the day was with my sister, I heard a news report that some people were tearing up and stepping on images of martyr Khaled Saeed at the voting stations. A political party that was for changing the constitution entirely had featured a picture of Khaled Saeed on its flier and posted the question under it, "Are you going to let him die in vain?"

The voters stepping on the fliers favored the existing Constitution with amendments and viewed Khaled's image on the fliers as a cheap ploy to get people to support a new constitution. In anger, they defiled one of the most potent symbols of the revolution and I felt inherently ashamed.

I hoped his mother hadn't witnessed it, as it was bound to tear her apart. I wondered how much of what we had once deemed sacred to the revolution would be trampled upon in the upcoming months. It became apparent that things would get far worse before they had a chance to get better.

❧　❧

I dropped off my children at my mother-in-law's house and headed out to meet Layla Marzouk, Khaled Saeed's mother. Schools in our area had not reopened yet, and I felt bad that I was leaving both of them in her care because it was a lot of work and I would not be back for the majority of the day. The drive alone was four hours round trip.

The whole way, I had butterflies in my stomach. I had spent all night reading articles and viewing videos of interviews with Marzouk and her daughter. The story of how Khaled was dragged out and beat to death in front of his friends and neighbors while his mother was visiting a friend was horrid and painful. Witnesses said his screams could be heard for miles and miles, and yet police held people back and forced them to bear witness.

Their fear castrated them, as they realized they had not witnessed a beating, but a murder. Witnesses had finally held a mirror to their own inability to stop the police, and the incident swelled and engulfed Alexandria's inhabitants until the guilt spilled over to the rest of Egypt.

What kind of a country lets this happen to their children and does not fight back? That is the question Wael Ghonim had packaged so well online on the "We Are All Khaled Saeed" Facebook page. We *were* all Khaled Saeed. None of us had the power to avoid a torturous death if we were unlucky enough to cross the police.

They need not use due process, read us our rights, or even take us to the station. They could kill us right then and there if they wanted to, and they didn't even care to hide it. They were unashamed of their power over us because they knew that our fear had shamed us into paralysis.

Khaled Saeed was our unspoken voice that cried out as his spirit left his body. Khaled Saeed was our martyred youth and our raped dreams. His broken face would remind us that our mothers had no rights and our dead had no dignity.

I could not believe I was about to meet with a mother who had withstood such pain. The policeman who carried out the murder got away with a farcical warning and the police proceeded to make Marzouk's life hell. Police stationed at her building's entrance often forbade her own family members from visiting her, and they heckled her and made horrible comments about her son every time she attempted to go out.

Marzouk was known to be a tower of strength, and she stood sad but proud in the face of her abusers. Her demeanor and fighting attitude that helped Khaled's story remain front and center motivated many to speak out.

I was about to sit with her in her daughter's apartment, and I was scared out of my mind. I was afraid I would break into tears and look like an idiot—or even worse, be unprofessional in my questions, fail at the interview, and succeed only in making her relive what she spent her days trying to forget.

As I rang the doorbell, my heart was beating hard in my face. She opened the door herself and gave me a big smile.

She said the most enigmatic thing as she pulled me in and kissed me. "There you are. I knew you would come."

I decided not to comment but definitely made a note to later attempt to find out what she could have meant by it. Greatly moved by her warmth, I hugged her for a minute before I let go and proceeded into the apartment.

The apartment was big and bright and heavily decorated with birthday party decorations, of all things. This was her daughter's home and I knew she had children, so I concluded that one of them must have had a party recently. Marzouk's heavy-set body, dressed in a loose fitting, black dress and a black veil, stood in stark comparison to the colorful decorations and the bright sunlight.

Like an epicenter of grief in this otherwise cheerful room, she was a reminder that in this beautiful world ugly things happen to good people all the time. A larger-than-life photograph of Khaled's face inhabited the wall in front of the seating area into which she guided me. His eyes would look at me for the next five hours.

She had eight cats running around the apartment, and it caught me off guard that they all seemed to be rubbing up against me.

"These are Khaled's cats," she explained with a smile as one of them jumped onto her lap. "His cats had a bunch of kittens and we are still trying to find homes for them. Would you like one for your children?"

I had not mentioned to her that I had any children. "Oh, they would have loved that, but I may be traveling soon, you see…"

My heart had begun to pound in my head from all the excitement. I proceeded to engage in friendly chatter as I set up my camera and my digital recorder.

She interrupted my small talk by interjecting, "Let me get you something for that headache first."

Something odd was taking place. She was acting like she knew me, and more importantly, what I was thinking. I had known that she was a strong woman from watching her composed and collected interviews, but I was not prepared for a crystal-ball-reader experience.

Her daughter, Zahra, came into the room with a glass of water and a pill and I shook her hand warmly and thanked her for the medicine. I immediately whispered to her, "I am so thankful that she agreed to talk to me. I have already read and viewed what happened to your brother online, and I promise I will not walk her through the murder itself again. I am more interested in learning about her life before and after, and hearing about the kind of person that Khaled was."

Zahra smiled kindly. She had a petite and welcoming face, fair skin and light brown hair, and looked like the portion of Egyptian society that had Turkish ancestors. "She tells the story every day, so don't worry about it," she said. "I will be out shopping and picking up my children from school, but she will take care of you, OK?" She collected her purse and keys from a nearby table.

As I watched her leave, I nervously popped the pill into my mouth and washed it down with water.

Marzouk came back into the room and sat down just a few minutes later. The cats followed her. They had all left with her except for one that stayed, as if to make sure I didn't run out.

Marzouk followed what was called the *Shazliya* Islamic tradition, which is akin to a sect in the sense that only a small percentage of Muslims believed in its teachings and practices. Followers of the *Shazliya* method believe in saints and the supernatural, and usually follow a sheikh who is believed to be a descendent of Prophet Mohamed.

During the interview I was unaware of all this and so her actions struck me as highly unusual and I began to wonder if the stress of her experience had rendered her unstable. I apologized to her one more time for coming to open wounds that she undoubtedly was trying to heal. Khaled had been killed June 6, 2010, so it had been less than a year since the horrifying tragedy.

She smiled peacefully and said, "I give interviews every single day, dear. But not all of *them* would understand what I am about to share with you."

In fact, few people would or could understand the story Layla Marzouk shared with me, but I felt very privileged to hear it, as it added an element that begged to be included in the story that I had secretly believed in my whole life.

The world had more magical things than we dared to admit.

Sure, one could use science to explain away everything, but what is science if not God's way of explaining his magic tricks?

If you are the type of person who immediately shuts down when faced with the supernatural, go ahead and skip this chapter, but think of this: How is it that in a country that tortured so many in its prisons, that America sent its hard-core suspects here to be interrogated, that this specific case got so much attention and seemingly mobilized so many people at once?

Many hypothesized that it was because the murder was so out in the open and Khaled was an upper-middle-class Egyptian with no record and no ties to any religious groups. It was absolutely clear that the killing was unjustified.

Although this explanation was mostly true, Khaled's story did so much in such little time that it merited closer investigation. It was the universe marrying two forces of energy together: Wael Ghonim's quest to find a path through which he could help his country, and Khaled Saeed's life, which was severed prematurely with such terror that his spirit seemed to haunt the Egyptian people.

His story would simply not go away after you put the paper down or turned off the TV. It stayed with you and visited you when you least expected it. It became the melancholy tune we couldn't keep out of our heads.

∽ ∽

Layla Marzouk's earlier life had most definitely prepared her for hardship. She married at the young age of eighteen to help her husband escape hardship. She selected him out of all her colleagues at work because he had recently lost his father and appeared burdened by grief.

She was moved by the overwhelming need to support and assist him in caring for his mother and his many brothers and sisters. Because her husband was the oldest male in the family, he was expected to remain in the family house to assist his mother as his father's replacement.

Consequently, that's where Layla lived and had her first child, Yehia. Their finances were not all that comfortable since her husband's money was shared with his mother and siblings, so she had to continue working. She took her baby with her to work, where there was a humble day care facility, and took the proper steps with her doctor to ensure she did not have another one any time soon. But fate would intervene, and she would end up having another boy, Ahmed.

She changed her contraceptive plan and made sure to be as careful as possible after Ahmed's difficult birth and her slow recovery. However, one day her sister called and said that she had dreamed that Layla was giving birth to a statue of Mother Mary (also revered in Islamic faith with the Quran naming her as the "greatest woman to ever grace the earth"). A voice in the dream whispered in her sister's ear that the statue of Mother Mary should be kept a secret from all, but Layla shared the dream with her mother-in-law, who advised her to see her gynecologist.

When she did, he informed her that she was pregnant even though she had an IUD in place. "Should I remove the child or the IUD?" he asked.

To which she replied, "The IUD, of course. Children are a gift that should never be removed."

Layla had a beautiful baby girl that she wanted to name Mariam, the Arabic name for Mother Mary, but her husband had a different plan. He had recently taken a job on a commercial cargo ship called *El Zahra* that traveled between Cairo and Nigeria. He loved that ship and wanted to name his daughter after it and so they did.

Layla seemed to be constantly expecting, despite her use of contraceptives. She had four children with a man who was only home about a quarter of the time. She had Yehia, Ahmed, Zahra, and finally Khaled.

When Khaled was born, he was so beautiful that her in-laws had thought she had gotten another girl. A group of French doctors who worked at the hospital at the time joked that they were holding a pageant for the cutest baby of the ward and her son had definitely won. The hospital had a small French publication that served as its quarterly journal and it had a picture of Khaled in it. He had fair skin and black hair and seemed to look straight at you even though he was merely a few days old.

She had such a good time with him when he was a baby and hoped that her husband could enjoy him with her. But her husband was out of reach, and she was left with his family.

She had a very close relationship with her mother-in-law, but the brothers and sisters seemed to lack affection when it came to her. Her many children were a burden to the household, and the atmosphere was never as warm as she hoped it would be. When she went on an outing with them, her eye would catch a couple dining out with their children and she would feel sad. She longed for the intimacy of living with a man and raising his children in his presence. She had rarely had that, and soon fate would ensure that she never would.

On one of his short stays home during his time off from the ship, her husband started complaining of sharp pains in his stomach, and a slew of tests ensued. The doctors shared with Layla and his family that he had stage-four cancer, and that his days with them were numbered. Khaled, her youngest, was only six years old and her eldest son had just turned twenty.

The family decided to keep the news from him and instead fed him daily lies about how he would get better. When Layla tried to be alone with him so she could tell him the truth and discuss matters that a husband and wife should discuss in such circumstances, the family would forcefully keep her away. She was only allowed to visit with him briefly in the morning and before she went to bed.

She was kept so busy with her work and caring for the four children that she barely had time to think about how she could work around what his siblings were doing. She kept hoping that he would get well enough for her to take him out somewhere and have a candid conversation with him, but that never happened.

Eventually, her husband began to wonder why she never cared for him or spent time with him though he was ill, and he'd almost started to believe that she didn't care.

One night she awoke with the urge that she had to find him. As she walked through the hallways of the large house and searched the rooms, she realized that he wasn't there. She quickly got dressed and told her eldest son that she was going to search for his father in nearby hospitals.

It took her a few hours but she eventually found him. He had taken a turn for the worse, and the doctors had to move him to intensive care. His siblings guarded his room protectively, but she begged them to sit with him. She needed to have one conversation with him before he was lost to her forever.

They reluctantly let her in and as she approached him, his eyes lit up and he motioned for her to sit down next to him.

"How about we run away together when I get out of here?" he whispered. "I do not want to go anywhere but Alexandria. Take me to Alexandria but keep me out of the hospitals."

She put her hand on his forehead and bent in closer to his ear. His siblings turned away and headed quietly out of the room. They reasoned that there was nothing she could tell him now that would make any difference.

"No hospitals, my love," Layla whispered into his ear. He looked up at her and gave her a big smile.

"Please get me a pen and paper," he said.

On the paper he wrote that everything he owned should go to his wife and children. He knew that the end was near, and he wanted Layla and the children to be taken care of. When he finished writing, he closed his eyes and she kissed him on the forehead and left him to rest.

When she walked out she showed his family what he had written.

"I have no intention of trying to take all of his money," Layla told them. "I am merely showing you what he wants for me and the children, and you can do what you see fit."

In the end, her husband's money was distributed among all of them and there was little left for Layla and the children.

Yehia had found a job in the American Embassy in Alexandria. He started out as an office assistant but slowly worked his way up to other administrative positions. He had a good command of the

English language and his supervisors liked how hard he worked and how pleasant he was.

When the embassy closed down the Alexandria office, he was offered a severance package and a visa to visit America.

Layla held his hand as Yehia cried at the funeral. "Let me recite the 'Fatha' with you here and now," she said. The recitation of the "Fatha," an opening verse in the Quran, was a tradition reserved for marriages and business deals.

"You and I are these children's parents," she told him as she pointed toward his two brothers and sister. "We will raise them together and remain together until we marry them off."

Yehia shook his head in agreement, still laden with the grief and shock, but knew that this was a promise to which he was too young to be committed. He would try his best, but Layla had just placed upon him the same burden that her husband's family had place on her husband.

She was too young to realize it at the time. She was blinded by how much trouble she was in, now that she would have to find her own place to live and keep all five of them afloat.

It wasn't long before the suitors, friends, and acquaintances of her husband started pouring in. Layla was in her late thirties, but she was very beautiful and most of them found that it would not be an awfully difficult duty to step in and "help" her by giving her a husband and a father to her children.

She refused them all and thought to herself, "If I accepted one of his friends, his family would accuse me of having it all planned while my husband was still sick." Their visits were also greatly disturbing her children, who had just lost their father and moved out of the family's house to an apartment in Alexandria.

Six-year-old Khaled was sleeping with a large knife under his pillow. When Layla found it and asked him why he had it he replied, "This is for all the men that have been coming for you. If they try to come in here again, I will shred them to pieces."

"There are no men in my life except for you and your brothers my love," she said. "The nails on your fingers are worth more to me than all of these suitors combined."

And so she became a widow who had never been with a husband on her own to begin with. She had missed out on the whole experience of father, mother, and children, and it was too late to correct it. She experienced loneliness so profound that it kept her from sleeping in her own bedroom.

She ended up selling her bedroom furniture for extra cash and sleeping on a couch in the dining room area. She bought a sewing kit and supplemented her income from work by selling clothes to friends and neighbors. It also saved her money on clothes for her four children.

Zahra was entering into her teen years and required a wardrobe befitting of her age. Layla had lost so much trust in people that she convinced Zahra that there was no need for her to have friends outside of school. She was to visit no one and no one was to visit her. Layla felt that friends brought trouble. Girlfriends always led to boyfriends. There would always be a brother, cousin, or male friend lurking around trying to get to her daughter, she believed.

She could not let that happen to Zahra. The girl didn't know what hardships the world may have in store for her. Zahra didn't seem to mind her mother's restrictions, as she regarded Layla as her best friend. They would sit together, clean the house together, and cook for the boys.

Life was simple but stable. There was a lot of love in that house. Everyone worked hard so that the whole family could stay afloat.

One night, when Layla had fallen asleep, exhausted at the sewing table, she dreamed that a large silver platter was descending from the sky and into her balcony. As it approached she realized how huge it was and wondered how it could possibly fit into her balcony, but it did.

On the silver platter was Prophet Mohammed's mosque from El Madina in Saudi Arabia, with its glorious eight minarets and spacious prayer areas. The mosque seemed to expand into the living room, covered in diamonds. It was followed by the Kaaba of Mecca, which floated in and landed in the center of her humble apartment. From this scene emerged a tall white man with eyes as wet and glistening as a scuba diver's suit. His hair was long, soft, and black, and he tossed it back as he walked toward her. In the dream, Layla was frightened and hid under the dining room table.

The man told her not to fear him, for he was an angel of God sent on behalf of Prophet Mohamed to be her guardian. He said that he would watch over her and protect her and her children. He reminded her that she had been visited before and that this had not been the first time that God had sent her a message.

The message he was referring to was another dream that Layla had had when her husband was still alive but away on one of his long trips. She had been visited by a beautiful woman who was hovering inside the minaret of a mosque that Layla had frequented as a child. Her long, blond hair floated about her and her bright blue eyes filled the mosque with light. The young beauty kept signaling to Layla to rise up and join her at the top, but Layla's feet could not leave the ground.

In fact, Layla was weighed down by her own embarrassment. She had felt that the woman and the mosque were so beautiful when compared to the dirty streets that surrounded them. She could not imagine rising up from all the ugliness around her. The more the woman told Layla to come join her, the more Layla realized the futility of her taking flight like the angelic being before her.

When she had shared the dream with her father, he told her that the woman was Mother Mary.

"How do you know that?" she asked.

"Because it is written in the Quran that Mother Mary was the most beautiful woman who ever lived, and that fits your description of her," he explained. "Have you ever seen a woman more beautiful than her?"

"No, I haven't," Layla said.

"Then that is her, my child," her father concluded. "Do you know who she visits? She visits those who have been dealt a grave injustice, as the one that she had been forced to bear when the villagers accused her of being impure when she was pregnant with our Prophet Jesus. When they questioned who his father was, she pointed to her baby that spoke out and said, 'My mother has been wronged for I have come from God as a messenger to the world.'"

Her father took Layla's hand in his and continued, "Congratulations, my child, for you will experience hardship like we all have, but you will be vindicated and your crises will turn into a great light for those around you."

It would take years for all the dreams to come together and make sense. However, in the meantime, on her desk at work, someone had left her prayer beads and a prayer booklet with the words "The Islamic *Shazliya* Tradition" printed in bold Arabic letters across its cover. She asked her colleagues who had left the booklet there, but all they knew was that a man had placed them on her desk and walked out. As she leafed through the booklet, she noticed that certain segments were highlighted for her to read.

The booklet's instructions explained that in the *Shazliya* tradition, one was chosen by a sheikh and taught the methods of the group. She was to recite the "Fatha" segment of the Quran to commemorate her intentions to follow through on this path. Certain pages held prayers that she was supposed to read in the morning, at night before she slept, and with every one of the five Islamic prayers that she was already executing. It was believed by followers of the *Shazliya* method that the Prophet himself had selected some of his closest supporters and had shared with them these methods.

Layla's parents had been in Sudan when she was born, and she had since found that she felt a sense of familiarity around people with darker complexions because of her childhood years there. In the booklet's cover was a brief history of the first chosen person to follow the specific prayers in the book. The man was very dark and very handsome, and she felt a spiritual link to him at once.

On the following page were his son and then his grandson and then his great-grandson—all followers of the same method.

Layla read the "Fatha" for all of their souls and held the booklet to her breast lovingly. This would be her solace for all the loneliness she had been feeling. The prayers would be her companions and her saviors. She felt better already.

Khaled would often look at her in amazement, sitting for hours on end on her prayer mat. Eventually, he asked, "What kind of a mother are you? Why don't I ever see you do what other women do?"

"What do you mean?" Layla said. "There isn't a thing that I don't do for you kids."

"Yes, but all I ever see you do in your spare time is read that booklet, or hold onto those beads or the Quran. If not that, then you are praying. What kind of a life do you have for yourself? Why don't you go out like other mothers? I have seen eighty-year-old women with more of a social life than you!"

"But God created us to pray to him and thank him for his gifts. This is what has kept us alive and well all these years."

"Really Mom," he answered, pointing to the apartment around them, his voice dripping with sarcasm. "Look at how good we have it. With all the time you spent on that prayer mat, we should have been millionaires by now."

She got up from her prayer rug and held him firmly but gently from both shoulders. He was already much taller than her. "When you want to compare us with other people, Khaled, look down before you look up. Look at what we could have had less, before you consider what more we could be gaining. Thank God, my son, for every day and every breath you have, or you will never be happy."

She made a point of taking him to bring food to the less fortunate and visit the sick in the hospital until he learned what the true meaning of being grateful for what God had given him meant.

The children grew bigger and stronger and were becoming successful in their own right. But Layla's pride in what she had achieved would soon be clouded by the flight of her eldest from the nest.

One morning she woke up to find him gone, his clothes packed and his bed made. He had left a note explaining that the children were doing well and he could not wait until they got married for him to have a life of his own. He used the visa the Americans had given him to go explore the possibilities of setting up a new life for himself there.

Layla cried for days as her other children consoled her and said the worst things about Yehia for abandoning them the way he did. But deep down, Layla knew that he had been too young to bear all the responsibility that she had poured upon him. He had done his share. He could not remain a father to his own siblings forever.

For years, out of fear and shame for what he had done, he did not make contact with his mother at all. She did not even know where he was or how he was doing. It upset her so much that she would tear at her skin with her fingernails and would have mysterious fevers that came and went. When Zahra took her to the doctor, he highly recommended that they find Yehia and get him in contact with his mother.

Layla had a cousin in Philadelphia but she could not find his number. So she turned to her *Shazliya* booklet and read certain prayers that were dedicated to sending messages to your loved ones. She would close her eyes and focus on her cousin's face in her head and say the prayers over and over.

After three days, the phone rang. It was a long-distance call from the United States. On the other end, she heard his voice say, "Layla, Layla what have you been doing? For three days all I could see when I closed my eyes was your face. I called all kinds of family members until I found someone who had your number. For God's sake, woman, what do you want?"

And so she explained to him her dilemma and he began his search for Yehia. He called the embassy and followed some leads from there, only to find that Yehia only lived forty-five minutes away from him.

Arrangements were made and Layla flew to the States to meet Yehia. In the airport she screamed *"Allah Akbar, Allah Akbar"* when she saw his face, and he fell to his knees crying and apologizing and kissing her hands." From then on our Yehia traveled back and forth to see his mom and sent her money to do the same. He married a woman from Egypt and took her with him and became a father to his own children.

Ahmed, her middle son, got a job in Nigeria first through his father's contacts, and then that job gave him an opportunity in America as well. Eventually the two brothers built a life in Philadelphia and when Khaled turned seventeen and finished high school, they sent for him to earn a two-year diploma in computer science.

Zahra got married and moved to Cairo with her husband. She was starting her own family and Layla's nest appeared to have become officially empty. It made her sad in a sense, but it also gave her a sense of completion of what she had tried so hard to accomplish on her own. As the years progressed it became apparent that Zahra was not happy in her union. Layla prayed that the couple would navigate their way out of it, as Zahra already had one child and was pregnant with her second.

Khaled completed his two-year program and was excited about finding his own way in America, but he had reached the end of his student visa and had to apply for a work visa. He returned to Alexandria and began the paperwork that included finishing or applying to be exempt from the obligatory Egyptian military service.

He asked around, and found that he had a good chance of getting out of it because his mother was a widow and both of his brothers were abroad making him her sole caretaker. That was a loophole he wanted to utilize to get out of the two-year commitment to the army. The sad thing was that he would use that specific excuse to leave Layla in Egypt, with no caretakers, and join his brothers.

When Layla's brother, an army lieutenant himself, heard of Khaled' plans, he became upset. He felt that yet another boy was abandoning his duties to the country and to his sister to flee and live abroad. He decided to take it upon himself to stop that from happening.

He told his sister that he would drive Khaled to the army base where they screened the drafted individuals to determine who would serve and who was exempt. Layla was happy and thought that for sure her brother would pull some strings to get Khaled out of the obligatory nightmare. On the way over, he told Khaled not to mention that he had any relatives in the States. He led him to believe that it would actually work against his plans and would make the army enlist him right off the bat.

So Khaled followed his instructions, though they went against his instincts, and in the end it turned out his instincts had been right. The army enlisted Khaled for two years and he was to be put in jail if he didn't comply. He came home angry and started telling his uncle that he hated him and that he had no right to interfere in his life.

His uncle said, "I wanted you to learn to be a man and to face up to your responsibilities toward your country and your mother!"

"That is just none of your business," Layla said, as she stood in front of him and looked at him with anger and reproach. "I sent you with him to help him, it is *my* duty to raise him, and you had no right to interfere with that."

Khaled and his uncle grew apart; another father figure uncer-emoniously stepped out of their lives.

Khaled's army base was in Cairo, so he would go to his sister's apartment when he had a short break and head out to Alexandria to his mother's apartment when he had a longer one. During this time, Layla grew lonely and decided to spend some time with Yehia in America as well.

She spent eight months in Philadelphia and communicated with Zahra and Khaled daily via the Internet. It was a calm and uneventful period of her life, in which the height of her worries was whether or not Khaled was being diligent about drinking the raw-eggs-with-milk concoction that she had insisted he drink every morning to ensure he got his adequate protein and nutrition for the day.

Generally, her visits to America were mini-vacations, where she enjoyed living in a beautiful environment and seeing her four grandchildren on a regular basis. Every time she grew tired of being alone, one of her children would send her a ticket.

Khaled made the best of his time in the army and soon he became very popular for his generosity. He had just returned from America and had a lot of packaged foods and clothes that he had brought with him in addition to what his brothers kept sending. He shared these coveted goods with his friends and some of the army officers.

One day, an officer complimented Khaled on his phone that he had bought from the States, so he gave it to him. Another time Khaled overheard another officer announcing that his daughter was getting married. He came home and told Layla, who was pre-paring to visit Saudi Arabia and do the *Omra* Islamic pilgrimage.

Layla bought the officer's daughter perfumes and lingerie, a prayer rug, and prayer beads. The officer was thrilled.

From that point onward they would let Layla send in as many things as she wanted to her son at the base. When she sent in food, she made sure to send in large trays that held enough food for everyone. The soldiers at the gate called her the "American Supermarket" because of all the gifts she gave them from there.

The Egyptian appetite for the American goods during Khaled's time in the army inspired him to want to go into the import business, and he approached his mother about making the Alexandria apartment his office and beginning a small business out of their home.

Layla was thrilled that he had decided to stay in Egypt and start his own business. She made sure he had everything he needed to make his dream come true. She transformed one of the apartment's rooms into an office and they set up an Internet DSL line, a fax machine, and all the stationary he needed. His brother Ahmed served as his supplier in the States, and they started out with computer-related products and spare parts.

Khaled's friends began to join him and they went to computer suppliers to identify areas of need and relayed the information to him, and he sent out to get what he needed through his brother. He researched and read more online to supplement his knowledge of computers that he had acquired in America. Little by little, his small business became a success, and he found himself earning enough money to help his mother and be completely self-sufficient.

He used his spare time to teach his neighbors and friends all about computers and how they facilitated life and opened one up to the educational experience of the Internet.

It was during this time, years after Layla had first received the *Shazliya* booklet and had been following its methods religiously, that she got summoned to visit Sheikh Saleh of the Zakazik governorate on the outskirts of Cairo.

Sheikh Saleh was a famous sheikh of the *Shazliya* method, and Layla had heard of him but had never met him. You did not elect to go to such a high profile sheikh. He had to send for you.

It happened one day when Layla was visiting with Zahra, who was having trouble with her husband and had recently separated from him. Layla received a phone call from an acquaintance of Sheikh Saleh. The voice on the phone said that Prophet Mohamed (Peace be Upon Him) had visited him in his sleep and told him to send for Layla.

Layla was thrilled. She had been hoping for someone to take her deeper than what the thin booklet offered. She asked the voice on the phone when she could come to see Sheikh Saleh, but he said, "There are obstacles in your way now, but it will be time soon. When it is time, we will call you."

Layla intensified her prayers until she felt that the booklet may fall apart. On one particularly hot night after Layla had fallen asleep with the booklet in her arms, she had a dream that felt so real that she wasn't sure if she was awake or asleep.

The ceilings and windows were pouring out water like waterfalls and Layla heard a voice order her to clean her house. She got large rags and mopped the apartment as the water poured down. The more the water flowed, the harder she cleaned until she felt her back would break.

When she woke up she was exhausted. Her back ached and her muscles were sore, but she was still in Zahra's apartment and it all had been a dream.

Zahra opened the bedroom door slowly and said, "Are you awake, Mama? The man from Sheikh Saleh is on the phone!"

When Layla picked up the phone, he said, "You have removed all the obstacles last night. How are you feeling?"

"I am exhausted! I spent the whole night cleaning!" Layla said, surprised.

"That is your job, you see," the voice said, "You will clean up a lot of the black elements that surround us. You will learn more as you know more."

The man instructed them to go to Obour Street, where he would be waiting to guide her to where el Sheikh Saleh was. He did not give a description of what he was wearing or what he looked like, and the street was full of men. Suddenly one particular man caught Layla's eye and she felt that she recognized this man without having ever met him before.

She told Zahra to stop by him, and he smiled. As Zahra opened her car window to speak to him, he said, "Your mom has the spirit within her and she just proved it."

Layla frequented El Sheikh Saleh regularly after that, and he helped her with her everyday problems. He taught her how to participate in "healing" sessions and showed her how to loosen negative energy from afflicted people who came to the sheikh and his group seeking help.

When Zahra's husband refused to grant her a divorce, Sheikh Saleh got her one. When Layla developed a hernia near her old C-section wound, Sheikh Saleh helped it close up when doctors had failed. They went to the sheikh for almost everything.

The sheikh then asked to see Khaled, but he would not go. He did not like the *hadras* that his mother and sister had started to frequent. In the *hadras*, they said the *zikr*, which is similar to a meditation mantra but is essentially the ninety-nine names of God in the Quran. Participants recited the names and swayed to the beat of drums and reportedly experienced a higher state of closeness to God.

The whole practice made Khaled uncomfortable, and there was no way Layla could convince him that these practices supplemented the five daily prayers that all Muslims agreed upon.

The sheikh instructed Layla to feed him from the food that they prepared in the *hadras*. Every *hadra* was held in a group member's home, and they helped whoever was the host prepare a big meal to be served after the *zikr*. Layla brought leftovers home every night and Khaled ate from the food not knowing its source.

One day, Layla asked Khaled if he wanted to come and he obliged much to his own surprise. He went with her cautiously and kept his guard up initially, but he found that he enjoyed the experience and it did not feel as strange as he had anticipated. Every time, he closed his eyes and said God's name over and over, he actually felt better. Any worries he had about work, his family, or the state of the country—which had begun to worry him lately—subsided with the *zikr*.

Layla felt that the house had been filled with light. However kind and giving Khaled already was, he became even kinder and more involved in making those around him happier. Even when he knew that someone was trying to take advantage of him and was only befriending him for selfish reasons, he would bring that person even closer. He would explain to his mother, "Let them show me their true colors so I have good reasons to cut them out of my life."

In the evening and sometimes late at night, neighbors and friends knew that if they wanted Khaled, they would find him seated at his computer on the balcony, which was his favorite spot. A friend passing by the balcony in the street below would call up to him and say, "Pray for me, Khaled, I am going to the military base tomorrow to see if I can get an exemption!"

To which Khaled would reply, "I will pray for you and, *insha Allah*, they won't take you!"

The next day the friend would come by with a couple of sodas and some sweets and say, "You were right, pal, they didn't take me! Your face brought me good fortune!"

Late one night a neighbor's twelve-year-old son started talking to Khaled from his nearby balcony. The boy's parents thought he was sleeping. He asked Khaled to teach him how to use a computer, but Khaled said, "Go to sleep and when you wake up, study hard and get good grades. If you do I will spend the entire summer tutoring you."

It was from this very same balcony that Khaled had overheard the corrupt officer in the coffee shop across the street brag about how he had distributed drugs confiscated in a police raid. When he went down and into the café to inch closer and hear more details. An acquaintance who he sat with at times told him that the police officer had the whole thing videotaped and saved to his cell phone.

Khaled hacked into the phone via the Bluetooth from his own cell phone and was able to obtain a copy of it. When he showed the video to Layla and Zahra after he had posted it to YouTube, he laughed lightheartedly.

Layla warned him. "Son, this is dangerous, take it down at once. You are not in the same league with these people!"

But Khaled laughed and said that they wouldn't be able to find out who posted it. He said it was important to expose police corruption; in fact, it was a religious duty. The cops were seizing the drugs and redistributing them for sale and then arresting those who bought it. The drugs were their capital and it kept coming back to them and making them more money. They did not care whether or not the Egyptian people battled addictions and drug-related crime. They only cared about their wallets.

The video was online for close to a year and nothing happened to Khaled. Everyone believed that he had gotten away with it. In fact, Ahmed had sent his mother a ticket to visit him, and she headed out to Philadelphia to spend a few months there. Ahmed's wife was visiting family in Cairo and he wanted his mother to keep him company.

A short twenty days into her visit, Layla began to experience panic attacks and feelings of desperation. She told Ahmed that she felt like she was suffocating and had to return to Egypt at once.

"But you have been here less than a month, Mom. I thought you promised to stay with me much longer. My wife isn't coming back for a couple of months still. She is spending the summer with her family."

Layla held her ground and insisted that she must return at once and she did.

Khaled was glad to have her home but sensed that she was going through some kind of turmoil. He had always been so intuitive when it came to how Layla felt. If she ever stood in the balcony sad and brooding, he would call out to her from his room and say, "Hey Mom, how far out have you gone in your head this time?"

He knew she was worrying about him and Zahra, or she was missing her husband or Ahmed and Yehia in the States...

"Don't go there, Mother, please!" he would say lovingly. "You know how much I love you!"

This time was no different. When he saw her face, he helped her into bed and got her a cup of tea. She had been in the room for about a half hour when he knocked on the door and burst in.

"Mom! You won't believe who just came! My brother Ahmed is here from the States!"

Layla jumped out of bed and ran to the living room. It was true! Ahmed, whom she had just left in America a few days ago, was standing before them.

"What happened, Ahmed? What made you come here and leave your work?" she asked, alarmed. She knew he oversaw the operation of several taxi cabs and was in the process of working on a house he was going to flip. His visit couldn't be good for his work.

"I left everything to Yehia, Mama. It is strange. I had the same feelings you were having, and had to leave and come here."

Layla welcomed him home and thanked God that she had the rare opportunity of having him so near. He and Khaled hadn't seen each other since Khaled served his military duty a few years before. As she fell asleep, she could hear them talking and laughing on the balcony. Ahmed was like a father to Khaled. He had done everything for him when Layla and Yehia had work. It was such a blessing to hear them enjoying each other.

$$\sim \quad \sim$$

That night when Layla slept, she dreamed that her bedroom lit up with a dim yellow light and she heard a voice fill the room.

The voice said, "I am Ahmed El Shafei, and I came to deliver a message to you. Something is going to happen and it will be of good fortune for Khaled, for your family, and for everyone, though you may not perceive it to be so."

Every Muslim knows that Sheikh Ahmed El Shafei has been dead for years upon years now. So Layla knew that this vision was indeed a message from a reputable spirit.

"I want you to listen to me, because I will not reveal myself to you lest I scare you. This thing that will happen to Khaled in the upcoming days will change the life you have grown accustomed to. His friends will no longer come around and his cats will no longer live in this apartment," the voice said.

"Is he going to America again?" Layla asked.

"Again," he said, "you are not paying attention, Layla. Something is going to happen and it will be of good fortune for Khaled, for your family, and for everyone, though you may not perceive it to be so."

The room became very bright and she found herself sitting next to Khaled, who was laid out on the ground naked, surrounded by a white light. He had no facial or body hair and he had no genitals. He lay there clean and pure and Layla found herself patting his forehead and his hair gingerly.

In the morning Layla took Khaled and went downstairs to consult Karim, a sheikh who had just moved into their building the previous week. He had visited with Khaled a lot, and the two developed a friendship rather quickly. The sheikh would often burst into tears for no reason and when Layla and Khaled tried to understand why, he would say that he didn't know why.

As Layla told him about her dream, the sheikh's eyes welled up. "I am afraid the dream means that Khaled will die soon," he said.

Khaled laughed nervously. "How could you say that to our faces? What is wrong with you, man?"

But sheikh Karim did not smile. He simply stepped away and said, "I am sorry but all the signs are there. The lack of body hair and the missing genitals...the fact that you were naked...those are all signs of death. God has his ways of preparing those who are close to him, to soften the blow." The sheikh then sat down in a corner and started crying.

Khaled took Layla aside and said, "You know, Mama, I think Karim is not very emotionally stable. You know what I am going to do? I am going to take him out fishing and maybe even take him for a quick swim."

Layla dismissed Sheikh Karim and the dream because it was too scary to consider. She tried to go about her day as normally as possible while the two headed out to the pier.

As they sat there fishing, a young beggar, who couldn't have been older than twelve, approached them asking for spare cash.

He was dirty and his clothes were worn and torn. Khaled playfully pulled him into the water and dove in with him. He cleaned him off with the salt water and wrapped him in a towel he had with him. He left him with Karim and ran home to his mother.

Once he was upstairs he elicited her help to find clothes in both of their wardrobes that could serve as a better outfit for the boy. He also heated up a plate of food for him and took everything back out to where Karim and the beggar were. Khaled dressed and fed the boy and gave him a pair of sports shoes that belonged to his mother but did not look particularly feminine. Khaled knew that his own shoes would have been too big.

He looked at the boy and his awkward outfit and said to him, "Come with me and I will show you where I live. You can come see me tomorrow and I will have a new outfit and a pair of shoes in your size."

The boy gave a wide grin that made Khaled's day.

As the evening turned into night, Khaled went into his mother's bedroom to wake her up from her long nap. "Mom," he said enthusiastically, "Auntie Amina called and said that she has just arrived in her Alexandria apartment all the way from Cairo. She wants you to go visit with her a little bit."

Layla looked at her watch; it was 9:45 p.m. "But Khaled," she said, "It is late. I never go out this late. This is when I rest."

"Oh Mom, live a little. It's summertime. Take one of those painkillers that do wonders for you and go have fun. I want you to—in fact, I am ordering you to."

Layla got up and got dressed and walked to her friend's nearby apartment. In the summer, Alexandria's streets stayed alive and crowded until the wee hours of dawn, so she felt safe and the walk was invigorating. She was happy Khaled had suggested it.

Khaled set himself up at his spot on the balcony and grabbed his computer and began to chat with some friends online and review some work-related items.

The acquaintance from the café across the street, who had been sitting with Khaled when he hacked into the officer's phone, called out to him from the street.

"Ya Khaled!" he yelled, "They need you in the cyber café down the street to fix something!"

"It's late, man." Khaled replied, "I am too tired now. How about in the morning?"

"It will only take a minute of your time!" the man said pleadingly.

Khaled felt obliged to help. He didn't like turning people down. In the café across the street, Khaled could see the officer whose phone he had hacked sitting with a group of other officers but thought nothing of it.

As he passed by on his way to the cyber café, he saw the man who had called him into the street signal to the officer. Apparently, he identified him to the police officer, who had previously not known what Khaled looked like.

The group of men who were with the officer sprang up and grabbed Khaled from his arms and pushed him into the cyber café. They grabbed him from his hair and smashed his face into the wall and the owner of the cyber café came rushing out.

"What are you doing?" he yelled at them.

"This is police business," the officer yelled back. "You stay out of it."

"Please," the owner said, "not here, I have customers…"

The police took Khaled into the entrance of the building adjacent to the cyber café. They pinned his arms behind his back and brought him down to his knees.

"We are here to kill you," the officer said to him as he grabbed his head and smashed it into the marble stairs. The doorman's wife screamed as blood gushed out from Khaled's nose and mouth. He cried out and asked why they were doing this to him, but he could barely get the words out before they lifted him from his head again and smashed his face into a marble counter. He could hear his bones crushing and felt his teeth fall into his mouth. He tried to cry out but his face was bashed into stone and marble until he couldn't breathe from the blood in his mouth.

He could make out feet surrounding him and could hear people screaming, but the blows continued. He tried to say that they were killing him, but by now he realized that that really was their intention.

This is what neighbors and witnesses told Layla about what happened. I would like to believe that at one point early on into the beating, he blacked out and could not feel the pain. No one can tell us about that but Khaled, and he died at the hands of police that day.

As Layla described how people stood by, shackled by fear, and watched the police beat the life out of a defenseless young man, I felt feverish and was going to throw up, but I did not interrupt her.

I had promised Zahra that we would not go into this segment of the story, but once we got near it Layla ploughed right through it as if she couldn't help herself. She told me how she had returned from her friend's house and found people in the street running toward her. They were all talking to her at once and from the bits and pieces of what people were telling her, she understood that Khaled was dead. Children in the street were crying and the wife of the doorman of the building where Khaled was killed was still mopping up his blood.

She told Layla that after he lay lifeless on the ground, a police officer smashed his skull with the butt of a gun to make sure he was dead. A child cried out to the officer, "He is already dead, just leave him!"

The officer looked the child in the face and said, "Would you like to join him?"

They then dragged him by his feet and threw him in the back of a police holding truck and threw his shoes onto his face.

Fifteen minutes later they threw him back in the spot where he had died and told the people on the street to call an ambulance if they wanted. Layla later found out that the police had inserted a drug capsule into his throat to "prove" that he was a drug dealer who died trying to swallow evidence, and they must have wanted him to go to the hospital to have that documented. But the ambulance refused to pick him up because he was already dead, so the police were forced to return and take his body to the station.

Layla called Ahmed and was crying and screaming when he came. Together they sobbed and cried out like someone had set them on fire. Zahra had been informed and she was on her way from Cairo to Alexandria.

When Layla went to the police station with Ahmed, they were met by a stone-faced officer who told them that Khaled was a drug dealer who had resisted arrest and choked on his own drugs. As the officer spoke, Layla was enveloped by a blanket of numbness. She realized that she was in the presence of pure evil and that that evil had claimed her son.

The officer asked her where her family's burial site was, as the police wished to bury him. She ignored his request and asked to see her son but the officer refused and told her that she needed to tell them where to bury him.

She said that he was no longer her responsibility. "As his mother, now that his soul has left his body my role to care for him and protect him has ended. You need to call his father's family for the information you are seeking." She said this because she wanted to buy time and she did not want them to bury him before she had the chance to see him. She looked to Ahmed, who was shocked by her answer, and asked him to take her home.

When they arrived at the house, they cried and cried until they felt that they had no more tears left. At 3:00 a.m., Layla finally said, "I have got to see him myself. I have got to see my boy and what they did to him. I cannot let him sleep there without holding him in my arms after what happened to him tonight."

Ahmed shared his mother's feelings entirely, and he accompanied her to the station that now had only one guard on duty. Layla grabbed the guard by the soldiers, looked him in the eyes, and said, "I have to see my boy, I have to see if he is OK. I know he is with God now, but I need to know that he is OK."

The guard's resolve seemed to melt beneath her fingers. "OK, but don't tell anyone that I did this," he said.

He placed his key in a large lock on a menacing black door. Why would a police station have a morgue to begin with? The room was big and bare and in the middle there was an iron table and Khaled was laid out on it.

They had changed his clothes and he was wearing a white T-shirt and black shorts that his mother did not recognize. There was a water hose next to him on the ground and he was soaking wet. They had tried to wash away all traces of blood from him, but a pool of red was still seeping out from the back of his head.

His face was frozen in an expression of intense and eternal pain. His teeth were broken and his lips were torn at the lower jaw. His eyes were open and full of fear. The last thing he had seen in this world was evil and ugliness.

Layla grabbed his hand and began kissing it and kept repeating, *"Ismallah Aleek ya habibi, Ismallah aleek"* ("In God's care, my poor darling"). Ahmed raised his shaking hand out and with his cell phone took a close-up picture of Khaled's face.

Layla left her son there in that cold room. She remembered how she had been wondering if he had eaten his salad when she was at her friend's house. It seemed like a thousand years ago. There would be no need for vegetables for him now, no need for the eggs and milk in the morning. He would never smile at her in the morning or kiss her goodnight.

Her son Ahmed realized that he had come back so he could be present at this moment.

Layla remembered her dream and how peaceful Khaled had looked laid out naked before her and she tried to hold onto it, but his image on the cold table, his contorted, anguished look, blinded her.

By the morning the police had realized that Khaled's father's family had come and their cousins were active politicians in northern Egypt. They would have to hand over the body, but they guarded it all the way to the burial site and sneered at Layla as she cried when they lowered him in.

Police heckled his friends who had come to help. "Did you bury him, oh noble friends? We can put you down there with him if you like."

They would not allow her take him to the mosque to pray for his soul nor have any other kind of funeral proceedings. He was buried under guard and in haste, and Layla returned home without him forever.

As she entered her home, she found that Sheikh Saleh and his group were already there waiting for her. They held a massive *hadra* for his soul and participants prayed, read the Quran, and then came together for a *zikr*. As the chants and *zikr* grew louder, a sheikh cried out, "I can see Khaled!"

The sheikh's eyes were closed and he continued, "He is surrounded by angels and he is riding on a big white horse!"

"*Allah Akbar*," the others said.

"He is dressed in white and he is smiling. The *Hassan* and the *Hussein*"— the grandchildren of Prophet Mohamed—"are with him and they are ascending into the sky."

Layla closed her eyes as tears streamed down her face. She focused on the image of Khaled on his horse and blocked out the rest of the ugly world.

Khaled would not spend the summer with the neighbor's child and teach him how to use the computer, and when that young beggar came around in the morning, he would realize that the angel he had spent the morning with yesterday was already in heaven today.

MUSTAFA EL NAGGAR AND A
REVOLUTION REVISITED

14.

had spent close to six hours in Zahra and Layla's apartment, and during that time my fever climbed to 101 degrees. I was more than two hours away from my mother-in-law's house and there was no way for me to get home other than to drive my own car back. Layla gave me some medicine to reduce my fever and prayed for me as we said our goodbyes.

Woozy and feverish with Khaled's horrible story in my head, I took wrong turn after wrong turn and got hopelessly lost in Egypt's back streets and shantytowns. I stopped and asked for directions several times, and my family tried to guide me over the phone.

In the end, it took me four hours to get to my in-laws' house, and they were all worried sick about me. I went into their house, barely talked to the children, and collapsed into bed. I never found

out what had been wrong with me but I was throwing up and feverish for three days and couldn't leave my mother-in-law's house.

My mother had a theory that the ugliness of the whole story
I collected in the interview had made me sick. After listening to
Layla's tales of the supernatural dimension of Egyptian culture, I
didn't know what to believe anymore.

As I later reviewed my recorded interview with Layla Marzouk
and took notes, I marveled at how she had risen afterward. She
took her son's story to the newspapers and refused to be quiet
about it or lay low, forcing authorities to hold a trial. The trial was
a sham and the police officer responsible would boldly raise his
middle finger at Layla in the middle of proceedings in the courtroom. The judge ruled Khaled's death a suicide, and the police
accused Khaled of being a rapist and a drug dealer who resisted
arrest. They even claimed that he had deserted his army duties
and had been on the run when the police attempted to "detain"
him, despite Layla having the paperwork that proved otherwise.
They deemed her documents a forgery and rewrote her son's life
in the papers.

Activists picked up on the story and began to show up at Layla's
house. They recreated a funeral and prayers for Khaled. Dr. El
Baradei and his family attended the commemoration services
without Layla knowing who they were.

A few days later they were formally introduced and Layla joined
Dr. El Baradei's campaign.

Khaled's twenty-ninth birthday would have been on January 27,
and the revolutionaries held a celebration for him in the square.
Layla stood on stage and talked to the youth, "What are you all
waiting for? How long can we be slapped around and not fight
back! Go get what is rightfully ours! Go avenge every mother who
has had her son killed and tortured! Go fight for our dignity!"

The crowds would be energized by her presence and cheer and
chant, and so she remained in the protests every single day until
Mubarak left.

A few weeks after the interview, I began to feel like I had all
the pieces of my book in place. I had assembled the general idea
of how protesters ended up in Tahrir, their various experiences

there, and the tragedies that occurred behind the scenes. I had experienced how it affected us at home and I had seen how the media was presenting as well as influencing it.

I wondered if there was much more to add to this picture. I still had Mustafa El Naggar's interview left and it kept getting postponed. Every time I was all set to go, I would receive a mysterious message from him canceling and saying he would reschedule.

Months past and Basil went back to California and I was due to catch up with him in less than a month.

I had tried to do some research on El Naggar online and found a few videos. He was often at Wael Ghonim's side in television interviews, but the focus never fell entirely on him. He did not attempt to pull the attention toward him, either. He seemed content to stay out of the spotlight.

At least two times I noticed in interviews that the interviewers referred to him as one of the chief instigators of the revolution, and I wondered why they said that since his name was not as well known as other key figures. Another curious thing I noticed was that in the very first infamous interview that Wael held when he was first released from custody, he said that Mustafa El Naggar and activists like him were the true heroes of the revolution and not himself.

Moez Masoud was the one who had insisted that I had to talk to El Naggar. He said he was integral to any book about the revolution and he had urged me to be patient about the scheduling issues.

Finally, about a week from my travel booking, El Naggar sent me a message saying that if I had the time to come into his office right away, at the headquarters of the new Justice Party, which he cofounded with notable activists in the field such as economist Mona El Baradei (Dr. El Baradei's sister), Egyptian poet and activist Abdul Rahman Yusuf (son of Islamic theologian Yusuf al-Qaradawi), and many more, he could give me the interview.

I called my mother-in-law and threw my kids in the car and raced over.

His office was located downtown right next to Tahrir, and the square had become the busiest and most chaotic place in town. It was June, four months after Mubarak's abdication, and protests were still taking place on Fridays as protesters grew impatient with the way that the Supreme Council of Armed Forces was handling the country's affairs.

Bloggers were still being arrested and key figures from Mubarak's regime remained in power in highly influential political posts. Egyptians developed an acute case of OCD (obsessive-compulsive demonstrating). It was the only mechanism that they had witnessed to be effective and to have brought about change, so they used it whenever they felt the need to make a statement. Minorities protested against the majority, women protested against men, students protested against university leaders, workers protested against their bosses…the list was endless.

Protesters and protests began to be viewed as a nuisance by a large segment of the Egyptian population and they, along with the scarce police presence, were generally blamed for the country's economic peril. People longed to see Tahrir Square evacuated of all the different people congregating for different and often unrelated causes and blocking the arteries of Cairo's downtown.

My father sent his driver by taxi to meet me there to take my car since there was no parking in the vicinity. The driver said I could call him whenever I was done and he would bring the car around, and I went into the heavily guarded building that held the Justice Party's main office.

It was rare to see police officers at this time in Egypt, but at this particular building's entrance there were a bunch. They seemed to stare at me as I waited for the elevator. When I looked back, one of them smiled a bit menacingly, and it made me very uncomfortable.

The building was nice, though the Justice Party's office was simple and unassuming. Mustafa greeted me personally at the door and showed me to his office. I noticed that he had a slight limp and looked much older than his thirty-one years. He also acted much older and walked slightly hunched over with the general demeanor of one who was carrying around a heavy burden.

I could already tell that he would be different than everyone else I had interviewed. He had the air of one who kept optimism in a bottle in his pocket, to brandish it in the face of those who may claim that he lost hope. He would access the bottle when it was appropriate, and made sure that he always had a supply. But for the most part, he looked at the world through skeptical eyes that gave me the impression that he half-expected everything to fall apart at any minute.

His story would prove that I had been indeed quite far from having a comprehensive account of the revolution and that, even after this interview, it would be naïve to claim that I could ever achieve that. Every story added a new element.

It was important to strive for one though. There was so much to this colossal Egyptian achievement that needed to be analyzed and studied. The facts would help rebuild Egypt and the truth—cliché as this may sound, could indeed set us free.

ᖃᖗ ᖃᖗ

Mustafa El Naggar is a dentist.

One cannot think of a stranger day job for such an avid activist. He is divorced and lives alone in an apartment in Cairo (which is unusual in Egyptian culture). His parents and siblings live in Alexandria, where they are all originally from.

After he finished his master's degree in dentistry, he became so interested in mass communication and how it affected societies that he studied it and earned another bachelor's degree in it from Cairo University.

He came from a family of heavily involved activists and politicians. Half of his family were members of the Muslim Brotherhood and the other half were leftist Marxists, a highly unusual combination to say the least.

His grandfather from his mother's side went to jail for his activism during President Abd El Nasser's rule, and remained behind bars for ten years because of his involvement with the Muslim Brotherhood. His father's brother went to jail for six years for being a communist. It was in this environment that Mustafa was born and raised and came to the realization that the situation in Egypt was not one he could be proud of or accept.

He spent his teenage years as a member of the Brotherhood, but as he grew into his twenties he began to feel that its mission did not represent the man he was growing up to be. He went through a period of political puberty in which he experienced a wide array of emotions and affiliations, and he emerged a fully grown and committed liberal with moderate religious views.

He had tested his willingness to die for a cause he considered just—and fearlessness in fighting oppressive powers—in his college days when he participated in the Palestinian *intifada* against Israel in addition to his joining of efforts to oppose the Iraqi invasion by troops from America, the United Kingdom, Australia, and Poland.

Egyptian authorities had already arrested him three times before the revolution. His first arrest was for trying to uncover corruption in the 2000 People's Assembly elections, the second was in 2003 for his participation in opposing the Iraqi War, and the third was in 2010 in the Egyptian governorate of Nag Hamadi, where he had traveled with a group from El Baradei's campaign who were there to pay their condolences and join Christian Egyptian families in their mourning for the victims of a sectarian conflict that had resulted in a massacre.

His fourth arrest would be on the 25th of January, 2011, for his role as a key organizer of the Egyptian revolution.

His take on the revolution was different than most. He did not believe it was a "sudden" revolution that appeared out of thin air or belonged to Egyptian youth, and it most definitely was *not* an "Internet" revolution.

It was not "sudden" because countless citizens had been working on it for over fifteen years and had in many ways paved the road for those who were assisted by fate to bring it to fruition.

It did not belong to the youth, although they were the spark. The people who carried the revolution through and molded it into what it became in the end were the entire Egyptian population across all age groups, economic statuses, and education levels. The Egyptian people, as a unified entity, were the heroes at the end of the day, and should be considered the revolution's true owners.

Most importantly, Mustafa believed this was not a Facebook or Internet revolution. The Egyptians had been utilizing the Internet with all its tools since 2004 to organize protests and coordinate activist activities, and it had never yielded the results that it produced on the twenty-fifth.

The early bloggers of Kefaya, Sixth of April, and El Baradei's coalition for change all tried to organize mass protests using the Internet and it had never worked before. Calling it an Internet revolution worked for the media and gave it the mythical quality it needed to keep people hooked on it, but Mustafa does not believe in romanticizing real life, as it seldom functioned in a "romantic" dimension.

There had been a need very early in the game to come up with a classification for this revolution so that people could come to terms with the miracle they had witnessed. Therefore, this whole affair between the spirit of activism and the breakthrough abilities of technology was a vicious rumor that people wanted to believe. Mustafa strongly felt that this was a *people's revolution*. Egyptian youth lit its spark and the Egyptian army secured its completion, it was as simple as that. Had these two variables been different, things could have gone in a very different direction.

The simplest proof is that on January 7, 2011, the same Facebook page, "We Are All Khaled Saeed," that called people out for the protests of the twenty-fifth had called for a mass protest against the Alexandria church bombing of New Year's Eve, and it failed to bring out more than fifteen hundred Egyptians across the entire country.

The main catalyst that mobilized and emboldened people to go through with the January 25, 2011, protests, was the televised triumph of the Tunisian Revolution.

In fact, in 2010, Mustafa had almost lost all hope that he would witness the country achieving change in his lifetime for several compelling reasons, which he had experienced firsthand through his own activist connections and efforts. Egyptian movements and opposition parties were weak and divided. In that sense, they worked against the country instead of working against the regime.

There was a negative, competitive spirit among the parties, and their leaders and every group claimed that the others were traitors.

The first figure to be successful in unifying the opposition behind a common agenda was El Baradei in February 2010. Prior to El Baradei, Mustafa had refused to buy into the notion that a single "hero" could save Egypt and lead all Egyptians to a victory. He had been turned off by the hordes of people who went to wait for him in the airport and had dubbed him "Egypt's next democratically elected president." Mustafa believed that El Baradei had been cleverly packaged to appear in that light by a Facebook group created by activist and poet Abd El Rahman Yousef. That Facebook group had a quarter-million members and had created a culture of its own that believed that this one person was a "savior."

However, Mustafa realized that what he had in common with these people was that they were all desperate for hope. In fact, in 2010, he had felt that his whole life in politics had amounted to little achievement. He had secluded himself from most of life's enjoyments at such a young age for no real gain as his political efforts had seemingly resulted in nothing productive for Egypt, which was the love of his life. He had wanted to believe in something, anything, to keep a glimmer of hope alive.

He began to read about El Baradei and fate would place El Baradei's nephew, Ahmed Shokry, a young dentist- turned-activist as well, in his path. The two bonded immediately, and Shokry introduced Mustafa to his famous uncle.

Dr. El Baradei had been actively becoming acquainted with Egyptian youth and celebrities in an effort to engage with Egyptians after a lifetime led abroad. El Baradei needed active youth to be part of his team and build his campaign, and he offered Mustafa a position as his assistant. Mustafa fit El Baradei's profile for those he wanted in his circle because he combined the criteria of being a researcher as well as an activist, which mimicked El Baradei's own youth.

Mustafa had landed a part-time research position in the American University's political science department as part of a scholarship he was awarded to study social movements and their political impact on societies.

He realized that as a leader, El Baradei lacked the charisma of leaders of the past such as Gamal Abd El Nasser, but he was proving to be an honest, educated, and loyal contender who loved Egypt as much as any member of his generation active in Egypt's political scene. Furthermore, he came to the table with a curriculum and a plan to tackle the current regime's hold on Egyptian territory.

Mustafa had long believed that struggling for the sake of "struggle" would not win back Egypt. Activists had been perishing for the cause for over a decade and attained nothing. He was convinced that they needed a scientific equation to get them to the level of public support they needed to build a mass, capable of bringing about true change, and he believed that El Baradei could teach it to them.

Along with Abd El Rahman Yousef, Mustafa became a leading organizer and coordinator for El Baradei's campaign. Another prominent member of the El Baradei team was young activist and Google executive Wael Ghonim, who was responsible for campaign branding, marketing, and Internet presence.

Wael created the very first official El Baradei campaign website and it quickly attracted over a quarter-million Egyptians. For close to a year, Wael was the main administrator of the page and had become quite successful at his job. However, he was becoming dissatisfied with El Baradei's campaign and his frustrations were making him restless.

Wael felt that the campaign could be organized more efficiently, and the fact that El Baradei himself was not available in Egypt most of the time made him the campaign's worst enemy. El Baradei would come to Egypt for two weeks and then be gone for two months. His other jobs and responsibilities rendered him to a great extent inaccessible. Mustafa agreed with Wael on this point, and failed to come up with the adequate arguments to convince him to remain on the team.

Wael broke away from his formal role in the campaign but maintained contact with Mustafa as a marketing consultant. Together they supported El Baradei's efforts to create a qualitative and quantitative critical mass capable of bringing about real change. The qualitative critical mass would need to consist of the educated, the specialists, the celebrities, and the businessmen who possessed the general characteristics that qualified them to inspire and lead the quantitative masses. To achieve this delicate equation that would lead Egypt to a boiling point in its near future, a lot of work needed to be done.

Mustafa and El Baradei's group studied the Latin American experience and the unfolding of events in Eastern Europe and Serbia, and they found them highly inspiring. The idea of civil disobedience and revolutionizing the streets through peaceful, nonviolent measures became their goal.

They systemized their efforts to cover all of Cairo's governorates and familiarized simple people with the mechanisms of nonviolent resistance and civic mobilization strategies. Eventually, they succeeded in having awareness teams in twenty Egyptian governorates across the country. The teams were structurally sound and taken together, extended the number of Egyptians working on El Baradei's pro-change awareness campaigns to fifteen thousand Egyptians.

The governorates with higher numbers of participants, such as El Mahala, El Suez, and El Gharbia, would later play larger roles in the revolution, and their youth would reportedly spark participation in marches in the streets.

Mustafa's life was completely consumed by this, and though it may have cost him his marriage, his parents couldn't have been prouder. They viewed his activism as a duty and not a favor he did for the country. In fact, in the past, when his mother had learned of his plans to go to fight in Palestine, she scolded him for not making arrangements to take his brother to fight alongside him.

He could afford to think or dedicate himself to little else beyond his work as a dentist and his work in the campaign. They were fighting against so many hidden forces in addition to the regime, such as power-hungry opposition parties that were not on board with El Baradei, the older generation of politicians and crony capitalists, the lack of funding, and more.

After years of working from Abd El Rahman Yousef's office, the campaign was finally able to secure enough regular funding to get its own office in the Mohandiseen area. It was illegal to fundraise from abroad for almost anything in Egypt if you were not a government entity, so El Baradei put some of his personal money into the campaign and the team was also able to secure a number of local patrons who gave what they could as regularly as they could.

It was under these circumstances that the team worked hard on creating its qualitative mass of active individuals who had not been tainted by previously politicized lives. They did not want seasoned politicians who came to the table with stubborn and stagnant beliefs—and perhaps even personal agendas.

They also avoided youth who viewed activism as a vocation, appeared to do little else and were not successful in their personal lives. The ideal candidate was a nonpartisan individual who was personally accomplished and believed in volunteering as a nationalistic duty.

Accordingly, with great effort, El Baradei's dream team was assembled with untainted values and little politically negative experience that could weigh down the movement with a sense of hopelessness or futility. This group believed they had enough fresh blood among them to save the hemorrhaging pride and faith of the current inhabitants of Egypt.

∽ ∽

When Khaled Saeed was murdered and Wael and Mustafa read about it, they became drawn to the story as a blatant example of how emboldened Egyptian police in general and Alexandrian police in particular had become.

Mustafa went to Alexandria himself and visited the police station where the perpetrators worked and began his own investigation. The facts were chilling and the police did not seem to care that their version of events clearly made no sense at all. It seemed that everyone who had a say in the case had taken part in the injustice, from the botched coroner's report to the miscarriage of justice on the judge's end. Khaled was regarded by authorities to be little more than a bug that was squashed by the big boots of those in power.

Wael came up with the idea of an anonymous Facebook page dedicated to the case that was not affiliated with any political movement or any specific individual who may take credit for it or suffer the consequences of spearheading it.

It was Mustafa who wrote the first article on the Khaled Saeed page, in Arabic, titled "We All Killed Khaled Saeed." The article was the first thing newly invited members and visitors read. It explained how all Egyptians were accomplices to the murder by their failure to stand up against it. Egyptians collective silence about similar crimes in the past encouraged police to push the bar every time making citizens as guilty as the officer who personally slammed Khaled's face against the marble steps of the apartment building where he was killed.

The article and the page saw so much activity within the first week of its presence that Mustafa was forced to tell Wael that he could no longer handle the responsibilities of being a co-administrator, given his commitment to the El Baradei campaign.

The page then fully became Wael's baby and his passion. He was constantly on it, observing people's comments, removing those who ruined the page's message, and managing its content in a way that kept visitors interested and gained their trust as readers.

The page's lack of affiliation with politics made it a comfortable cause to join. The tragedy was capable of uniting people in a way that no political campaign or set of slogans could even come close to achieving. When the El Baradei campaign went to Alexandria to join in the protests instigated by the page, the page's number of friends and participants surged almost overnight.

Mustafa, Abd El Rahman Yousef, and an activist by the name of Abd El Moneim Imam all advised El Baradei in a private meeting to pay his respects to Khaled's mother without drawing attention to who he was by bringing along his wife and children. But the press had learned which hotel El Baradei was staying in and followed him there. El Baradei took the reporters aside and told them that they could not enter the apartment building or conduct any kind of interview with him in the Saeed residence, and instead promised them that he would talk to them after the visit if they stuck to his instructions.

Dr. Ayman Nour, another leading opposition figure, had arrived with a lot of fanfare, and Khaled's family had already respectfully declined to meet him. Accordingly, El Baradei and his group were at the forefront of a Friday prayer service to pray for Khaled's soul in the Sidi Gaber Mosque next to his house. Word quickly spread of El Baradei's presence and people started coming to the mosque in droves.

Ironically, perhaps, security forces came in to regulate the crowds and a full-force protest condemning Saeed's attackers erupted without much recourse from the police. The "We Are All Khaled Saeed" Facebook group members, who were dressed in black and lined Alexandria's beach promenades holding the Quran and the Bible and praying in silence in a show of nonviolent, resistant solidarity, joined the protest as well. The protest moved from the mosque to Khaled's residence, where protesters, took turns visiting Khaled's mother and paying their respects.

Khaled Saeed's mother finally gave her son the proper service he deserved.

As the protest came to an end, El Baradei was almost crushed by people attempting to come near him to thank him and shake his hand. Alexandrian activists had done their homework and distributed thousands of fliers with El Baradei's biography and his efforts for reform listed on them. People battled each other to shake his hand and even tried to hug and kiss him. The numbers increased around him to such an extent that his handlers had to extract El Baradei from the situation for his own safety.

It was moves like these that began to resonate with Egyptian youth and make them see the possibilities of how their voices can reach out and connect to each other. Inspired by the success of this experience, Mustafa, along with his team, decided to conduct an experiment to gauge the scope of public response that his team could command at will.

The chosen experiment was an exercise in what is known as "creative chaos," and had been utilized in the Chilean resistance efforts. In essence, it encouraged activists to come together publicly on a specific date and time and produce a minor but noticeable disturbance and have it recorded on videotape and uploaded online.

Mustafa was very excited and the possibilities of success elevated his spirits. He believed that if the movement focused its effort on four or five governorates and trained citizens to come out in protest together, Egypt would have its revolution.

Some members of the team disagreed with this methodology, reasoning that it could mobilize those with financial grievances and become a revolution based on the poor against the rich and result in full-blown mayhem. But Mustafa had seen the futility of all the other political venues. He felt that Mubarak's regime had created its own constant mayhem that kept getting worse every year. Other methodologies had to be tested.

In September 2010, after Mustafa returned from Washington, DC where he attended a conference held by the American-Egyptian association, he began to gather covert funding to train the necessary individuals in select governorates to participate in the Chilean experiment, Day of Anger, as the movement called it.

Prominent figures in Egyptian society, such as Dr. Mohamed Abu El Ghar and Dr. Mohamed Ghonim, participated in secret money drops to supply the movement with the cash it needed. Mustafa would receive phone calls that explained, in code, that money had been left in specific locations and Mustafa would drive to these personally, park far away from the drops, and go in on foot to collect the packaged funds. He took a grave risk every time he did it.

On November 26, 2010, a couple of months before the revolution, the first test drive for a Day of Anger took place. The theme of this day was for activists to create a certain level of noise as a way of expressing their stance against injustice and torture, capture it on tape and share it online. Ten governorates were ready to participate and El Baradei's movement coordinated its efforts with the Sixth of April youth opposition movement in what could be considered a test drive for the January 25th protests.

Wael Ghonim's Facebook project, "We Are All Khaled Saeed," was used as the main announcer of the planned event so that Egyptians unaffiliated to any oppositional movement could participate if they felt it made sense to them. This was an important coordinating effort that gave the El Baradei movement a lot of information about reaching beyond the activists' and into the bulk of the Egyptian people.

A division of labor took place between Mustafa and the Sixth of April's main coordinator, Ahmed Maher. Sixth of April was heavily involved on the streets and was responsible for photocopying and distributing fliers about the event, while El Baradei's campaign focused on the online efforts, the management of security-related issues, and the complex process of selecting fake venues and real venues to throw off the police.

The day was a success and it lifted the spirits of all of those involved. Sixth of April mobilized participants in six governorates, while El Baradei's movement utilized its participants in twenty governorates and the "We Are All Khaled Saeed" enabled regular citizens to participate. In unison, Egyptians briefly stood in the streets and in balconies, banged on pots and pans, whistled, yelled, and created any kind of noise they could manage for ten minutes, and then retreated.

The movement proved that it could mobilize if it chose to and it began to gain some confidence. It also began to build a reputation that its sole focus was *change*—and not necessarily making Dr. El Baradei president.

Two distinct entities were in place when it came to El Baradei and his movement. The first was the National Association for Change, which was viewed as a campaign for him personally. The second was the Popular People's Movement to Support Dr. El Baradei and His Efforts for Change, which was joined by people who may not have necessarily wanted El Baradei to be the next president but realized that he had the know how to help Egyptians bring about true change. The latter group had a substantial following.

When the Alexandria church bombing took place, Mustafa and Wael Ghonim came together to see how their Chilean-inspired experiment worked when there was a true call for people to take to the streets. They were disappointed by the low turnout, of a total of only 1500 participants, across Egypt and began to question the experiment's initial findings. While they were busy dealing with their frustration in their failure to mobilize the Egyptians, the Tunisian revolution took place.

Mustafa and his team were further perturbed that another Arab country had seemingly beat them to their goal with relative ease. Up until Tunisia's efforts became successful, the plan had been to attempt an Egyptian revolution at the end of 2011 as a reaction to the farcical elections expected to take place. If the government did not make the demanded changes in the Constitution to ensure a fair and democratic election process, the movements would call for collective civil disobedience that would not end until Egyptians had a democratically elected president in office.

The Tunisian triumph moved that go-date forward, to the 25th of January instead. The twenty-fifth had already been designated as a yearly day of protest against police brutality in Egypt by activists, but this year all elements were coming together to make youth want something much bigger than a mere protest. Several posts on the "Khaled Saeed" page declared the twenty-fifth to be the selected date of the Egyptian revolution. Mustafa laughed when he saw this on his computer screen and was surprised that Wael Ghonim believed in this as a strategy.

According to Mustafa's research, there was no such thing as a preplanned revolution that announced the date of its occurrence. That defeated the element of surprise, rendering the whole effort useless. Activists were not superheroes perched on the edges of buildings who were going to descend from the sky screaming, "We are here to save the day!" Mustafa argued to his colleagues.

Many were disappointed in his reaction.

But none of those with true experience in activism believed that this method could prove successful. Mustafa wrote two analytical articles about the situation. One, on Masrway.com, urged people to not take the word "revolution" lightly, and by doing so make light of a very difficult task that could easily fail creating a sense of defeat that may prove to be irreversible. Instead, he recommended that people approach change in its proper stages to ensure success.

The second was a more optimistic piece published on January 22 in the opposition paper *El Destour* under the headline, "Mr. President, This Is Why We Are Choosing the 25th of January." In the article, Mustafa made comparisons between President Mubarak's regime and that of fallen Tunisian President Zein El Abideen, and deduced that Mubarak's regime had indeed already fallen, but neither the president nor his people had realized it yet.

The same strategies tested for the Chilean experiment were utilized by Mustafa, Wael, and the Sixth of April movement for the protests of the twenty-fifth. Fake locations were posted along with real locations; key participants knew the difference and had their way of spreading the word in the streets as marches moved along.

Chants were preselected by leaders, including Mustafa, Wael Ghonim, and Ahmed Maher, and were organized in a specific order to garner particular reactions. They were posted to the "Khaled Saeed" page with some explanation of their relevance and expected outcome.

The movement stationed members at important geographical locations to start chants and suggest directions for the crowds to follow. The real locations for the mass gathering were posted a mere thirty minutes before everything took place, and none of them actually included Tahrir Square. The Mustafa Mahmoud Mosque and Kasr El Eini Street were supposed to be the main areas of mass protest.

El Baradei's team's protest headquarters was in the Kasr El Eini area, and Sixth of April was responsible for the Gameat El Dowal area that surrounded the Mustafa Mahmoud Mosque. The initial plan was for all crowds to end up at the main building of Egypt's Supreme Justice near Kasr El Eini Street and create a sit-in there that was to remain in place until the government removed the Minister of Interior Affairs. At 1:00 p.m., there were about two thousand people from El Baradei's campaign there, and the police quickly formed a cordon around them. As phone calls informed

Mustafa and other leaders that massive crowds were gathering and coming in, they became increasingly motivated to break through the police cordon.

The women in the group were the ones who ended up succeeding in this first. They threw themselves at the police with unabashed bravery and miraculously broke through as if they were possessed by beings stronger than their small bodies. The others pushed in after them and started running down El Kasr El Eini Street with gusto. The police, some in riot garb and some in regular clothes, were running toward them with equal strength, with sticks and Tasers drawn.

The police began beating people up mercilessly, women and men alike, with little regard for how severe their onslaught was. Mohamed Diab and Amr Salama were among this first group of protesters, and the police captured Amr Salama and beat him within an inch of his life and left him for dead on the ground.

As the protesters ran through the Garden City area downtown with the police on their tails, they began to encounter the so-called "protestors of the educated elite," which included medical school students in their white coats, law school students in their robes, engineering students, pharmacy students, and more, who were all invited to participate in the Kasr El Eini vicinity. They were also joined by unions of workers, actors, and artisans. It was a beautiful sight to behold.

As the crowds came in from all across Cairo and El Baradei's supporters ran back to their original stations after incessant efforts of the police to beat, arrest, and disperse them, it became apparent that the only space that would take them all was Tahrir Square.

As Mustafa walked into the square with Ahmed Maher, Abd El Rahman Yousef, and Wael Ghonim in a daze, completely dumbfounded by the massive turnout, they realized that they had no idea what the next step should be. People would ask them where to go and Wael would reply, "I honestly do not know. This crowd is too big to move around. Never in our wildest dreams did we ever think it would get this big."

Protestors and leading members alike begun hugging and weeping and the mood quickly turned festive. They had triumphed over the police's oppressive efforts and ended up in this symbolic square with its symbolic name. Egyptians would watch the spectacle that was Tahrir that day, unaware of the battle that took place that made it possible.

This was the open invitation to Egypt's people to revolt, and the real revolution was expected to be a continuous event that took place over the upcoming weeks, until the regime responded in an acceptable manner.

Wael looked around him and announced to his friends that they had all succeeded in everything they had set out to achieve. They had built an untouchable group of people in a mostly peaceful manner and now all the authorities could do was stand by and observe. He was obviously elated and he began to sing loudly and clap his hands. Mustafa pulled out his cell phone and called El Baradei in America and filled him in. "You must come to Egypt right away," Mustafa said forcefully.

"I will begin speaking to CNN and the international media and then..." El Baradei began.

Mustafa cut him off. "No, you do not understand, I am standing in Tahrir among what must be close to one hundred thousand people. You must come and be part of this at once!"

Mustafa painted the picture to him that the media was not yet sharing with the rest of the world. He told him how this was everything they had ever dreamed of. El Baradei hurriedly gathered his belongings, and headed for the airport.

In preparation for the massive strike that they had hoped for, Abd El Rahman Yousef suggested that they create a podium with loudspeakers in the square so they could address and unify the people toward certain objectives. He took out two thousand pounds and gave it to a member of the movement to go and get the necessary equipment. However, when the first set of equipment arrived, it malfunctioned, and they were still short a communication system to address the crowds.

Mustafa then gave the movement fifteen hundred pounds he had on him and pooled the rest from other members. When the second set of equipment arrived, they discovered that they needed an electrician to install it. So they searched the protesters for an electrician and found one who helped use an electricity line from a street lamp to set up the microphone and speaker set.

Abd El Rahman Yousef grabbed the functioning microphone and announced, "This is the first broadcast of the radio for change channel, set up by the free Egyptian people!"

The crowd cheered and clapped and you could hear "Allah Akbar!" reverberating throughout the square. The moment was beyond description.

"We are here and we are immovable," Abd El Rahman Yusuf said, as the crowd cheered in agreement. "We have broken the boundaries of fear and Egypt will never be the same."

The radio show had begun and Mustafa took over the microphone, rallying the crowds and calling in poets, writers, singers, and celebrities. Gamila Ismail, Dr. Alaa El Aswany, and Hamza El Namira all exercised their rights to speak to a free crowd about coming together to fight for the betterment of Egypt, and the protesters loved it.

As the hours passed, they began making plans to spend the night. They called their contacts to provide them with blankets and supplies and perhaps even back-up protesters, as some protestors who had not included a sit-in in their plans had started to go home. Some of those leaving were actually families with children who came into the square after the numbers had swelled because they had felt that it had become a safe environment for children.

Other opposition parties, such as the Wafd, The Ghad, and the National Association, began to make plans to join. They had not had a role earlier but had realized now that this was an event that required their participation.

Sadly, they would not have the chance to reach the square, at least not in its current state. A few minutes after midnight, Abd El Rahman Yousef informed Mustafa that he sensed a strange shuffling and repositioning of the police forces surrounding the square and at some of its entrances.

Mustafa announced into the microphone that the radio show would be suspended for a half hour to check the security of the square and reassess the safety of the situation. There were still a number of families with children present, and Mustafa had begun to feel an immense sense of responsibility.

Mustafa and Abd El Rahman Yousef took it upon themselves to walk around the perimeter of Tahrir to get a general feel of the situation. As they walked through Kasr El Aini Street, it became apparent that they were being followed. Mustafa wasn't overly concerned because he still believed they were protected by the sheer number of people in the square.

However, within minutes they began to hear the tear gas canisters being shot into the square. The very first spot hit was the stage. Abd El Rahman Yousef told Mustafa that they should split up so that authorities wouldn't get them both. Separately, they both headed back to Tahrir from different routes.

When he reached Tahrir, Mustafa was heartbroken by the scene, which resembled the memories he had from the Palestinian war. The police were shooting rubber bullets and tear gas into the crowds, and the injuries began mounting. Mustafa had just passed the Egyptian museum when he felt like his leg was set ablaze. When he looked down, he realized that a rubber bullet was lodged in his lower leg. He fell to the ground next to the museum's wall, as a tear gas canister landed next to him. Mustafa, who has asthma, began to choke on the canister's fumes and was unable to get up to kick it across the street or move away from it.

As he became dizzy from the lack of oxygen, he watched the Egyptians run for cover in what once was, for a brief period of time, his crowning achievement. Police began to spray the crowds with pellet bullets and Mustafa, unable to move, was being grazed by the shots. *"Ash had Ana la ilea ill Allah way Ana Mohamad rasul Allah"* ("I proclaim that there is only one God and that Mohamed is his prophet"), Mustafa said to himself, which is the prayer Muslims say at death's door. In his heart, Mustafa was happy. He could not think of a better way—or a better day—to die.

Just then, three concerned young men approached. They picked Mustafa up and steadied him on their shoulders. They told him they would save him and discussed rushing him to the nearest hospital. They carried him all the way to the Sixth of October Bridge to Abd El Moneim Riyad Street, where there was a small garage. In the garage a Peugeot 405 sedan was parked with its doors open. Without warning, the men pulled out a blindfold and covered Mustafa's eyes, tied his hands behind his back, and shoved him into the car.

It dawned on Mustafa that these were the men that had been following him and he almost laughed out loud. He had been tricked in an almost comical manner that made him feel like a complete and utter fool.

"Where are you taking me?" Mustafa asked.

"You just shut your mouth!" the men, who had faked concern so well, replied.

They were pretending no longer.

～♋ ♋～

The car drove a short distance and Mustafa was shoved out and forced to walk on his leg in the direction in which they were pushing him. He was still having bouts of uncontrollable coughing caused by the tear gas inhalation and the amount of stress he was under. He felt something being tied above the wound in his leg and figured it was to stop the bleeding. He figured that had to be a good sign. If they were attempting to stop the bleeding, they probably weren't out to kill him.

Shortly, after he was seated, Mustafa could hear and feel someone standing in front or beside him. The individual seemed to linger there a little bit. Suddenly, without any warning Mustafa was struck hard by a thick stick across his chest. The blow caused sharp, resonating pain and triggered the coughing once more. With every cough, the pain from the blow seared across his upper torso.

In such situations, the body immediately secretes massive amounts of adrenaline and one's internal fear mechanisms are elevated to the level of "panic". Anticipating the pain becomes almost as bad as experiencing it. As blow after painful blow landed, Mustafa began to assume that they had stopped the bleeding in his leg so they could slowly torture him to death.

There was a slight pause in the beating as an officer sat down and began to play some audio tapes. It was like they had every phone call he ever made on tape. They played phone calls between him and Ahmed Maher, and Dr. Abu El Ghar, and El Baradei...the list went on and on.

After every conversation they played for him, they cursed and yelled at him, and then the beatings would start again. At one point they played back footage of him standing on stage in Tahrir talking to the crowd less than an hour before.

"You think you are made for theater, you son of a whore," the voice would say as the thick stick came down. He began to feel as if he was fading again and repeated to himself the death prayer over and over.

The human body can withstand more than we can imagine.

Mustafa's beating and interrogation started at 1:00 a.m. on the twenty-sixth and continued until close to the same time the following night. The near twenty-four hours, were designed to badger him on three things: Firstly, they wanted to know who the administrator of the "We Are All Khaled Saeed" page was. Secondly, they demanded that he sign a confession stating that the Muslim Brotherhood had been behind the whole thing and that El Baradei had enlisted its services to create the mass protest that did not reflect the will of the Egyptian people. Finally, they wanted a list of names of people and/or entities that were funding El Baradei's campaign.

Mustafa refused.

In moments in which Mustafa was almost traveling outside of his body to escape his present, he would remember when he used to joke with Wael about this very situation. Wael used to say, "If they catch you and torture you, Mustafa, will you tell them who I am?"

Mustafa used to joke, "It all depends, Wael, really...are you going to share that sandwich?" and they would shrug the whole thing off.

He wondered what Wael would think of him now. Mustafa was conditioning himself to believe that there was no exit from the pain so there was no use considering confessing. In his mind, to give them what they wanted was not an option, so his sole focus would be withstanding the pain and dying with dignity.

They laid Mustafa out on a table, fastened him to it and began to focus their beating on the bullet in his leg. "I am going to cripple you so you can't walk in another protest again," one of the interrogators yelled in Mustafa's ear.

They bashed the leg incessantly with a thick stick.

It was an endless period of constant, immeasurable pain in a room surrounded by compassionless people who took sadistic pleasure in Mustafa's plight.

Torture is an agonizing, isolating, and emotionally crippling practice designed to break your very spirit from deep inside. It breaks you while it is taking place, and stays with you the rest of your life. What they do to you in the torture room remains with you in every room you are in, always, like a little reminder that no matter how peaceful the current moment may be, evil is just around the corner.

At first, when Mustafa still had it in him, he would try to tell the officers that what they were doing would be held against them in a new and reconstituted Egyptian judicial system. He told them that Mubarak's regime was on its last leg and that they would be the patsies if the regime fell.

The officers just told him to shut up and admit which foreign entity or branch of the Brotherhood had set him up to do this. As time passed, Mustafa became too weak to speak, and all of the possible arguments escaped him. Late that Wednesday night, as Mustafa lay with his face on the ground, his hands still tied behind his back, he could feel his soul trying to leave his body. He began to shiver as he felt the room getting colder.

He could hear the officers, standing not too far away, discussing his condition and squabbling among themselves.

"This one is as good as dead, you know," one said.

"So what? Won't be the first one ..." the other replied.

"You moron," the first snapped. "This one will bring too much attention. Let's just throw him somewhere, let him die someplace else."

"How about he dies first and then we get rid of him?" the second suggested.

They went back and forth before settling on throwing him out before he died.

Mustafa's hands were untied and his blindfold removed, and a few minutes later he was thrown to the ground from a moving car. As he drifted in and out of consciousness, he recognized that he was in a secluded area near the Abdeen Palace neighborhood. He may have picked up a money drop in this location before. He decided to move himself in whatever way he could towards an area that had pedestrians in it. It took him a while, because he was slowly crawling on his hands and knees, but he finally reached a street where he pulled himself up with the help of a street lamp and attempted to stop cars.

The cars were afraid of him and a few sped away. A taxi driver finally stopped and Mustafa told him what had happened. The man took him to Mustafa's apartment – in Cairo you do not head to the hospital without money – and helped him call friends to come and get him to a hospital. Wael and Abd El Rahman Yousef were with Mustafa in the hospital. Mustafa was afraid to stay because he feared the police would come back to get him when they found out he survived.

Though he had suffered broken ribs, blood loss, and a severely wounded leg, Mustafa insisted that he collect the medicine prescribed to him, check himself out, and head to one of his friends' homes. He kept what happened to him a secret from his family. He was determined to be a part of the rest of the fight for freedom. There would be time to recover when Egypt was free.

Mustafa and Wael did not discuss what had happened to him and instead all their conversations were focused on what they would do on Friday. They would finally have a real Friday of Anger.

On that same Wednesday night, Mustafa's friends practically carried him to the Al Jazeera channel, where he appeared on air and reported what had happened to him in detail. He invited all the viewers watching to join in on the Friday of Anger and help the Egyptians break free of this regime or die trying. That would be the last time Mustafa saw Wael before his abduction.

By Thursday morning, El Baradei had arrived in Egypt and Mustafa insisted on attending the emergency meeting with him as

well. He was carried there by his friends, but he showed up nonetheless and participated in the planning process. Dr. Abu El Ghar,
Dr. Essam El Erian (of the Muslim Brotherhood), Abd El Rahman
Yousef, Dr. Katatny (of the Muslim Brotherhood), and Mustafa put
their brains together to plan for Friday.

                                                                                     ⚭ ⚭

As Mustafa told his story, he once again took me through how
brutal and bloody the Friday of Anger was, as did all the others
who I had interviewed before, reminding me that my family was
lucky to have Basil still among us.

The timeline and highs and lows of the days of revolt were
the same: the Friday of Anger, the first million-man march, the
Battle of the Camel, and so on. But like Moez had mentioned,
Mustafa's experience *was* unique in that he had become one of
the key figures that the regime was negotiating with while the protests continued. His interactions, along with Wael Ghonim, were
like a, behind-the-scenes, version of all the other stories I collected
before him.

He would receive phone calls asking him to come meet officials to discuss protester demands. Their long term surveillance of Mustafa had highlighted the significance of the role he
played along with El Baradei's group. At one point Mustafa met
with Ahmed Shafiq, the newly appointed prime minister, and
that meeting was followed by an interrogatory hearing led by
Vice President Omar Suleiman and attended by representatives
from opposition parties, the Muslim Brotherhood, and a group
of six young activists that included Mustafa and Abd El Rahman
Yousef.

When the Brotherhood and other opposition representatives
spoke, they addressed Suleiman by his title and afforded him all
the respect that his position carried. However, when it became
Mustafa's turn, the stress of his experience descended upon him
and he found himself speaking aggressively. He told the VP that
after the twenty-fifth, Mubarak may be Suleiman's commander and

chief but he wasn't Mustafa's president. He told him that there was no negotiation without the president leaving.

This angered Suleiman, and though he let Mustafa continue his rant, he told him that the end he was seeking, namely a militarily run country, would not produce a happy ending for Egypt. Suleiman repeated the regime's theory that the youth in Tahrir had been brainwashed by foreign entities and that Egypt was bigger than that and would not fall under the misguided pressures of inexperienced youth such as himself.

The accusations flew back and forth, and Mustafa began to fear Suleiman and his subtle, threatening insinuations. He could see that his eyes were dead and devoid of any true compassion. The VP appeared to be bred to be doubtful of any inherent "good" and he did not believe that what the youth were demanding was as innocent as it seemed. Still, Mustafa strived to attain *any* measure of cooperation from the regime's end that signified a tangible sign of true negotiation.

"At the very least," Mustafa said at one point, "we should be afforded the same rights as prisoners of war and be given access to food and medicine."

"What are you talking about?" Suleiman asked.

"The army is keeping vital supplies from entering the square." Mustafa stated, a bit taken aback by Suleiman's sudden interest in his statement. The VP appeared to be oddly offended by this specific claim regardless of all the other atrocities that Mustafa had listed.

"The Egyptian army is more honorable than your mind can even imagine," Suleiman responded. "Take my cell phone number and if that situation you mentioned does not change tomorrow morning, then you call me."

Encouraged, Mustafa quickly pulled out a paper with Wael's name on it and handed it to Suleiman. "My friend Wael Ghonim is missing and we think he has been arrested but the police won't confirm or deny it. Can you help us?"

Suleiman took the paper and raised it above his head, signaling to the man standing behind him to take it. "This boy is to be released tomorrow."

Just like that.

Wael's wife and parents had been searching frantically for him, the media had been calling for any information about him and Mustafa had had this awful feeling that he must have been killed. Yet the whole thing appeared to end with that piece of paper? If Wael was still alive, his ordeal was as good as over.

Mustafa could not imagine Wael withstanding torture and he felt that he was likely to die at the hands of his captors if they employed the same level of torture they had used with him. Now, there was hope that all his loved ones would finally know his fate in a matter of hours.

Interactions like these indicated to Mustafa that there was something different about Egypt's handling of these things. Even with the tyrannical regime that ruled the country, Egyptian officials seemed to have their own code of honor. When compared to the Ghadaffi of Libya or Bashar al-Assad of Syria, Egyptian officials seemed to have a cutoff point when it came to how crazy they would allow things to get or how low they would actually go.

Wael was released the next day at seven o'clock in the evening.

The irony of Wael's situation was that it was revealed that he had not been arrested for being the administrator of the Khaled Saeed page. He had been arrested for being in a meeting with a Jewish Google executive who had been under surveillance because of his work as a lecturer in a series of "Resistance through Nonviolence" seminars. In fact, Moez Masoud was supposed to attend this meeting but had luckily got detained by a prior engagement.

During Amn El-Dawla's interrogation, the police discovered that they had unknowingly caught the administrator of the "Khaled Saeed" page. The techniques used to break Wael focused on accusing him of being a spy for Israel out to create havoc to tear Egypt down.

He was blindfolded for the entirety of his detainment and he was beaten. He would deny the authorities mistreatment of him to the press in an effort to unify Egyptians against the regime itself as opposed to fixating the people on the officers in particular. Wael personally believed that Egypt needed its police and army intact in order to survive.

He also believed his captors when they stated that they were doing their jobs to maintain the safety and sovereignty of Egypt.

By the end of his interrogation, Wael had shared the names of everyone he had ever been in contact with. This was always part of the plan that Wael had agreed upon with Mustafa. (Mustafa had told him that if the police tortured him, he should go ahead and name names since the police were already onto Mustafa and others.)

When Amr Salama, Mustafa, and Mohamed Diab met with Wael in the street before his famous interview, he was reportedly acting understandably wild and illogical. He was defending the police's actions adamantly, and kept repeating that together they had to save Egypt from chaos. Mustafa grabbed his shoulders and tried to steady him and remind him of the game that was being played on him and the rest of Egypt.

"Wael, people died in droves and we cannot let that go." Mustafa had said.

But it did not appear to sink in. The police had broken him. They alternated between the good-cop-bad-cop routine for so long, with the "bad cop" going as far as threatening him with rape, that they had him convinced that his activism was putting Egypt at risk.

It was not until the TV host showed him the pictures of the martyrs who had been killed that Wael finally broke down, realizing the extent of the regime's guilt in the senseless killings of peaceful protesters. He walked off the set and into his friends' arms off camera, where they all cried like babies.

∾ ∾

The night before the president's abdication, Wael called Mustafa and announced, "We are going to meet President Mubarak."

To which Mustafa replied, "Have you lost your mind?"

But Wael insisted that it was the right move and that they should band together and go as a unit. Mustafa had previously rejected this idea on principle, but Wael insisted that he needed support.

Mustafa met Wael at the Sonesta Hotel. Wael explained that he and Amr Salama had met with Amn El-Dawla the previous night, and were told that the president wanted to leave but wanted to exit in an honorable manner. They had him convinced that they could even be as involved as being part of the process of selecting the correct wording and manner of Mubarak's departure.

"Wael, they are stringing you along to get you to cooperate," Mustafa explained, but that just made Wael angry.

"You have always been a pessimist, Mustafa! Why can't you just believe that we all want to save the country and resolve the situation?"

It was Mustafa's gut feeling that that Wael was currently coming apart at the seams in his post-traumatic state. In addition to his harrowing experience, certain coalition movements from Tahrir Square and the media had begun to label Wael, Mustafa, Mohamed Diab, and even El Baradei as spies for America who wanted to steal the efforts of the Egyptian people who had fought the true battle. They cited their recent trips abroad to attend conferences and their constant contact with individuals beyond Egypt, and all that negativity must have been taking its toll.

Mustafa decided to go along for support and to stop Wael from doing anything under duress. He called Ahmed Maher of Sixth of April to join them as well. Amr Salama and Khaled El Baramawy, the administrator of Masrawy.com, met up with them, too, and they all went to the Amn El-Dawla office to meet with the Chief Director Hassan Abd El Rahman. El Rahman instructed them to follow him in their car to meet with Prime Minister Ahmed Shafiq, and that they would then head to the presidential palace.

On the way over, Mustafa announced, "I cannot see myself shaking Mubarak's hand. I see him as a mass murderer."

"You have to be open to new beginnings if you want us to move forward, Mustafa," Wael replied. "We have forced them to shift gears, and now that the situation has changed from their end we must try to achieve our goals and move the country beyond this." On that note Wael's spirits began to gradually rise and he began singing, *"Ya ahla ism fi el wogood ya Masr"* ("The most beautiful name in the world is Egypt"), an old nationalistic song from the eighties and Amr Salama pitched in as well. The refrain filled the car and threatened to push all negativity out. Mustafa watched and listened to them in silence and willed himself to believe.

As the five of them sat before Prime Minister Ahmed Shafiq, Amn El-Dawla's Chief Director Hassan Abd El Rahman, and Minister of Interior Affairs Mahmoud Wagdy, all the optimism they had felt earlier in the car began to melt away. In fact, the group's rhetoric and tone of voice managed to make all of Mustafa and Wael's memories of their incarceration and torture come flooding back. Mustafa inadvertently found himself interrupting Hassan Abd El Rahman and blurting out, "I was tortured in your prisons and so were millions of Egyptians and I want retribution! Give me retribution!"

As Abd El Rahman began to casually explain that certain officers took it upon themselves to use torture methodologies but not all officers should be held responsible, nor addressed in this manner, Mustafa could not get a hold of how he felt and watched himself in horror as he burst into tears in the middle of the room. Wael began sobbing as well.

Then, in a totally unexpected move, Ahmed Shafiq got up and took the two young men in his arms and comforted them. Wael and Mustafa were shocked into silence and eventually pulled away, the tears dry and feeling utterly uncomfortable.

The move did not reconcile the group, nor did it remove the mistrust that was rampant between the two sides. But for a few seconds in history, Ahmed Shafiq saw the revolutionaries as his sons and they, in a moment of vulnerability, had accepted his embrace.

In mere minutes they would fall back into their separate worlds and what they believed about each other, and they would never take a step toward one other again.

In fact, it appeared that even the president had changed his mind about meeting them, and the meeting ended by a phone call from Dr. Hossam Badrawy, a prominent NDP member who was reportedly in direct contact with the president, stating that Mubarak would not meet with the activists as planned.

At this point in recalling the story, Mustafa paused and looked at me sadly.

You know, Hoda, about the crying. During these times my tears would flow at the slightest provocation, and it was not because of the 24 hours of torture I had recently endured.

The true experience that hurts me now as I sit before you just as much as it did when it happened, I have yet to share with you. You see, on the night of the Battle of the Camel there was a young man who had introduced himself to me as I stood by the Sixth of October Bridge. His name was Ahmed and he was a student in Cairo University. He had recognized me from television and asked me, "Do you think they will shoot at us and try to kill us at this point?"

I looked at him confidently and said, "No, I think they are just trying to scare us away. They are Egyptians just like us. They wouldn't go that far, why would they?" I said, "You just stay close to me and you will be fine."

A few minutes later, he was shot in the chest by a sniper and literally fell into my arms. I felt like he and I were being punished for being so naïve. I picked him up and ran with him as blood poured out of his chest. I could see he was fading fast and all color was draining from his face. He did not panic or cry or anything like that. When I lay him down at the makeshift hospital they had set up, and it was obvious even to him that he was dying, he looked at me calmly but weakly and asked, as if his life depended on it, and it did, "Mustafa, are we right or wrong in what we did?"

I answered with all the conviction I could muster, "We are right and you are right and you will be a martyr who will live in heaven and we will follow you, God willing." He died a few minutes later and I live with the fact that I was the reason that this young man lost his life.

The question of who is right, what methodology is just and what is considered acceptable as a price to pay for change, is what all of us need to consider on a daily basis.

Mustafa struggled to keep his voice steady and to my surprise he suddenly appeared to be uninterested in continuing the interview. He hurried through the rest of it with little of the intimacy of the first few hours of our talk.

He told me I could contact him if I had any questions, but wanted to leave me with a song, that he had recorded on his laptop. He had personally written the lyrics to the song for the young man that had died in his arms and a friend of Mustafa's had written the music.

He said his goodbyes and left me in his office to hear it as he retreated to a meeting in a nearby room.

As I sat alone in his office in the Justice Party's building and listened to the lyrics of loss and sacrifice, I started to cry.

When the song ended, I gathered my notes and equipment and exited quietly into Cairo's downtown. We drove through Tahrir on our way home. Sparse tents, signs and sad, listless individuals were scattered across its historical square. It lay there like a vacant womb welcoming those who would undoubtedly choose to inhabit it time and again for months to come hoping to have their dreams come to fruition.

I would be leaving Egypt in days. All my problems, plans and efforts that I had imagined to be worth anything for Egypt, suddenly felt like nothing. They paled in comparison to the selfless sacrifices of the young men and women who gave their life during those 18 days of dreams.

Would writing about it in a book truly be of any use? Would the words on these pages convey what this country had been through and answer questions about how or when it can rise above it?

Can Egyptian youth lead Egypt out of it or will they be damned for trying?

Were we right to dare to want something different? Could our strategies or timing have been improved upon?

She or he who claims he has the answers to these questions lies.

They lie because the world is not about getting it "right." Our hours spent are not graded on a "pass" or "fail" basis. What is "right" for us all is a quest ... compassion and understanding our propelling ores.

Words in print are nothing if people do not seek the knowledge and desire a well-informed heart. We need to seek beyond what our eyes and ears are offered by the media and the circles of people that surround us. We must learn about each other and sample the struggles of cultures seemingly removed from ours.

I had a plane to catch and an Egyptian family I would leave behind and I had these stories in my purse and a fear of the unknown in my heart. But, I had stopped looking for answers and was finally content in being grateful for every human story I had and will hopefully continue to have the honor to learn about.

Let us all learn from what happened to Egypt and be part of her effort to rise above her current challenges. Keep her in your prayers, if you can do nothing else. Look at her with admiration and compassion, for she shall, God willing, rise into her full potential and be the beautiful country that the world has always admired.

EPILOGUE

One of the greatest challenges I faced when trying to capture the spirit of the Egyptian revolution into a story on paper was attempting to do this while on American soil. Not just any "American soil," but *Californian* soil.

I cannot think of a place farther removed from the stories of Tahrir Square than the San Francisco Bay Area of California. With a temperate climate almost year-round and my life revolving around soccer practices and outdoor activities, it was like writing about solitary confinement from the ocean view suite of a luxury sea liner.

Although I did most of my writing at night, during the day I existed in another realm. While preparing my son for school, cooking, cleaning, caring for my daughter and juggling home-work and practices, my nine characters and their recorded voices were always funneling around in my head.

I listened to Moez's voice while I did the dishes and was plagued by nightmares of Shawky's torture in my sleep. Wael El Zoghby's story, which intersected with mine, reminded me of how close to being an activist I had come. And Shahinaz's juggling of mother-hood and the protests motivated me to not give up on the project when it seemed I couldn't handle it with all my chores.

They became my friends and my muses and their messages were a grave responsibility that I was eager to spill onto paper and delegate to the world. For the most part, I thought that I was writing about an era of atrocities that was over and done with and that this book would be part of the healing process.

Consequently, it was painful to hear of Egypt falling into a second wave of apparent oppression that began in March of 2011 and has since continued to escalate against peaceful protestors, field doctors, journalists and innocent bystanders without discrimination. The world has borne witness to a slew of charges against the Supreme Council of Armed Forces (SCAF) including "virginity tests," torture, maiming and murder of protestors. No definitive action has been taken to investigate these crimes or their perpetrators and for many the revolution has not yet attained its goals.

I maintain the belief that the revolution was the beginning, not the end of our road to freedom. Consequently, each generation will take us forward for as far as it can manage, serene in the knowledge that our success lies in the fact that we have agreed to embark on this difficult journey to begin with. God bless Egypt and all oppressed people around the world.